$21-

THE
REAL LINCOLN

FROM THE TESTIMONY OF HIS CONTEMPORARIES

BY

CHARLES L. C. MINOR, M. A., LL. D.

Fourth Edition, Revised and Enlarged
(Edited by M. D. Carter)

Harrisonburg, Virginia
SPRINKLE PUBLICATIONS
1992

Sprinkle Publications
P.O. Box 1094
Harrisonburg, Virginia 22801

CONTENTS

PUBLISHER'S NOTE

"History is bunk" says Henry Ford. Had he qualified this statement with "as it is written," his assertion would have been more readily accepted by the reading public. Unfortunately, history—which is merely the recorded lives and acts of the individuals comprising the citizenry of any given unit of government—has been unreliable, as a general thing, because past historians, many of them, could not rise above or go beyond their likes, dislikes, pleasures or disaffections. They were not content with presenting the actual truth. The historian felt it his duty to chronicle the good; or, if mentioning the evil, to gloss it or explain it away. Frequently he went so far as to invent pretty stories that served to bolster up a tottering hero.

Recently there has been a decided change. Biography —the handmaiden of history—as written in America and published by American firms for American readers has become the antithesis of biography as heretofore universally written. There has been an about-face from the heights to the depths, from apotheosis to demonification, from the sublime to the ridiculous, from one extreme of untruth to the other. The present vogue "inters the good" and then, with hammer and tongs, tears down the idol and leaves the reader the shattered remnant of a once-glorious figure. Each of these types of biography has its ardent proponents as well as its no less dogmatic opponents.

However, there is one noteworthy sign of the times. The present generation of readers is eager for biography. This is amply proven by the avidity with which each new volume of this character is appropriated and by the vast and ever increasing number of such books coming regularly from the press. The record of the lives and achievements of real flesh-and-blood is more interesting than imaginary fairies. Truth is ever stranger than fiction. Such study, moreover, is instructive, enlightening, provocative of thought. Hence this eagerness is a good sign.

The publishers of this fourth edition of ''The Real Lincoln'' have the firm conviction that it is built on neither of these extremes but ploughs a straight furrow through the truth. It is their belief that a careful reading of this book in North and South alike will serve to establish in the mind of America a truer knowledge and a clearer understanding of the real Lincoln that occupied the most important position in the government of the United States at one of her most crucial periods.

With the exception of a few minor corrections and the inclusion of two articles in the appendix this book is identical with the second edition published shortly after the author's death.

THE PUBLISHERS

Gastonia, N. C., Jan. 1, 1928

INTRODUCTION BY THE EDITORS

The manuscript of this volume was completed by Dr. Minor only a few days before his death. After the issue of the first edition, in 1901, he began this, thinking that a second edition would be needed. When the call for a second edition came, he had gathered and worked in much new matter, so that it has become a book now instead of a pamphlet.

To the undersigned was committed the charge of editing it—a labor of love in a double sense, for it is hard to say which they love most, the writer or the cause of political and historic truth so ably championed by him. It is all his work—his last work—to which might be appended the words of the Roman gladiator: *moriturus vos saluto.*

It is unnecessary for the editors to say anything as to the purpose for which this book was written; for this is fully stated in the preface by the author, and the concluding words of the second chapter show how the facts set forth, and so fully proved in this book, tend to allay rather than to excite sectional feeling between North and South. If in doing this it has been necessary for the writer to set forth facts which compel Lincoln's admirers to esteem him less, let not the reader blame the author for lack of charity; but rather consider that truth is a very precious thing, and that only truth could come from such an array of unwilling witnesses as has been marshalled here.

No man ever lived more willing than the author to give due homage to worth, and more unwilling to take from a hero any portion of his meed of praise; but to restore in some measure that goodwill between the sections which he had known in youth and early manhood, was an object with him beyond all price, and well worth his utmost efforts in the cause of truth, even though it should compel the world to place one of its heroes on a lower pedestal.

True here, as of all truth, are the words of the Master, "Ye shall know the truth, and the truth shall make you free," from prejudice, passion, and all uncharitableness.

The editors are under obligations to Mr. Paul S. Whitcomb, of Portland, Oregon, for permission to use his article on "Lincoln and Democracy" which originally appeared in Tyler's Quarterly Magazine; to Capt. Samuel A'Court Ashe, of Raleigh, N. C., for condensing said article and supplying very valuable marginal notes thereto; and to Mrs. Beulah Johnson Howell, of New York City, for valuable suggestions.

BERKELEY MINOR,
M. D. CARTER.

SKETCH OF THE AUTHOR

Charles Landon Carter Minor was the eldest son of Lucius H. Minor of ''Edgewood,'' Hanover County, Virginia. His mother was Catharine Frances Berkeley. He was born December 3, 1835. He received the degree of Master of Arts at the University of Virginia in 1858.

The beginning of the War between the States found him teaching at Bloomfield, LeRoy Broun's School, in Albemarle County, Virginia. He volunteered very shortly after the secession of his native State, and for some time served as a private in the Second Virginia Cavalry, Munford's regiment, seeing much active service about Manassas and in ''Stonewall'' Jackson's Valley Campaign; but later by competitive examination received a captain's commission in the Ordnance Department, and served on General Sam. Jones' staff in Southwest Virginia, and was his chief of ordnance when in command at Charleston, South Carolina. Captain Minor's last assignment was with General Gorgas as executive officer at the Richmond Arsenal, where he was when the war ended.

After the war he conducted a school in Lynchburg, Virginia, for some years. Then he held a chair in the University of the South at Sewanee, Tennessee, till he was called to be the first president of the Virginia Agricultural and Mechanical College, now the Virginia Polytechnic Institute, at Blacksburg, Virginia, where he was for eight years. He subsequently conducted the Shenandoah Valley Academy, at Winchester, Virginia, for a good many years, and finally, while assistant principal of the Episcopal High School, near Alexandria, Virginia, an attack of grip so injured his health that he was able thereafter only to take private pupils in Baltimore.

During these later years he gave much time to historical and political studies, particularly of the times of the Civil War, and wrote a good deal on these subjects in Baltimore and Richmond papers.

In 1874 Dr. Minor received the degree of LL.D. from William and Mary College.

In 1860 he married Miss Fanny Ansley Cazenove, of Alexandria, Virginia. Two children survive him, Fanny, wife of Rev. James F. Plummer, of Clarksburg, West Virginia, and Anne, wife of Rev. A. G. Grinnan, of Weston, West Virginia.

Dr. Minor died suddenly, Monday, July 13, 1903, at "Beaulieu" in Albemarle County, Virginia, the residence of his brother-in-law, R. M. Fontaine, Esq.

Dr. Minor was a devout Christian and loyal churchman; for many years of his life a vestryman, sometimes a delegate in the Councils of the diocese; always striving to do his duty in that state of life unto which it pleased God to call him. The writer knows none who have more fully illustrated the character of the Christian gentleman as drawn by Thackeray in the "End of the Play."

> "Come wealth or want, come good or ill,
>   Let young and old accept their part,
> And bow before the awful will,
>   And bear it with an honest heart.
> Who misses or who wins the prize,—
>   Go, lose or conquer as you can;
> But if you fail or if you rise,
>   Be each, pray God, a gentleman."

PREFACE

Since the publication of a pamphlet called *The Real Lincoln,* the author has found in the *Official Records of the Union Army,* published by the United States War Department, and in other works by people of Northern sympathies, much that is interesting and curious to corroborate the points made in the pamphlet, and to establish other points of no less value for the vindication of the cause of the South, and for the establishment of the conclusion arrived at on the 57th page of the pamphlet that "the North and West were never enemies of the South" —a conclusion as little expected and as surprising to the author as it can be to anyone else. The final result of these studies is herewith given in a volume with the same title as the pamphlet, meeting the demand for a second edition of that work, but largely increased by part of the accumulations above described.

Some explanation is needed of the nature and aim of the work, and it is submitted, as follows:

A mistaken estimate of Abraham Lincoln has been spread abroad very widely, and even in the South an editorial in a leading religious paper lately said as follows: "Our country has more than once been singularly fortunate in the moral character and the admirable personality of its popular heroes. Washington, Lincoln and Lee have been the type of character that it was safe to hold up to the admiration of their own age and the imitation of succeeding generations." In the North the paean of praise that began with his death has grown to such extravagance that he has been called by one eminent popular speaker, "a servant and follower of Jesus Christ," and by another "first of all that have walked the earth after the Nazarene," and on his late birthday a eulogist asked us to give up aspirations for a heaven where Lincoln's presence is not assured. A very distinguished preacher, on Easter succeeding the Good Friday on which Lincoln was assassinated, called him "A Christian man—a servant and follower of Jesus Christ— . . . one whom we have revered as a father, and loved more than we can love any human friend," set forth a comparison between his death and that of the Saviour of Mankind, likening Wilkes Booth to Pilate, and ended with, "Shall we not say of the day, it is fit?" It was on Good Friday that Lincoln was shot, and in a theatre.

To try to reawaken or to foster ill-will between the North and the South would be a useless, mischievous and most censurable task, and it will be seen at pages 13–14 of this book that it has an exactly opposite purpose, but it is a duty to correct such misrepresentations, for the reason that they make claims for Lincoln entirely inconsistent with the concessions of grave defects in him that are made by the closest associates of his private life; by the most respectable and most eulogistic biographers and historians of his own day and of this day, at home and abroad, who have described his character and career, and equally inconsistent with the estimates of him by the greatest and closest associates of his public life, and by a very large part of the great Northern and Western Republican leaders of his own day. The fact that the evidence submitted comes from such witnesses, and such witnesses only, is the chief claim that this book has upon the interest and confidence of its readers, and attention is called to the extraordinary cogency of such evidence, and to the fact that not a word of testimony is offered out of the mass that might be offered from the eminent writers, speakers, statesmen, and soldiers who took the Southern side.

In the Appendix will be found, in alphabetical order, the names of all the witnesses whose evidence is submitted. Reference is invited to that Appendix, as each witness is reached by the reader, and especially in every case where the reader finds it hard to believe the evidence, and it will be found that each is included in one of the above indicated classes. Only old and exceptionally well-informed men of this day are likely to know the ample authority with which these witnesses speak. See Lincoln himself; see Generals U. S. Grant, and Wm. T. Sherman; see Lincoln's greatest Cabinet Ministers, Seward, Chase, and Stanton; see, among the foremost leaders of thought and action of their day, John Sherman, Ben Wade, and Thaddeus Stevens; see representatives of the highest intellectual and moral standards, Richard Dana, Edward Everett, Charles Francis Adams, and Robert Winthrop; see the most ardent and prominent Abolitionists, Senator Sumner, and Wendell Phillips; see Horace Greeley, whose lofty integrity extorted admiration from thousands on whose nearest and dearest interests his *Tribune* newspaper waged a war as deadly as it was honest; see the correspondent of the London *Times*, Russell; see the most 1902, up-to-date historians of our own day, Ida Tarbell, A. K. McClure, Schouler, Ropes, and Rhodes; and see the most intimate associates of Lincoln's lifetime, Lamon and Herndon, who give such reasons for telling not the good only, but *all* they know about their great friend, as win commendation from the latest biographers of all, Morse and Hapgood, whose books have received only praise from the American reading public.

The following objection has been made to the first edition of this work: "What has the author himself to say about Lincoln? Nothing is found from the author himself; only what other people have said or written.'' It was the author's purpose to submit the testimony of certain classes above described, and to leave the reader to draw his own conclusions.

Another objection has been offered, that this book gives only the bad side of Lincoln, and not the good. The author makes the acknowledgment that the largest measure of every excellence—intellectual, moral, and spiritual —has been claimed for Lincoln, and very generally conceded to him, and space need not be given to reciting those claims, because they are familiar to all who have given the least attention to Lincoln's place in the world's esteem, and because to give them any adequate statement would require a space like the ten very large volumes in which Nicolay and Hay have done that work so ably and with such jealous protection of their hero's good name. Not only does the author concede that these comprehensive claims have been made and have been generally admitted, but the Appendix shows that even the strongest of these claims have been made, in whole or in part, by most of the very witnesses whose testimony is quoted in this book. To reconcile the damaging concessions with the contradictory claims by the same witnesses is not the duty of the author of this book. An examination of the chapter headed *Apotheosis of Lincoln* will, however, discover some explanation of these contradictions. It was a saying of Lord Somers that often the most material part of testimony is that on which the witness values himself the least.

A third objection has been made, that this book gives the testimony of Lincoln's enemies. Who were Lincoln's friends, if they are not included among these witnesses, and which of these witnesses was not on his side in the great contest?

THE REAL LINCOLN

CHAPTER I

APOTHEOSIS OF LINCOLN [1]

FEW who read this book will escape the conclusion that The Real Lincoln was a very different man, in his private and in his public life, from what the world's verdict has pronounced him to be. The question then must arise in the mind of every one interested in his history, how so false an estimate of him was impressed on men's minds. The way it was done has been described more or less fully by several of his eulogists, as is now about to be shown; and a name, *Apotheosis,* has been given to the process of deification by four of his ardent eulogists.[2] *The Century Dictionary* defines the word apotheosis as "deification; excessive honor paid to any great or distinguished person; the ascription of extraordinary virtues or superhuman qualities to a human being."

Allen Thorndike Rice describes[3] the process as

---

[1] In previous editions this chapter and the one immediately following, entitled "What This Book Would Teach," appeared as the last two chapters. As explaining why the book was written and what it hopes to accomplish, they logically belong at the first, hence the change of position in this edition.— Editor.

[2] Horace White, John Russell Young, Ward H. Lamon and Vice-President Hamlin.

[3] Introduction to *Reminiscences of Lincoln, &c.,* p. 18.

1

follows: "Story after story, and trait after trait, as varying in value as in authenticity, have been added to the Lincolniana until at last the name of the great War President has come to be a biographical lode-stone, attracting without . . . discrimination both the true and false." Horace White says,[4] "The popular judgment of him is in the main correct and unshakable. I say in the main, because in this judgment there is a tendency to *apotheosis* which, while pardonable, is not historical, and will not last." And he goes on (p. 21), "The popular conception of Mr. Lincoln as one not seeking public honors . . . is a *post bellum* growth; . . . he was (p. 22) in hot, incessant competition with his fellows for earthly honors."

Horace White goes on (p. 26), "What Mr. Lincoln was after he became President can best be understood by knowing what he was before. The world owes more to Mr. William H. Herndon for this particular knowledge than to all other persons taken together."

As late as September 14, 1901, the *Church Standard,* of Philadelphia said of McKinley that "like Abraham Lincoln five and thirty years ago, he was hardly known for what he was until he died." General Keifer said (*Slavery and Four Years of War,* p. 178), "But President Lincoln was not understood in 1861 nor even later during the war, and not fully during life, by either his enemies or his personal or party friends." Schouler says of Gen.

---

[4] Introduction to a later book claiming to be Herndon's *Abraham Lincoln.* See the Appendix at the name of Herndon.

William T. Sherman's first interview with Lincoln (*History of the United States,* Vol. VI, p. 23) that he "left the mansion . . . silenced and mortified," and General Sherman himself says of the interview (*Memoir,* Vol. I, p. 168), "I was sadly disappointed, and remember that I broke out on John,[5] d——ning the politicians generally, saying 'you have got things in a hell of a fix.'" Rhodes says (*History of the United States,* Vol. IV, p. 211), "The hand that draws the grotesque trait of Lincoln may disappoint the hero-worshipper, but the truth of the story requires this touch which . . . and . . . serves as a justification for these who could not in the winter of 1862–'3 see with the eyes of to-day." . . .

The biographer of Ex-Vice-President Hamlin says,[6] "Indeed Mr. Hamlin was of the opinion that no man ever grew in the executive chair in his lifetime as Lincoln did. . . . Lincoln's growth has long been a favorite theme with writers and speakers; . . . his extreme eulogists made the mistake of constructing a Lincoln who was as great the day he left Springfield as when he made his earthly exit four years later. Lincoln's astonishing development was thus ignored, and . . . There is no intention of reviving an issue that once caused wide discussion. . . . Mr. Hamlin came to the ultimate opinion that Lincoln was the greatest figure of the age. . . . But he saw two Lincolns." . . .

In these last extracts the biographer makes us

[5] His Brother, Senator John Sherman, had introduced him to the President.
[6] *Life and Times of Hannibal Hamlin,* by C. E. Hamlin, p. 393.

aware of two things—that Lincoln's Vice-President was long in discovering his greatness and that efforts were made to check the apotheosis when it began. No one who knows the history of the time, as told by the most ardent Northern historians, such as Rhodes, or Ropes, or Schouler, will wonder that the contest ceased on the "issue that once caused wide discussion." Lalor's Cyclopaedia quotes the official records to show that thirty-eight thousand men and women had been dealt with by courts-martial. Many incurred imprisonment, often long and torturing, and not a few the death sentence and execution.[7] No doubt some who had disapproved the conquest and the emancipation were tempted to join in the *io triumphe*, and to share the monstrous spoils. The vast number who had opposed the whole war could hardly do else than despair and acquiesce. Fresh from a system that placed provost marshals wherever needed, and furnished veteran soldiers to repress resistance, only very bold men would venture to provoke the dominant powers by criticising him who had won the victory and the title of martyr. No protest could get a hearing over the din of triumph. From the South protest was hopeless. It was the *Reconstruction Period,* a time now regarded with complacency by none or very few.

Hamlin's biographer, his son, further goes on to say (p. 489), "The truth should be emphasized that it is a great mistake to judge public men of this time by their attitude toward Lincoln," and he names among those who opposed and bitterly cen-

[7] See page 141 of this book.

sured Lincoln (p. 50, p. 51 and p. 449), Chandler, Wade, Sumner, Collamer, Trumbull, Hale, Wilson, Stevens, H. Winter Davis (p. 454), Grimes, Julian, Governor Andrew, of Massachusetts, David Dudley Field, John Jay, Wendell Phillips, Horace Greeley, Wm. Cullen Bryant, and Secretary Chase. Schouler says (*History of the United States,* Vol. VI, p. 21), "Yet Lincoln was long believed by contemporaries secondary in point of statesmanship. . . . Lincoln, as one of fame's immortals, does not appear in the Lincoln of 1861, whom men outside of the administration[8] likened in ridicule to *the original gorilla.*"

Morse says (Lincoln, Vol. I, p. 75) of Lincoln's "elaborate speech" in Congress on his resolutions nicknamed "the Spot Resolutions," which Congress did not notice by any action: "It may be not a very great or remarkable speech, but it was a good one," . . . and says the resolutions "were sufficiently noteworthy to save Lincoln from being left among the nobodies of the House." This is *faint praise* for Lincoln's career in Congress.

John Russell Young is quoted[9] as follows: "I have never read a description of him that recalls him as I knew him. Something always beyond and beyond. Nor has fame been kind to him in the sense that fame is never kind unless it is just. There is little justice in much that is written of Lincoln. Then comes the dismal fear that he is to live in an

---

[8] His Chief Cabinet Ministers, Stanton and Chase, were not outside of the administration. See what they called him, page 39 of this book.

[9] *Review in N. Y. Times* for January 18, 1902, p. 34.

apotheosis. His sad fate may invite this; assassination is ever a consecration, for thus do the gods ap-
point their compensations. . . . The figure van-
ishes into mists; incense vapors a vision, not a man.
For of such is human sympathy and human love."

And the reviewer goes on, "If Lincoln could have
chosen, Mr. Young thinks, and justly, that he would
have desired to be remembered as he was, and not
looked at through any distorting medium like the
aureole and crowning flame of martyrdom. . . .
Mr. Lincoln did not impress the capital as a welcome
personal force. Living in an element of detraction,
he was not a popular man. It would be hard to recall his friends."

No longer ago than February, 1902, a journal as
strongly Republican as *Leslie's Weekly* published a
paper called *Mr. Lincoln's Habits and Tendencies,*
which contained the following: "Mr. Lincoln's
neighbors in Springfield cannot yet realize that he
was a marvelously great man. . . . They think
there has been a mistake made, somehow; as he
presented himself to them, he was decidedly *of the
earth, earthy.*"

In order to express his regret for the fact that [10]
"the men whose acquaintance with Lincoln was intimate enough to form any just estimate of his character, . . . did not more fully appreciate his
statesmanship and other great qualities; . . .

---

[10] Rhodes, in his *History of the United States*, Vol. III., p. 368, note,
records that R. Fuller, a prominent Baptist preacher, wrote Chase: "I
marked the President closely. . . . He is wholly inaccessible to Christian
appeals, and his egotism will ever prevent his comprehending what patriotism
means."

that they did not recognize him as the greatest patriot, statesman and writer of his time," Rhodes makes the important concession (*History of the United States,* Vol. IV, p. 211, *et seq.*), "We cannot wonder that his contemporaries failed to perceive his greatness."

How ve.ṛy far this "failure to appreciate his greatness" prevailed among the many eminent literary men of the North is noteworthy, for the world has been much misled about it. Horace Scudder, long editor of the *Atlantic Monthly,* says of the sixth stanza of the famous *Commemoration Ode (Biography of Lowell,* Vol. XI, p. 70), "Into these three score lines Lowell has poured a conception of Lincoln which may justly be said to be today the accepted idea which Americans hold of their great President. It was the final expression of the judgment which had been slowly forming in Lowell's own mind, and when he summed him up in his last line, 'New birth of our new soul, the first American,' he was honestly throwing away all the doubts which had from time to time beset him."

The words "the judgment which had been slowly forming" and "doubts which had from time to time beset him," can be understood from the following extracts, and others that might be made from the *Biography.* Vol. XI, p. 29, records that Lowell wrote a friend in December, 1861, "I confess that my opinion of the government does not improve. . . . I guess an ounce of Frémont is worth a pound of Long Abraham." Three years later he wrote Mr. Norton (Vol. XI, p. 55), "I hear bad things about Mr. Lincoln, and try not to believe them.'' How very late Lowell did throw away the doubts about Lincoln which had beset him is curiously shown by Scudder's reluctant concession of the fact (Vol. XI, p. 70) that Lincoln was not referred to at all in the ode as delivered (July 21, 1865) by Lowell on Commemoration Day at Harvard, but was subsequently introduced into it. Scudder says (Vol. XI, p. 70), ''The sixth stanza was not recited, but was written immediately, afterward.'' Laboring to explain this, he is obliged to call it ''an after-thought,'' and to say, ''one likes to fancy the whole force of the ode behind it,'' though he has shown that any such *fancy* would be entertained in defiance of the facts he records. If this ''after-thought'' did occur to Lowell ''immediately'' after, it did not occur to him, according to Scudder's own dates, sooner than ninety days after Lincoln's assassination; and it is a curious additional example of his *apotheosis,* that this ''conception of Lincoln'' should have become, as Scudder says, ''the accepted idea which Americans hold of their great President.'' The *New York Nation,* November 28, 1901, says, reviewing Scudder's *Life of Lowell,* ''Lowell's growing appreciation of Lincoln is an important trait. A good many will be grieved to learn that the great Lincoln passage in the *Commemoration Ode* was not a part of it when it was first read by its author, but was written subsequently.'' The same *Nation* reveals that but for Lowell's wife, he would have gone ''hopelessly wrong on the main question of his time.''

However late Lowell's favorable judgment of Lincoln was formed, Scudder quotes (Vol. XI, p. 71) from a paper in the *Century Magazine* for April, 1887, headed *Lincoln and Lowell,* as follows: "Lowell was the first of the leading American writers to see clearly and fully and enthusiastically the greatness of Abraham Lincoln."

All of this testimony to the fact that people found in Lincoln before his death nothing remarkably good or great, but on the contrary found him the reverse of goodness or greatness, comes from witnesses the most trustworthy possible, they being what lawyers call *unwilling witnesses.* So far, however, as they testify, either directly or by suggestion, that a marvelous change, intellectual, moral and spiritual came over Lincoln after his entrance on the duties of President, their evidence has no such weight as that recorded by them against him, and has a strong presumption against its truth.

Gen. Donn Piatt presents very effectively his view of how the change of the American world's feeling toward Lincoln, and of its estimate of him, came about. In *Reminiscences of Lincoln* (p. 21) he says: "Lincoln was believed by contemporaries secondary in point of talent" and "Lincoln as one of Fame's immortals does not appear in the Lincoln of 1861, whom men . . . likened to 'the original gorilla.' " [11] "Fictitious heroes have been embalmed in lies, and monuments are being reared to the memories of men whose real histories, when they

---

[11] Schouler, in his *History of the United States,* Vol. VI., p. 21, uses without quotation marks the exact words of Piatt above quoted.

come to be known, will make this bronze and marble the monuments of our ignorance and folly.'' And again he says (*Reminiscences of Lincoln, &c.,* p. 477): ''With us, when a leader dies, all good men go to lying about him, and, from the monument that covers his remains to the last echo of the rural press, in speeches, sermons, eulogies and reminiscences, we have naught but pious lies.'' . . . ''Poor Garfield . . . was almost driven to suicide by abuse while he lived. He fell by the hand of an assassin, and passed in a moment to the rôle of popular saints. . . . Popular beliefs in time come to be superstitions and create gods and devils. Thus Washington is deified into an impossible man, and Aaron Burr has passed into a like impossible monster. Through this same process, Abraham Lincoln, one of our truly great, has almost gone from human knowledge (the *Reminiscences* are dated 1886). I hear of him and read of him in eulogies and biographies, and fail to recognize the man I encountered for the first time in the canvass that called him from private life to be President of the United States.'' Piatt then goes on to describe [12] a conference that he and General Schenck had with Lincoln in his home in Springfield. ''I soon discovered that this strange and strangely-gifted man, while not at all cynical, was a sceptic; his view of human nature was low; . . . he unconsciously accepted for himself and his party the same low line that he awarded the South. Expressing no sym-

[12] *Reminiscences of Lincoln, &c.,* p. 480: ''Lincoln had just been nominated for the first time.''

pathy for the slave, he laughed at the Abolitionists [13]
as a disturbing element easily controlled, without
showing any dislike to the slave-holders. . . .
We were not (p. 481) at a loss to get at the fact and
the reason for it, in the man before us. Descended
from the poor-whites of a slave State, through many
generations, he inherited the contempt, if not the
hatred, held by that class for the negroes. A self-
made man, . . . his strong nature was built on
what he inherited, and he could no more feel a
sympathy for that wretched race than he could for
the horse he worked or the hog he killed.[14] In this
he exhibited the marked trait that governed his public life. . . . He knew and saw clearly that the
people of the free States not only had no sympathy
with the abolition of slavery, but held fanatics, as
Abolitionists were called, in utter abhorrence.
While it seemed a cheap philanthropy, and therefore popular, to free another man's slave, the unrequited toil of the slave was more valuable to the
North than to the South. With our keen business
instincts, we of the free States utilized the brutal
work of the master. They made, without saving,

[13] Mrs. Lincoln was present, and General Piatt adds, "One of Mrs. Lincoln's
interjected remarks was, 'The country will find how we regarded that Abolition
sneak, Seward.'" Rhodes says, in his *History of the United States,* Vol. II.,
p. 325: "Lincoln was not, however, in any sense of the word, an Abolitionist."
Whitney, too, says in his *On Circuit with Lincoln,* p. 634, "He had no intention to make voters of the negroes—in fact their welfare did not enter his
policy at all." Rhodes quotes, in his *History of the United States,* Vol. IV.,
p. 64, note, testimony of General Wadsworth, who was in daily communication, frequently for five or six hours, with the President and Stanton, as
follows: "He never heard him speak of anti-slavery men otherwise than as
'radicals,' 'abolitionists'; and of the 'nigger question' he frequently spoke."

[14] "Herndon's *Lincoln,* Vol. V., p. 74, *et seq.,* tells a story of Lincoln's
barbarous cruelty, *etc.*"

all that we accumulated. . . . Wendell Phillips, the silver-tongued advocate of human rights, was, while Mr. Lincoln was talking to us, being ostracised at Boston and rotten-egged at Cincinnati. . . . The Abolitionist was (p. 482) hunted and imprisoned under the shadow of Bunker Hill Monument as keenly as he was tracked by bloodhounds at the South.''

Then General Piatt candidly repudiates the false pretensions that are so often made to lofty, benevolent purpose in those who ''conquered the rebellion,'' and ends as follows: ''We are quick to forget the facts and slow to recognize the truths that knock from under us our pretentious claims to high philanthropy. As I have said, abolitionism was not only unpopular when the war broke out, but it was detested. . . . I remember when the Hutchinsons were driven from the camps of the Potomac Army by the soldiers, for singing their Abolition songs, and I remember well that for nearly two years of our service as soldiers we were engaged in returning slaves to their masters when the poor creatures sought shelter in our lines.''

CHAPTER II

IN VIEW of what this book presents, those who have learned to rate Lincoln highest can hardly refuse to modify their estimation of him, and it was with the purpose to effect such a change in men's minds, in the interest of truth, that the task was undertaken. But the search in Northern records has taught the writer another truth, and a more important one, that he was far from seeking. To gain the ear of the people of Northern prejudices by presenting no testimony but that of Northern witnesses was the plan adopted in seeking materials for this sketch. To win more patient hearing from people of Southern prejudices, it had been contemplated to put on the title page as motto *Fas est ab hoste doceri*. But the search showed that the North and the West were never enemies of the South; that those who disapproved, deplored, bitterly censured secession, for the most part disapproved yet more coercion of sister States and emancipation of the negroes, while a vast part thought the South was asking what she had a right to ask.

Should we forget these things as matters of reproach upon our country's past? Should we not rather recall them now and earnestly weigh them and take courage from the recollection that not in

13

the border States only, but in every State, many men were found ready to make formidable resistance with loss of fortune, liberty, and life to what its most ardent eulogists call a complete military despotism? May their sons work with us to prevent or, if need be, to resist like evils in the future!

So it is to forgetfulness of the sad quarrel—to love, not to resentment or hate—that the lessons of this book would lead its readers. Those who taught that there was "an irrepressible conflict" between the North and South were but a handful of fanatics —the same who denounced the Constitution of the United States as a "covenant with hell, and a league with death."[1]

Is it not shown in this book that it would have been nearer the truth to say that the North and the South were essentially of one accord on the two questions, whether a State might, at least as a revolutionary right, withdraw from the Union, and whether the negroes should be emancipated?

Is it not an immense gain to know that the facts were as set forth above, rather than go on believing the story that has spread so widely—that one side carried fire and sword into the homes of the other as a punishment they believed the sufferer well deserved? Can those who suffered the great wrong really forgive and forget while events are so recorded in history?

[1] Such, Gen. B. F. Butler says, was . . . "the proposition of the Free-Soil party, as enunciated by William Lloyd Garrison," as late as 1849.

CHAPTER III

WAS LINCOLN HEROIC?

BEFORE considering the testimony as to Lincoln's moral and religious character that is furnished by the two intimate friends of his whole lifetime, Ward H. Lamon and William H. Herndon, readers should examine carefully what is told of them in the Appendix under their names, in order to see the extraordinary conclusiveness of their testimony. Besides this, the reader will find proof there that when no one of the many distinguished eulogists of Lincoln had ventured to try to controvert or even to contradict what Lamon and Herndon call their "revelations" and "ghastly exposures" about Lincoln, although Lamon's book was published as long ago as 1872 and Herndon's as long ago as 1888, defenders of Lincoln were reduced to the strait of publishing as late as the years 1892 and 1895 two books with titles similar to the genuine books of Lamon and Herndon, which new books make no reference to the existence of the earlier books, contain the frank avowals of Lamon and Herndon that they mean to tell all the gravest faults of their hero along with his virtues and omit the "revelations" and "ghastly exposures."

Among the heroic traits claimed for Lincoln is personal courage. This claim is hard to reconcile with his carefully concealed midnight ride into

Washington a day or two before his inauguration. A. K. McClure[1] has been at no small pains to apologize for it, describes the midnight journey, and says: "His answer to solicitations at a dinner given him by Governor Curtin in Harrisburg—to go as he did go to Washington—was substantially, and I think exactly, in these words: 'I cannot consent. What would the nation think of its President stealing into the Capital like a thief in the night." McClure calls these words "painfully pathetic." Lamon describes (*Recollections of Lincoln, &c.*, p. 39, *et seq.*) a conference with his friends in Harrisburg in the evening of the same day, in which conference Lincoln decided to make the midnight journey, though warned by Colonel Sumner that it "would be a damned piece of cowardice." Lamon says (*Life of Lincoln,* p. 526, *et seq.*): "Mr. Lincoln soon learned to regret the midnight ride. His friends reproached him, his enemies taunted him. He was convinced that he had committed a grave mistake in yielding to the solicitations of a professional spy, and of friends too easily alarmed. He saw that he had fled from a danger purely imaginary, and felt the shame and mortification natural to a brave man under such circumstances. . . ." The Hon. Henry L. Dawes says (*Tributes from his Associates,* p. 4): "He never altogether lost to me the look with which he met the curious and, for the moment not very kind gaze of the House of Representatives on that first morning after what they deemed a pusillanimous creep into

[1] *Lincoln and Men of the War Time,* p. 46, *et seq.*, and *Our Presidents and How We Make Them,* p. 180 to 181, *et seq.*

Washington." Lamon was (see Appendix, at his name) then and thereafter to the end of his life the intimate friend of Lincoln, had come with him from Springfield, and was chosen[2] as the one heavily-armed companion of the midnight journey; but (*Life of Lincoln,* pp. 512-513) he expressly declares that "it is perfectly manifest that there was no conspiracy—no conspiracy of a hundred, of fifty, of twenty, of three; no definite purpose in the heart of even one man to murder Mr. Lincoln at Baltimore."

Dorothy Lamon's book, *Recollections of Abraham Lincoln by Ward H. Lamon,* though its object seems to be (see Appendix at name of Lamon) to conceal some of Lincoln's most evil traits, quotes him as saying to Lamon, "You also know that the way we skulked into this city in the first place has been a source of shame and regret to me, for it did look so cowardly." Horace Greeley (*American Conflict,* Vol. I., p. 421) likened Lincoln to "a hunted fugitive." Rhodes says of the midnight journey (*History of the United States,* Vol. III., p. 304): "This drew ridicule from his enemies and expressions of regret from many of his well wishers." Nicolay and Hay devote a chapter (XX of Vol. III) to it, but do not claim that there was any danger. Morse, as jealous to defend Lincoln as any other, concedes that there was no danger at all, and that "Lamon's account of it . . . is doubtless the most trustworthy," and records Lincoln's regret and shame for what he had done.[3]

---

[2] A. K. McClure's *Lincoln and Men of the War Time,* p. 46, *et seq.*

[3] See Appendix at Morse's name, and his *Life of Lincoln,* p. 197, *et seq.*

Ida Tarbell describes (*McClure's Magazine* for January and February, 1900) Lincoln's progress through the city to his inaugural ceremony—the strong military force, including artillery, assembled to protect him—"platoons of soldiers" at the street corners, "groups of riflemen on the housetops," and shows how he passed through a board tunnel into the Capitol building, "with fifty or sixty soldiers under the platform," and that "two batteries of artillery were in adjacent streets and a ring of volunteers surrounded the waiting crowd." Dr. E. Benjamin Andrews (*History of the United States*, Vol. III, p. 324) gives nearly the same account but does not mention the tunnel.

Schouler says (*History of the United States*, Vol. VI, p. 6, *et seq.*): "The carriage in which Lincoln and Buchanan came and returned over Pennsylvania Avenue had been closely guarded in front and rear by a military escort of regulars and the District militia. Cavalry detachments protected the crossings at the great squares; skilled riflemen were posted on the roofs of convenient houses with orders to watch windows from which a shot might be fired. On Capitol Hill the private entrance and exit of the presidential party was through a covered passageway on the north side, lined by police, with trusted troops near by, ... with a battery of light artillery on the brow of the hill." . . . The story of the midnight journey and of the inauguration make quite comprehensible what Vice-President Hamlin (*Hamlin's Life of Hamlin*, p. 389) and the above quoted historians record that Lincoln was

bitterly ashamed ever afterward of what he had done
on these two occasions.

When Baltimore had stopped the Massachusetts
soldiers, and Maryland had stopped all soldiers going to Washington, Ida Tarbell, Nicolay and Hay,
Schouler and Rhodes, give singular accounts of Lincoln's state of apprehension. Rhodes and Tarbell
quote his words: "Why don't they come? Why
don't they come? I begin to believe there is no
North. The Seventh Regiment is a myth."[4] Schouler
quotes almost the same words (*History of the United
States*, Vol. VI, p. 45). Rhodes says he was "nerv-
ously apprehensive," and sympathetic. Ida Tarbell
says the words were uttered "in an anguished tone."
Curtis's *Life of Buchanan* gives a letter of Edwin
M. Stanton to the Ex-President describing this panic
in the city, which he says (Vol. II, p. 547) "was increased by the reports of the trepidation of Lincoln." . . .

Russell wrote (*My Diary, North and South,* p. 43)
in Washington, July 22d, the day after the first
Union defeat at Bull Run, "General Scott is quite
overcome; . . . General McDowell is not yet arrived; the Secretary of War knows not what to do;
Mr. Lincoln is equally helpless;" and again he wrote
later (p. 185) that Lincoln, "stunned at the tremendous calamity, sat listening in fear and trembling
for the sound of the enemy's cannon."

In the second great panic in Washington, when the
Union Army under General Pope was utterly routed

---

[4] Rhodes' *History of the United States*, Vol. III., p. 368, and Tarbell in
McClure's Magazine for February, 1899, p. 325.

and close on Washington in retreat, Gorham and
Rhodes describe Lincoln in such distress and perplexity as to say to Chase and Stanton, of his
Cabinet, that ''he would gladly resign his place.''
General B. F. Butler censures the account of Lincoln's condition given by Nicolay and Hay, as follows: ''A careful reading of that description would
lead one to infer that Lincoln was in a state of abject fear.''[5]

Russell says (*My Diary, etc.*, p. 15) that in March,
1861, in Washington, there was ''little sympathy
with, and no respect for, the newly-installed government,'' and that ''the cold shoulder is given to Mr.
Lincoln,'' and that (p. 36) ''personal ridicule and
contempt for Mr. Lincoln prevail in Washington.''

The *Life of Charles Francis Adams* describes (p.
120, *et seq.*) Adams's visit to the new President to
get his instructions as Minister to England. He got
none whatever, was ''half amused, half mortified,
altogether shocked,'' and got an impression of ''dismay'' at Lincoln's behavior and his unconsciousness
of ''the gravity of the crisis,'' or his insensibility to
it, and perceived that Lincoln was only ''intent on
the distribution of offices.'' The biographer, his son,
says that this impression had not faded from the
mind of Mr. Adams twelve years later, when he made
a *Memorial Address* on the death of Seward, as indeed plainly appears in that address, which describes
Lincoln (p. 48, *et seq.*) as displaying when he entered

---

[5] See Gorham's *Life of Stanton*, Vol. II., p. 44, *et seq.*; Rhodes' *History of
the United States*, Vol. IV., p. 137, *et seq.*, and p. 497; and *Butler's Book*,
p. 219.

on his duties as President, "moral, intellectual, and executive incompetency." The biographer goes on (p. 181, *et seq.*): "Seen in the light of subsequent events, it is assumed that Lincoln in 1865 was also the Lincoln of 1861. Historically speaking, there can be no greater error. The President, who has since become a species of legend, was in March, 1861, an absolutely unknown, and by no means promising, political quantity;" . . . and again, "none the less the fact remains that when he first entered upon his high functions, President Lincoln filled with dismay those brought in contact with him. . . . The evidence is sufficient and conclusive that, in this respect, he impressed others as he impressed Mr. Adams in this one characteristic interview." "Disgust" is the word used by Schouler (*History of the United States*, Vol. V, p. 497) to indicate the impression made by Lincoln on "the members of the Peace Conference" when they paid their respects to the President in February, 1861. Rhodes refers to them scornfully as "polished patricians," but it would be hard to name more competent judges in the matter than they were, as, for example, Ex-President Tyler.

A. K. McClure says (*Lincoln and Men of the War Time*, p. 123, *et seq.*): "Lincoln's desire for a renomination was the one thing ever apparent in his mind during the third year of his Administration," and he draws a pitiful picture (pp. 113 to 115) of Lincoln as he saw him in fits of abject depression during a considerable time after his second nomination, when he and all the leaders of the Republican party thought his defeat inevitable. McClure, describing in his later book, (*Our Presidents and How We Make Them*, p. 184) an interview with Lincoln, says, "A more anxious candidate I have never known. . . . I could hardly treat with respect his anxiety about his renomination;" and gives other details betraying contempt for Lincoln's behavior. Fry,[6] too, tells (*Reminiscences of Lincoln, etc.*, p. 590) of "a craving for a second term of the presidency," which he could not overcome, and confessed he could not, and quotes Lincoln's words, "No man knows what *that gnawing* is till he has had it."

Rhodes[7] records contempt for Lincoln expressed by his Secretary of the Treasury, Salmon P. Chase, afterwards made by Lincoln Chief Justice of the Supreme Court, and says that Chase "was by no means alone in his judgment," and that "in many Senators and Representatives existed a distrust of his ability and force of character;" and he further quotes so high an authority as Richard H. Dana, who said in a letter to Thornton Lothrop, February 23, 1863, when on visit to Washington, "The lack of respect for the President in all parties is unconcealed;" and wrote in March, 1863, to Charles Francis Adams, Minister to England, that Lincoln "has no admirers, . . . and does not act, talk, or feel like the ruler of a great empire in a great

[6] Chapter by James B. Fry in *Reminiscences of A. Lincoln by Distinguished Men of His Time*, collected and edited by Allen Thorndyke Rice (N. Y. 1886) p. 390. The full quotation is, "I observed but one craving that he (Lincoln) could not overcome; that was for a second term of the presidency. He was fully conscious of the grip this desire had upon him and once said in the way of apology for it, 'No man knows what that gnawing is till he has had it.' "

[7] *History of the United States*, Vol. IV., p. 205 to 210, *et seq.*, and note on p. 210.

crisis. . . . If a Republican convention was to be held tomorrow he would not get the vote of a State. . . . He is an unspeakable calamity to us where he is."

No heroic trait has oftener been claimed for Lincoln than tenderness of heart. General Donn Piatt (*Reminiscences of Lincoln, etc.*, pp. 486 to 489) denies the claim made for Lincoln that he was "of a kind or forgiving nature," or of any gentle impulses, and shows (p. 493) his extraordinary insensibility to the ills of his fellow-citizens and soldiers when the miseries of the war were at their worst. He says (p. 486), "There is a popular belief that Abraham Lincoln was of so kind and forgiving a nature that his gentler impulses interfered with his duty. . . . The belief is erroneous. . . . I doubt whether Mr. Lincoln had at all a kind, forgiving nature. . . . (p. 487). I heard Secretary Seward say in this connection, that President Lincoln 'had a cunning that was genius.' As for his steady refusal to sanction the death penalty in cases of desertion, there was far more policy in the course than fine feeling. . . . . As Secretary Chase said at the time, 'Such kindness to the criminal is cruelty to the army, for it encourages the cowardly to leave the brave and patriotic unsupported.' " General Piatt says referring to the leading members of the Cabinet, Seward, Chase, and Stanton, "While all these were eaten into and weakened by anxiety, Lincoln ate and slept and jested. . . . (p. 493, *et. seq.*) He faced and lived through the awful responsibility of the situation with the high courage that came of indifference. At the darkest period, for us, of the war, when the enemy's cannon were throbbing in its roar along the walls of our Capitol, I heard him say to General Schenck, 'I enjoy my rations and sleep the sleep of the innocent.' '' (P. 484.)

A delicate refinement of feeling is one of the traits often claimed for Lincoln. What he was capable of in his dealings with women is conclusively illustrated by his letter to Mrs. Browning about Miss Owens. Lamon copies it, and so do Herndon and Hapgood; Nicolay and Hay concede its authenticity in trying to make light of it; Hapgood copies, besides, another letter, in which Lincoln asks Miss Owens to marry him. Morse calls the letter to Mrs. Browning ''one of the most unfortunate epistles ever penned,'' and elsewhere calls it ''that most abominable epistle.''[8]

Acknowledging that he had lately asked Miss Owens to marry him and had been refused by her, Lincoln writes to Mrs. Browning that one of his reasons for asking her to marry him was the conviction that no other man would ever do so. Lamon speaks (page 181) of ''its coarse exaggeration in describing a person whom the writer was willing to marry, its imputation of toothless and weather-beaten old age to a woman young and handsome.''

Evidence of the marriage of Lincoln's parents has been found since Lamon's *Lincoln* was published in 1872, and like evidence of his mother's legitimate

---

[8] Lamon's *Life of Lincoln*, p. 181, *et seq.*, and Herndon's *Abraham Lincoln*, Vol. I., p. 55, and Hapgood's *Lincoln*, pp. 64 to 71, and Nicolay and Hay's *Abraham Lincoln*, Vol. I., p. 192.

birth since Hapgood's *Lincoln* was published in 1900. But Lincoln himself was capable of bringing shame upon the birth of his mother to escape the reproach of being of the unmixed "poor white" blood of the Hanks family. Herndon's *Lincoln* (Vol. I, p. 3) says: "It was about 1850, when he and I were driving in his one-horse buggy to the court in Menard county, Illinois. . . . He said of his mother . . . . that she was the illegitimate daughter of Lucy Hanks and of a well-bred Virginia farmer or planter, and he argued that from this last source came his power of analysis, his mental activity, his ambition, and all the qualities that distinguished him from the other members of the Hanks family, ... and he believed that his better nature and finer qualities came from this broad-minded, unknown Virginian." [9]

[9] "Abraham Lincoln, a North Carolinian, With Proof" by Dr. J. C. Coggins (see Appendix A) is attracting widespread attention because of startling revelations it purports to make relative to the parentage of Lincoln and the place of his birth. The author publishes many affidavits from old people in support of his claim that Lincoln was not born in Kentucky but in Rutherford county, North Carolina. A similar claim is made by James H. Cathey, of North Carolina, in a book published a few years ago under the title, "Truth is Stranger Than Fiction; True Genesis of a Wonderful Man".

CHAPTER IV

ALMOST all the Christians of Springfield, his home, opposed him for President. He was an infidel, and "when he went to church, he went to mock and came away to mimic." (Lamon's "Life of Lincoln," p. 487.) He wrote and talked against religion in the most shocking words. He never denied the charge, publicly urged, that he was an infidel. His wife and closest friends attest all this. He became reticent about his religious views when he entered political life, and thereafter indulged freely in pious phrases in his published documents and passionate expressions of piety began to abound in his speeches; but he never denied or flinched from his religious opinions and never changed them.

As to Lincoln's attitude towards religion, Dr. Holland in his *Abraham Lincoln*, says (p. 286) that twenty out of the twenty-three ministers of the different denominations of Christians, and a very large majority of the prominent members of the churches in his home, Springfield, Illinois, opposed him for President. He says (page 241): . . . "Men who knew him throughout all his professional and political life" have said "that, so far from being a religious man, or a Christian, the less said about that the better." He says of Lincoln's first recorded religious utterance, used in closing his farewell address to Springfield, that it "was regarded by many as an evidence both of his weakness and of his hypocrisy, ... and was tossed about as a joke—'old Abe's last.'"

Hapgood's *Lincoln* (page 291, *et seq.*) records that the pious words with which the Emancipation Proclamation closes were added at the suggestion of Secretary Chase, and so does Usher (*Reminiscences of Lincoln, &c.,* p. 91), and so does Rhodes; and Rhodes shows him "an infidel, if not an atheist," and adds, "When Lincoln entered political life he became reticent upon his religious opinions." (*History of the United States,* Vol. IV. p. 213 *et seq.*). Of his words that savor of religion, Lamon says (*Life of Lincoln* p. 503): "If he did not believe in it, the masses of 'the plain people' did, and no one was ever more anxious to do what was of good report among men." Lamon further says (page 497) that after Mr. Lincoln "appreciated . . . . . the violence and extent of the religious prejudices which freedom of discussion from his standpoint would be sure to rouse against him," and "the immense and augmenting power of the churches," . . . . (page 502), "he indulged freely in indefinite expressions about 'Divine Providence,' 'the justice of God,' the 'favor of the Most High,' in his published documents, but he nowhere ever professed the slightest faith in Jesus as the Son of God and the Saviour of men." (Page 501, *et seq.*) "He never told any one that he accepted Jesus as the Christ, or performed one of the acts which necessarily followed upon such a conviction." . . . "When he went to church at all, he went to mock, and came away to mimic." (Page 487.) Leland says (*Abraham Lincoln,* Vol. II, p. 55, *et seq.*): . . . "It is certain that after the unpopularity of free-thinkers had forced itself upon his mind, the most fervidly passionate expressions of piety began to abound in his speeches." Lamon tells in detail (*Life of Lincoln,* p. 157, *et seq.*) of the writing and the burning of a "little book," written by Lincoln with the purpose to disprove the truth of the Bible and the divinity of Christ, and tells how it was burned without his consent by his friend Hill, lest it should ruin his political career before a Christian people. He says that Hill's son called the book "infamous," and that "the book was burnt, but he never denied or regretted its composition; on the contrary, he made it the subject of free and frequent conversations with his friends at Springfield, and stated with much particularity and precision the origin, arguments, and object of the work." Rhodes (*History of the United States,* Vol. IV, p. 213) tells the same story, with confirmation in another place. (Vol. III, p. 368, in note.)

Herndon describes the "essay" or "book" as "an argument against Christianity, striving to prove that the Bible was not inspired, and therefore not God's revelation, and that Jesus Christ was not the Son of God." Herndon says that Lincoln intended to have the "essay" published, and further quotes one of Lincoln's associates of that day, who says that Lincoln "would come into the clerk's office where I and some young men were writing, . . .

and would bring a Bible with him; would read a chapter and argue against it."[1]

A letter of Herndon (Lamon's *Lincoln,* p. 492, *et seq.*) says of Lincoln's contest with the Rev. Peter Cartwright for Congress in 1848 (page 404): "In that contest he was accused of being an infidel, if not an atheist; he never denied the charge; would not; 'would die first,' because he knew it could be and would be proved." And Lamon further says (page 499): "The following extract from a letter from Mr. Herndon was extensively published throughout the United States about the time of its date, February 18, 1870, and met with no contradiction from any responsible source: 'When Lincoln was a candidate for our Legislature, he was accused of being an infidel; of having said that Jesus Christ was an illegitimate child. He never denied the opinions or flinched from his religious views.' "

On pages 487 to 514 Lamon's *Lincoln* copies numerous letters from Lincoln's intimate associates, one from Davis,[2] a Justice of the Supreme Court, and one from Lincoln's wife, that fully confirm the above as to his attitude of hostility to religion. Lamon copies (*Life of Lincoln,* p. 495) another letter of Herndon, as follows: "When Mr. Lincoln left this city"—Springfield, Illinois—"for Washington, I know that he had undergone no change in his religious opinions or views." And Lamon gives (page 480) a letter of Nicolay, his senior private secretary throughout his Administration, which states that he

---

[1] Herndon's *Lincoln,* Vol. III., p. 39, *et seq.,* and 439, *et seq.,* and Lamon's *Lincoln,* p. 492.

[2] The Appendix shows that he was an intimate friend of Lincoln.

perceived no change in Lincoln's attitude toward religion after his entrance on the presidency. The *Cosmopolitan,* of March, 1901, says that Nicolay "probably was closer to the martyred President than any other man; . . . that he knew Lincoln as President and as man more intimately than any other man." . . .

CHAPTER V

RHODES is everywhere jealous to defend Lincoln, but he thinks fit to record the following (*History of the United States,* Vol. IV, p. 471, note and p. 518), prefacing it with the statement that the *World* was then the organ of the best element of the Democratic party; that the *New York World,* of June 19, 1864, called Lincoln "an ignorant, boorish, third-rate, backwoods lawyer," and reported that the spokesman of a delegation sent to carry the resolutions of a great religious organization to the President publicly denounced him as "disgracefully unfit for the high office"; and that a Republican Senator from New York was reported to have left the President's presence because his self-respect would not permit him to stay and listen to the language he employed. Rhodes further sets down "a tradition" that Andrew, the great War Governor of Massachusetts, when pressing a matter he had at heart, went away in disgust at being put off by the President with "a smutty story."

Dr. Holland's *Abraham Lincoln* says of the indecency of his jokes and stories: "It is useless for Mr. Lincoln's biographers to ignore this habit; the whole West, if not the whole country (he is writing in 1866), is full of these stories, and there is no doubt at all that he indulged in them with the same freedom that he did in those of a less objectionable character.'' Again he says (page 251): . . . "Men who knew him throughout all his professional and political life . . . have said that he was the foulest in his jests and stories of any man in the country.''

This is a comprehensive indictment from one of Lincoln's most loving worshippers, as is shown at Holland's name in the Appendix, and is fully sustained by testimony submitted below from Morse, Hapgood, Piatt, Rhodes, and—most shocking testimony of all—from Lamon and Herndon.

Norman Hapgood, a very late biographer of Lincoln (of the year 1900) and Morse, the next latest (of the year 1892), confirm the ''revelations'' and the ''ghastly exposures'' about Lincoln that are described below as recorded by Lamon and by Herndon. Morse says that a necessity and duty rested on those biographers to record these truths, as they both claim was their duty, and Hapgood says, ''Herndon has told the President's early life with refreshing honesty and with more information than any one else.'' [1]

General Donn Piat records (*Memories of the Men who Saved the Union,* p. 35) an occasion when he heard Lincoln tell stories ''no one of which will bear printing.'' Lamon adds to all this his testimony (*Abraham Lincoln,* pp. 480 and 430) that this habit of Lincoln's ''was restrained by no presence and no occasion,'' and General Piatt refers to him as ''the

---

[1] Hapgood's *Abraham Lincoln*, Preface, p. 8; Morse's *Lincoln*, Vol. I., p. 13 and p. 192, *et seq.*

man who could open a Cabinet meeting called to discuss the Emancipation Proclamation by reading aloud Artemus Ward,'' and refers to Gettysburg as ''the field that he shamed with a ribald song,'' ''Picayune Bother,'' making reference to a song that Lincoln asked for and got sung on the Gettysburg battlefield the day he made his celebrated address there. (Nov. 20, 1863.) This behavior has been much discussed by his eulogists, and defended as a relief necessary for a nature so sensitive and high-wrought.''[2] ''Was ever so sublime a thing ushered in by the ridiculous?'' says Rhodes (*History of the United States,* Vol. IV, p. 167). The mood in which Lincoln issued the Proclamation is hereinafter described as set forth by his eulogists.

Herndon gives (*Abraham Lincoln,* Vol. I, p. 55, *et seq.*) a copy of a satire written by Lincoln, *The First Chronicle of Reuben,* and an account of the very slight provocation under which Lincoln wrote it, and in two footnotes describes the exceedingly base and indecent device by which Lincoln brought about the events which gave opportunity for this satire; and Herndon copies some verses written and circulated by Lincoln which he considers even more vile than the *''Chronicle.''* Of these verses Lamon says, ''It is impossible to transcribe them.'' (*Life of Lincoln,* pages 63 and 64.) Decency does not permit the publication of the *Chronicle* or the verses here.

In neither of A. K. McClure's books, *Lincoln and Men of the War Time,* published in 1892, or *Our*

[2] *Reminiscences of Lincoln, &c.,* p. 481, *et seq.,* and p. 485, *et seq.*

Presidents and How We Make Them, published in 1900, does he offer any contradiction of the "revelations" and "ghastly disclosures" that Lamon and Herndon had published to the world so long before, but McClure does say in the earlier of the books, in the preface (p. 2), "The closest men to Lincoln, before and after his election to the presidency, were David Davis, Leonard Swett, Ward H. Lamon, and William H. Herndon." Letters of the first two named are among the letters referred to above, published by Lamon as evidence of Lincoln's attitude toward religion.

If any would take refuge in the hope that the responsibilities of his high office raised Lincoln above these habits of indecency, they are met by authentic stories of his grossly unseemly behavior as President by the evidence of Lamon, the chosen associate of his life time, as given above, that his indulgence in gross jokes and stories was "restrained by no presence and no occasion."

CHAPTER VI

ESTIMATES OF LINCOLN

THE evidence thus far submitted concerns chiefly the personal character of Lincoln. Let us proceed to consider evidence to show that his conduct of public affairs provoked the bitterest censure from a very great number of the most conspicuous of his co-laborers in his achievements.

A. K. McClure says (*Lincoln and Men of the War Time*, p. 51) of Lincoln, "If he could only have commanded the hearty co-operation of the leaders of his own party, his· task would have been greatly lessened, but it is due to the truth of history to say that few, very few, of the Republicans of national fame had faith in Lincoln's ability for the trust assigned to him. I could name a dozen men, now[1] idols of the nation, whose open distrust of Lincoln not only seriously embarrassed, but grievously pained and humiliated him."

Ben Perley Poore shows (*Reminiscences of Lincoln, &c.*, p. 348) Henry Ward Beecher's censures of Lincoln, and so do Beecher's editorials in the *Independent* of 1862, of which Beecher says himself (*Reminiscences of Lincoln, &c.*, p. 249) . . . "they bore down on him very hard." Beecher's contemptuous censures are recorded by Rhodes, too (*History of the United States*, Vol. IV, p. 462); and

---

[1] McClure's title page is dated 1892.

he shows, besides, that Senator Wilson, of Masachu-
setts, was among the great body of leading Republicans who, as will be shown, bitterly opposed
Lincoln's renomination for President in 1864. He
says, too, of Wilson that his open assaults were
amazing; . . . that he was loud and bitter even
in the President's house.

Hapgood quotes (*Abraham Lincoln,* p. 164) Wendell Phillips about Lincoln: "Who is this huxter
in politics? Who is this county court lawyer?"
Morse, too, gives (*Lincoln,* Vol. I, p. 177) severe censures of Lincoln by Wendell Phillips. A. K. McClure
(*Lincoln and Men of the War Time,* p. 117, and p.
259 and p. 54, *et seq.,* and p. 104) records bitter censure of him by Thaddeus Stevens, and shows the
hostility to Lincoln of Sumner, Trumbull, Ben
Wade, and Chandler, and of his Vice-President,
Hamlin. Ida Tarbell [2] calls Senator Sumner, Ben
Wade, Henry Winter Davis, and Secretary Chase
"malicious foes of Lincoln," and makes the remarkable and comprehensive concession that "about all
the most prominent leaders . . . were actively
opposed to Lincoln," and mentions Greeley as
their chief.

Frémont, who eight years before had received
every Republican vote for President, charged Lincoln (Holland's *Abraham Lincoln,* p. 259, p. 469,
and p. 471) with "incapacity and selfishness," with
"disregard of personal rights," with "violation of
personal liberty and liberty of the press," with

[2] *McClure's Magazine,* Vol. XIII., for July, 1899, p. 277, and for July,
1899, p. 218, *et seq.*

"feebleness and want of principle"; and says: "The ordinary rights under the Constitution and laws of the country have been violated," and he further accuses Lincoln of "managing the war for personal ends."

Dr. Holland shows (*Abraham Lincoln,* p. 469, *et seq.*) that Frémont, Wendell Phillips, Fred Douglass, and Greeley were leaders in a very nearly successful effort to defeat Lincoln's second nomination, and quotes as follows, action of the convention for that purpose held in Cleveland, May 21, 1864, that "the public liberty was in danger"; that its object was to arouse the people, "and bring them to realize that, while we are saturating Southern soil with the best blood of the country in the name of liberty, we have really parted with it at home."

Colonel Theodore Roosevelt, in a speech at Grand Rapids, September 8, 1900, said that in 1864 "on every hand Lincoln was denounced as a tyrant, a shedder of blood, a foe to liberty, a would-be dictator, a founder of an empire—one orator saying, 'We also have our emperor, Lincoln, who can tell stale jokes while the land is running red with the blood of brothers.' Even after Lincoln's death the assault was kept up."

A. K. McClure (*Lincoln and Men of the War Time,* p. 54), recording the hostile attitude toward Lincoln of the leading members of the Cabinet, makes a concession as comprehensive as Miss Tarbell's above: "Outside of the Cabinet the leaders were equally discordant and quite as distrustful of the ability of Lincoln to fill his great office. Sumner, Trumbull, Chandler, Wade, Winter Davis, and the men to whom the nation then turned as the great representative men of the new political power, did not conceal their distrust of Lincoln, and he had little support from them at any time during his administration''; and McClure says again (p. 289, *et seq.*): "Greeley was a perpetual thorn in Lincoln's side . . . and almost constantly criticized him boldly and often bitterly. . . . Greeley labored (p. 296) most faithfully to accomplish Lincoln's overthrow in his great struggle for re-election in 1864." (Morse's *Lincoln,* Vol. II, p. 193.) And Edward Everett Hale shows (*James Russell Lowell and His Friends,* p. 178, *et seq.*) that even the circumstances of Lincoln's death did not for a day abate Greeley's reprobation.

The careful reader will not fail to observe that Lincoln's first term of four years was at this time nearly over, so that all this bitter censure from his associates was based on full knowledge of him.

Very few other persons, if any, were so competent to estimate Lincoln's character as the three great leaders in his Cabinet, Seward, Stanton and Chase, whose testimony we are now to examine; certainly no others had so good an opportunity to form an estimate.

Secretary Seward's estimate of Lincoln is furnished by Ida Tarbell,[3] as follows: "A less obvious perplexity than the office-seekers for Mr. Lincoln," when he entered on his duties, "though not a less real one, was the attitude of his Secretary of State

[3] *McClure's Magazine* for March, 1899, p. 448, *et seq.*

—his (Seward's) cheerful assumption that he, not Mr. Lincoln, was the final authority of the Administration; . . . he believed (p. 267), as many Republicans did, that Lincoln was unfit for the presidency, and that some one of his associates would be obliged to assume leadership . . . a sort of dictatorship; that if he, Seward were absent eight days . . . the Administration . . . would fall into consternation and despair." And Ida Tarbell quotes from Seward's letters to his wife at the time full proof of this.

Seward has been much criticised and accused of rare presumption for a letter that he wrote to the President, as Secretary of State, one month after his first inauguration, because the letter manifested a sense of superiority and condescendingly offered his advice and aid and leadership. It is possible that Seward did feel some of the contempt for Lincoln that his brethren in the Cabinet, Chase and Stanton, never ceased to express freely for Lincoln throughout their long terms of office and very frequently showed to his face, as is shown below. Like them, Governor Seward was a man of the highest social standing, and of large experience in the highest public functions. The Lincoln whom so many now call a hero and a saint is exceedingly different from the Lincoln that the people who came in contact with him knew up to the time of his death, as is frankly avowed in this sketch by Adams and Piatt, and reluctantly conceded by Crittenden and Rhodes. What he was capable of in personal habits, manners, and morals has been shown in the account

of the *"First Chronicle of Reuben,"* and his submission to humiliations such as are described below,
and elsewhere in this book, from such men as Seward, Stanton, Chase, and General McClellan, is
not at all unaccountable.

Few were more ardent Abolitionists than Seward,
as shown in Bancroft's late life of him, but he was
no tyro in statecraft, and knew the exceedingly
small number of voters in the United States who
would hear patiently of abolition.[4]   The policy Seward so authoritatively suggested was—to use the
very words of his letter[5]—"to change the question
before the public from one upon Slavery for a question upon Union or Disunion."   Lincoln at once
adopted that policy, as shown in Chapter X of this
book, and by means of it precipitated the war."
Its astuteness in distracting men's minds from the
matter of slavery has been much commended, and
Seward might well say, as he did,[6] that Lincoln "had
a cunning that was genius."   (Gen. Donn Piatt.
See p. 23 of this book.)

How successfully the *issue* was *changed* is proved
in a quotation from Lowell by Scudder (*Atlantic
Monthly* for February, 1861), as follows: "Slavery
is no longer the matter in debate, and we must be-
ware of being led off on that issue.   The matter now
in hand is . . . the reaffirmation of National
Unity."   Yet Lowell was an ardent Abolitionist, and

[4] General Butler says in *Butler's Book*, p. 293, that as late as July, 1861,
no one in power was in favor of emancipation.

[5] William Elery Curtis says in his *True Lincoln*, p. 204, an ardent eulogy,
published in 1903, that this letter of Seward's did not come to light till "nearly
thirty years after."

[6] *Reminiscences of Lincoln, &c.*, Allen Thorndike Rice, N. Y., 1886, p. 487.

not an admirer of Lincoln, as will be shown at p.
(7–8) of this book, until long after this; not, indeed,
until Lincoln's *Apotheosis* began, the *Commemoration Ode* to the contrary notwithstanding.

A. K. McClure says (*Lincoln and Men of the War
Time*, p. 151, *et seq.*): "Secretary Stanton had been
in open malignant opposition to the Administration
only a few months before." (This was in January,
1862.) "Stanton often spoke of and to public men,
military and civil, with a withering sneer. I have
heard him scores of times thus speak of Lincoln
and several times thus speak to Lincoln." . . .
"After Stanton's retirement from the Buchanan
Cabinet, when Lincoln was inaugurated, he maintained the closest confidential relations with Buchanan, and wrote him many letters expressing the
utmost contempt for Lincoln. . . . These letters, . . . given to the public in Curtis's *Life of
Buchanan,* speak freely of the painful imbecility of
Lincoln, the venality and corruption which ran riot
in the Government"; and McClure goes on: "It is
an open secret that Stanton advised the revolutionary overthrow of the Lincoln government, to be
replaced by General McClellan as Military Dictator.
. . . These letters, published by Curtis, bad as
they are, are not the worst letters written by Stanton to Buchanan. Some of them are so violent in
their expression against Lincoln . . . that they
have been charitably withheld from the public."

Hapgood refers (*Abraham Lincoln,* p. 164) to
Stanton's "brutal absence of decent personal feeling" towards Lincoln, and tells (p. 254) of Stan-

ton's insulting behavior when they met five years earlier, of which meeting Stanton said that he "had met him at the bar and found him a low, cunning clown." See also Ben Perley Poore in *Reminiscences of Lincoln, &c.,* p. 223. Morse says (*Lincoln,* Vol. I, p. 327) that Stanton "carried his revilings of the President to the point of coarse personal insults," and refers (p. 326) to his "habitual insults." Yet to a man of President Buchanan's character and standing Stanton showed an excess of deference; for Mr. Buchanan complained in a letter to his niece, Miss Harriet Lane (Curtis's *Life of Buchanan,* Vol. II, p. 533), that Stanton, when in his Cabinet, "was always on my side and flattered me *ad nauseam.*"

Schouler says of Stanton (*History of the United States,* Vol. VI, p. 159), "He denounced Lincoln in confidential speeches and letters as a coward and a fool."

Of Secretary Chase, A. K. McClure says (*Lincoln and Men of the War Time,* p. 8), "Chase was the most irritating fly in the Lincoln ointment." Ida Tarbell says (*McClure's Magazine* for January, 1899), "But Mr. Chase was never able to realize Mr. Lincoln's greatness." Nicolay and Hay say (*Abraham Lincoln,* Vol. IX, p. 389, Vol. VI, p. 264) of Chase, "Even to complete strangers he could not write without speaking slightingly about the President. He kept up this habit to the end of Lincoln's life." . . . . "But his attitude towards the President, it is hardly too much to say, was one which varied between the limits of active hostility and benevolent contempt." Yet none rate Chase higher than Nicolay and Hay do for character, talent, and patriotism. Rhodes says (*History of the United States*, Vol. IV, pp. 205 and 210) that Chase's "opinion of Lincoln's parts was not high," and that he "dealt unrestrained censure of the President's conduct of the war."

CHAPTER VII

DID LINCOLN EVER INTEND THAT THE MASTERS BE PAID FOR THEIR SLAVES?

CONSPICUOUS among the baseless claims made for Lincoln is the allegation that he proposed and really had the purpose to compensate the masters for emancipation of their negroes. Rhodes sets forth the plan (*History of the United States,* Vol. III, p. 631), and there and elsewhere labors to vindicate the claim, but he shows by a letter of Lincoln's (p. 632) that Lincoln did not himself expect that it could take any effect anywhere but in Delaware, Kentucky, Missouri, and the District of Columbia. And Rhodes acknowledges that it did take effect nowhere but in the District of Columbia, and there with compensation to "loyal" masters only. He further explains (Vol. IV, p. 218) that the slaveholders of the Border States were saved from any temptation to accept what was offered by "the belief that it was impossible for the North to conquer the South."[1] Rhodes goes on to say that the alternative was "separation of the sections with strong guarantees for slavery in the Border States which remained with the North; that the remark which it is said Lincoln made to Crittenden, 'You Southern men will soon reach the point where bonds

[1] That Lincoln's belief then was the same is shown abundantly elsewhere in this book, and that fact bears strongly on his claim for credit.

will be a more valuable possession than bondsmen,'
was far from a self-evident proposition in February,
1863; in truth, the reverse was the estimate of the
Democrats.'' And Rhodes says further (Vol. IV,
p. 68), that ''one other objection must have weighed
with them. . . . It was a part of the plan that
payment for the slaves should be made in United
States bonds; and while negro property had become
notoriously precarious, the question must have suggested itself whether, in view of the enormous ex-
penditures of the Government, the recent military
reverses, and the present strength of the Confederacy, the nation's promises to pay were any more
valuable.'' And Rhodes goes on still: ''The whole
conquered part, at least, could be counted on to resist
a payment from which themselves were excluded
—any computation of the amount to which their
slaves added would bring the compensation will
show that no one could ever dream of including
them.'' Rhodes quotes from *McPherson's Political
History* the answers, to the above effect, given by
''a majority of the Representatives in Congress of
Kentucky, Virginia, Missouri, and Maryland,'' who
gave as an additional reason that they ''did not
think the war for the Union could possibly hold out
another year, or that the offer would be carried out
in good faith; . . . that they doubted the sincerity of Congress [2] in making the offer.'' Referring
to what he calls ''current expressions'' of opinion
in England, Rhodes says (p. 79, *et seq.*): ''Lincoln's
plan of compensated emancipation was pronounced

[2] And Rhodes concedes that he does, too.

chimerical, and its purpose insincere,'' and that it was ''issued for the purpose of affecting European opinion.'' Rhodes' desire to vindicate his hero's claim betrays him into inconsistencies. Ida Tarbell, with even greater zeal, calls Lincoln's plan for emancipating the slaves ''simple, just, and impracticable,'' and says[3] ''nothing ever came of it.'' . . . .

Henry J. Raymond says,[4] ''The bill was referred to a committee, but no action was taken upon it in Congress, nor did any of the Border States respond to the President's invitation.'' And Rhodes gives a similar account of it.

Boutwell says,[5] ''It is not probable that Mr. Lincoln entertained the opinion 'that these measures, one or all, would secure the abolition of slavery.' ''

Gorham shows (*Life of Edwin M. Stanton*, p. 185) his impression of Lincoln's purpose, as follows: ''The result of this so-called Border-State policy seems to have been meagre in the way of proselyting slaveholders to the Union cause.''

A. K. McClure (*Lincoln and Men of the War Time*, p. 223) and Nicolay and Hay (*Abraham Lincoln*, Vol. X, p. 132) tell of Lincoln's offering to his Cabinet a written plan for emancipation with compensation to the amount of $400,000,000, which plan was unanimously disapproved by the Cabinet. Like the paper elsewhere described in this book, which expressed Lincoln's purposes in view of the

[3] *McClure's Magazine*, Vol. XII., April, 1899, p. 525.
[4] *Life and Public Services of President Lincoln*, p. 239.
[5] *Abraham Lincoln Tributes from His Associates*, p. 86.

almost certainly expected election of McClellan to the presidency, this plan for emancipation was sealed up by Lincoln and committed to the care of one of the Cabinet members, and this would seem the only purpose with which it could have been prepared. Rhodes quotes (*History of the United States,* Vol. IV, p. 407 and p. 409) an account of the matter in Lincoln's own words, published in a letter which Rhodes says "may be called a stump speech," as follows: "I suggested compensation, to which you answered that you wished not to be taxed to buy negroes."

It will be seen that after Lincoln's failure thus to secure the support of the Border States, he fell into despair, until new measures were devised to enlarge his powers and force on the people his re-election.

CHAPTER VIII

BEFORE treating the subject indicated by the heading of this chapter, it is convenient to state here precisely a widespread, erroneous belief which this book undertakes to correct.

The impression upon the minds of thousands of people about the War Between the States may be formulated as follows: That at the firing upon Fort Sumter, the people of the Northern States rose with one mind, and for the four years of the war ungrudgingly poured forth their treasure and shed their blood to re-establish the Union and to free the slaves. Let us consider how much foundation there is for this popular impression.

In order to show the enormous difficulties overcome by their hero, Lincoln, in accomplishing his two notable achievements, his eulogists have furnished much evidence that shows that both the coercion of the South and the emancipation of the negroes were accomplished against the will of the Democratic party and of no small part of the Republican party in the North and West, and their evidence to that effect will now be submitted.

As there had been agitation of abolition long before any one ever suggested seriously the possibility of coercion in case States should secede, as was not seldom threatened, not in the South only, but by

New England earlier and quite as earnestly, it is best to consider first how far the North and West approved of abolition.

Dr. E. Benjamin Andrews records the fact[1] that abolition was opposed by an overwhelming majority of the Northern people and the Western people, not only down to the war, but during the whole of it, and as long as opposition to it was at all safe. Bitter as his reprobation of this public sentiment is, he frankly concedes it, and says that between 1830 and 1840 "there was hardly a place of any size where any one could advocate emancipation, and that in 1841 there were but two pronounced anti-slavery men in the House of Representatives. The Rev. Edward Everett Hale says,[2] "As lately as when I left college, in 1839, my classmate, the Rev. William Francis Channing, was, I think, the only man in our class who would have permitted himself to be called an Abolitionist. I should not, I am sure."

The Life of Charles Francis Adams, by his son of the same name, records (p. 29) that Garrison was mobbed in Boston in 1835 for being an Abolitionist. See, also, page 33 and page 58. Page 105 and thereafter shows how ill-esteemed and shabby the Republican party in Washington was as late as 1859. In Edward Everett Hale's lately published book, *"James Russell Lowell, etc.,"* he names (page 22,

[1] Andrews' *History of the United States,* Vol. II., p. 15. It describes besides the destruction of charitable schools for negroes and even of their homes, by people regarded as the most respectable classes of society in Connecticut and elsewhere in New England and the prohibition by laws of schools for negro children.

[2] *Memories of a Hundred Years,* in the *Outlook* for August 2, 1902, p. 872.

et seq.) a classmate who was, he thinks, the only Abolitionist in Harvard College in 1838, and says (p. 21), "Boston, as Boston, hated Abolitionism" as the stevedores and longshoremen . . . hated "a nigger;" that Dr. Palfrey, once of the Divinity Faculty of Harvard, "like most men with whom he lived, had opposed the Abolitionists with all his might, his voice, and his pen;" and he adds that "the conflict at the outset was not a crusade against slavery." James Russell Lowell said (Scudder's *Life of Lowell*, Vol. I, p. 187) that "when Garrison showed strength in his agitation against slavery . . . a prolonged shriek of execration and horror quavered from the Aroostook to the Red river." The prominent place now given in Longfellow's works to his Abolition poems does not prepare us to hear from Scudder (*Life of Lowell*, Vol. I, p. 183) that the well-known Philadelphia publishers, Cary & Hart, brought out a handsomely illustrated volume of Longfellow's works from which this group of poems was omitted, and on the same page is a letter of Lowell's in which he refers to "Longfellow's suppression of his anti-slavery pieces."*

Schouler says (*History of the United States,* Vol. VI, p. 216), "Scarcely had an American bard struck his lyre to another chord of patriotism save the courageous Whittier;" . . . and again (p. 337, *et seq.*), "Hawthorne died, despondent of his country, in 1864. Of our galaxy of great poets Whittier alone could forge fitly in such a lurid flame."

* For Lowell's own attitude, see page (7–8) of this book.

The Rev. Henry Ward Beecher said in an address to the people of Manchester, England,[4] that in the North "Abolitionists were rejected by society, . . . blighted in political life;" that to be called an Abolitionist caused a merchant to be avoided as if he had the plague; that the "doors of confidence were closed upon him" in the church. Dr. Holland says (*Abraham Lincoln,* p. 67) that in 1830 the prevailing sentiment of Illinois was "in favor of slavery;" . . . "the Abolitionist was despised by both parties." And George William Curtis reproaches his own people (*Orations and Addresses,* Vol. I, p. 146) as follows: "We betrayed our own principles, and those who would not betray them we reviled as fanatics and traitors; we made the name of Abolitionist more odious than any in our annals. (Vol. I, p. 28.) If a man . . . died for liberty, as Lovejoy did at Alton, he was called a fanatical fool." Of the same death the editor of the book says (Vol. I, p. 131), "And the country scowled, and muttered, 'Served him right.' "[5] Curtis goes on, "The Fugitive-Slave Law was vigorously enforced in Ohio and other States." He quotes (Vol. I, p. 75, *et seq.*) a declaration of Edward Everett as Governor of Massachusetts that "discussion that leads to insurrection is an offence against the Commonwealth," and quotes Daniel Webster

---

[4] See a collection of his speeches in the Pratt Library, Baltimore, marked 53866–2557.

[5] Lovejoy was killed by a mob for incendiary agitation for Abolition—not in the South, but in Alton, Illinois, in 1836. Edwin Earle Sparks, in his *Man who Made the Nation,* quotes, at page 36, the Attorney-General of Massachusetts as saying to the public meeting that assembled in Faneuil Hall on the occasion of Lovejoy's death, "He died as the fool dieth."

that "it is an affair of high morals to aid in enforcing the Fugitive-Slave Law." He quotes (Vol. I, p. 88) a speech in 1859 of Stephen A. Douglas that fully justified slavery, and he quotes him as saying (p. 51), "If you go over into Virginia to steal her negroes, she will catch you and put you in jail, with other thieves." In the same spirit of scornful denunciation as the above, Curtis sets forth (Vol. I, pp. 80 to 82) the purpose the North entertained not to interfere with slavery. "In other free States men were flying for their lives; were mobbed, seized, imprisoned, maimed, murdered." . . . And all this was as late as 1850. "The Southern policy (Vol. I, p. 130, *et seq.*) seemed to conquer. The church, the college, trade, fashion, the vast political parties, took Calhoun's side. . . . In Boston, in Philadelphia, in New York, in Utica, in New Haven, and in a hundred villages when an American citizen proposed to say what he thought on a great public question . . . he was insulted, mobbed, chased, and maltreated. The Governor of Ohio (Vol. I, p. 131) actually delivered a citizen of that State to the demand of Kentucky to be tried for helping a slave to escape." He gives (Vol. I, p. 132) Seward's picture of the entire unanimity of the Washington Government both at home and abroad in supporting the Southern side, and says (p. 139), "Fernando Wood and the *New York Herald* were the true spokesmen of the confused public sentiment of the city of New York, when one proposed the secession of the city and the other proposed the adoption of the Montgomery

Constitution''—that is, the Constitution of the Confederate States, which was adopted at Montgomery, Alabama. And Curtis goes on: ''If the city of New York in February, 1861, had voted upon its acceptance, it would have been adopted.'' Referring to the enlistment of negroes for soldiers, Curtis says (p. 174), ''But I remember that four years ago there were good men among us who said, 'If white hands can't win this fight, let it be lost.' '' Does not Curtis here concede that ''white hands'' did not win the fight? Whether he does or not, did not Lincoln, in justification of the Emancipation Proclamation, say[6] that ''white hands'' could not or would not win the fight, and did not Lincoln frequently say afterwards in defense of his autocratic action, that but for his emancipating and arming the negroes the fight would not have been won? And—finally—did the ''white hands'' of the great North and West lack numbers or wealth or courage to win the fight, with such odds in their favor, if it had been their will?''

It is not uncommon to hear bitter reprobation of the Fugitive-Slave Laws and of the South for daring to ask the North and West to execute them. As late as the year 1902 *Harper's Weekly* said,[7] ''Some laws appeal to the human conscience for violation, such as the Fugitive-Slave Law, . . . which

[6] Rhodes' *History of the United States*, Vol. IV., p. 69, gives Lincoln's statement of the state of the case, from the diary of Secretary Welles, given in a drive with Seward and Welles, Sunday, July 13, 1862, as recorded by Nicolay and Hay, that the President ''had about come to the conclusion that it was a military necessity, absolutely essential for the salvation of the nation, that we must free the slaves or be ourselves subdued.''

[7] Editorial of March 8th, p. 293.

was merely legislated atrocity.'' The Fugitive-
Slave Laws required citizens of States to which
slaves escaped to arrest the fugitive by the hands
of their town and county police officers and surrender him to his master. It was *dirty work* which
gentlemen in the South did with great reluctance,
if at all, for their neighbors. Joel Chandler Harris
pictures faithfully, in his *Aaron in the Woods,* the
sympathy, and aid and comfort too, that the run-
away had and the reprobation of the master who
did not keep his negroes happy and content at
home. Better proof can hardly be imagined to
show how far the North and West were from favor-
ing emancipation than the following facts about
the Fugitive-Slave Laws.

As to the attitude of the people, Dr. E. Benjamin
Andrews, who is still an ardent admirer of the Abolitionists, concedes, as a bitter reproach to the North
and West (*History of the United States,* Vol. III, p.
240), that the Fugitive-Slave Laws were passed by
a Congress that had a decided majority of Northern
men. George William Curtis says (*Orations and
Addresses,* Vol. I, p. 29), ''The Fugitive-Slave Bill
was passed. . . . The North seemed to be eager
for shame. The Free States hurried to kiss the
foot of the monstrous power that claimed the most
servile allegiance.'' . . . The Fugitive-Slave
Law was vigorously enforced in other States. The
Life of William Lloyd Garrison quotes, in a note on
page 60, from a letter from Washington in the *New
York Herald* of May 16, 1862, as follows: ''The
Fugitive-Slave Law is being quietly enforced in this

district today, the military authorities not inter-
fering with the judicial process. There are at least
four hundred cases pending." Observe that this
was nine months after the first battle of Manassas,
or Bull Run.

As to Lincoln's own attitude towards the Fugitive-Slave Laws, we have the following testimony
from the following witnesses: Dr. Holland
(*Abraham Lincoln,* p. 347) and Markland tell us
(*Reminiscences of Lincoln, &c.,* p. 317) that Lincoln
repeatedly pledged himself to the execution of them;
that he promised a prominent Kentucky Democrat
that "the Fugitive-Slave Law will be better admin-
istered than it has ever been under that of my
predecesors;" that "he voluntarily and frequently
declared that he considered the slaveholders entitled
to a fugitive-slave law." Ida Tarbell quotes from
a letter of Lincoln's (*McClure's Magazine* for December, 1898, p. 162), "You know I think that the
Fugitive-Slave clause of the Constitution ought to
be enforced—to put it in the mildest form, ought
not to be resisted." She gives, too, in another copy
of the same magazine, a letter of Lincoln's to
Alexander H. Stephens, late Vice-President of the
Confederate States, referring to fears entertained
by the South that he might interfere directly or
indirectly with the slaves, and assures Stephens
"that there is no cause for such fears. The South
would be in no more danger in this respect than in
the days of Washington." Even Nicolay and Hay
concede (*Abraham Lincoln,* Vol. III, p. 253 and p.
258) that he "backed the Fugitive-Slave Laws fully,

in writing." His Inaugural gave a fresh promise that he would execute them.

As to Lincoln's views about abolition, we have his own full and distinct avowal, made in his speech in reply to Douglas at Peoria, Illinois, October 16, 1854:[8]

"Before proceeding let me say that I think I have no prejudice against the Southern people. They are just what we would be in their situation. If slavery did not now exist among them, they would not introduce it. If it did exist among us, we should not instantly give it up. This I believe of the masses, North and South. Doubtless there are individuals on both sides who would not hold slaves under any circumstances, and others who would gladly introduce slavery anew if it were not in existence. We know that some Southern men do free their slaves, go North, and become tip-top Abolitionists, while some Northern ones go South and become most cruel slave-masters.

"When Southern people tell us they are no more responsible for the origin of slavery than we are, I acknowledge the fact. When it is said that the institution exists, and it is very difficult to get rid of it in any satisfactory way, I can understand and appreciate the saying. I surely will not blame them for not doing what I should not know how to do myself. If all earthly power were given me, I should not know what to do as to the existing institution. My first impulse would be to free all the slaves, and

---

[8] Abraham Lincoln's complete works, edited by Messrs. Nicolay and Hay, Vol. I., p. 186.

send them to Liberia, to their own native land. But a moment's reflection would convince me that whatever of high hope—as I think there is—there may be in this in the long run, its sudden execution is impossible. If they were all landed there in a day, they would all perish in the next ten days; and there are not surplus shipping and surplus money enough to carry them there in many times ten days. What then? Free them all, and keep them among us as underlings? Is it quite certain this betters their condition? I think I would not hold one of them in slavery at any rate, yet the point is not clear enough for me to denounce people upon. What next? Free them, and make them politically and socially our equals? My own feelings will not admit of this, and if mine would, we well know that those of the great mass of whites will not. Whether this feeling accords with justice and sound judgment is not the sole question, if indeed it is any part of it. A universal feeling, whether well or ill founded, cannot be safely disregarded. We cannot make them equals. It does seem to me that systems of gradual emancipation might be adopted, but for their tardiness in this I will not undertake to judge our brethren of the South.

"When they remind us of their constitutional rights, I acknowledge them—not grudgingly, but fully and fairly; and I would give them any legislation for the reclaiming of their fugitives which should not in its stringency be more likely to carry a free man into slavery than our ordinary criminal laws are to hang an innocent one."

David R. Locke says (*Reminiscences of Lincoln, &c.*, p. 445) that in Lincoln's contest with Douglas for Congress in 1858, the imputation of abolition was what "it was Lincoln's chief desire to avoid," as appears in the following words, which show, too, the attitude of that district in Illinois towards abolition: "The Republican leaders, and Lincoln as well, were afraid of only one thing, and that was having imputed to them any desire to abolish slavery. Douglas, in all the debates between himself and Lincoln, attempted to fasten abolition on him, and this it was Lincoln's chief desire to avoid. Great as he was, he had not then reached the point of declaring war upon slavery; he could go no further than to protest against its extension into the Territories, and that was pressed in so mild and hesitating a way as to rob it of half its point."

Leland (his *Lincoln*, p. 50 *et seq.*) quotes from Lamon and from Holland to show that Lincoln's anti-slavery protests before the war were very mild, and confirms their statements about it.

The *Nation* of October 7, 1899, quotes from James R. Gilmore's *Personal Recollections of Abraham Lincoln and the Civil War* what Lincoln said to Gilmore in May 1863. The Southern people "think they have a moral and legal right to their slaves, and until very recently the North has been of the same opinion." The same book, at page 57, says that Gilmore said to Lincoln, in November, 1861, "You told me eight months ago that after thirty years of agitation the Abolitionists were merely a corporal's guard, not a party." All of which shows that it would have been what is now called "bad politics" for Lincoln to avow abolition sentiments, though it is but justice to say that further evidence tends to show that he never entertained any such sentiments, although they have been attributed to him almost universally, like heroism, refinement, and personal piety, his claims to which virtues have been hereinbefore discussed. Rhodes gives,[9] without comment, a letter from the *New York Tribune's* correspondent to the managing editor, Sydney Howard Gay, giving details of a talk with General Wadsworth, who had been with the President and Stanton every day at the War Department—frequently for five or six hours—during several months. He says, "The President is not with us; has no anti-slavery instincts." This is in 1862 that he speaks of anti-slavery men as "Radicals, Abolitionists," and frequently speaks of "the nigger question."

A memorial addressed to the President by the *Meeting of the Christian Men of Chicago,* held September 7, 1862,[10] shows their impression about Lincoln's attitude to emancipation by quoting from the Bible Mordecai's threat to Queen Esther, "If thou altogether holdest thy peace at this time, . . . thou and thy father's house shall be destroyed."

Dr. E. Benjamin Andrews says:[11] "Mr. Lincoln and the Republican party resorted to arms not in-

---

[9] *History of the United States,* Vol. IV., p. 64, note.
[10] See *Fund Publication* of the Maryland Historical Society, p. 14.
[11] *History of the United States,* Vol. II., p. 190.

tending the slightest alteration in the constitutional status of slavery.''

Allen Thorndike Rice says [12] ''Lincoln did not free the negro for the sake of the slave, but for the sake of the Union. It is an error to class him with the noble band of Abolitionists to whom neither Church nor State was sacred when it sheltered slavery.''

[12] Introduction to *Reminiscences of Lincoln, &c.,* p. 14.

CHAPTER IX

SECESSION LONG THREATENED—COERCION NEVER SERIOUSLY THOUGHT OF TILL 1861

THE authorities we quote have put on record ample proof of a widespread conviction in the North and West in 1861 that the use of force to retain States in the Union was not only inadmissible under the Constitution, but abhorrent to the principles on which their political institutions rested.

Mr. Charles Francis Adams asked, in a late address to the New England Society of Charleston, South Carolina, referring to secession, "What at different epochs would have been the probable outcome of any attempt at withdrawal? . . . I hold that it was merely a question of time, and that such a withdrawal as then took place would never have failed of success at any anterior period in our national history." The same very high authority says [1] that "up to the very day of the firing on the flag the attitude of the Northern States, even in case of hostilities, was open to grave question, while that of the Border States did not admit of a doubt;" . . . "that Mr. Seward, the member of the President's Cabinet in charge of foreign affairs, both in his official papers and his private talk, repudiated not only the right, but the wish even to use armed

---

[1] *Life of Charles Francis Adams,* his father, Lincoln's Minister to England, p. 49, *et seq.*

force in subjugating the Southern States against the will of a majority of the people, and declared that the President willingly accepted as true the cardinal dogma of the seceding States, that the Federal Government had no authority for coercion;'
. . . and all this time (p. 150) the Southern sympathizers throughout the 'loyal' States were earnest and outspoken.''

General B. F. Butler records (*Butler's Book*, p. 298) that Henry Dunning, Mayor of Hartford, called the City Council together ''to consult if my troops should be allowed to go through Hartford on the way to the war. He was a true, loyal man, but did not believe in having a war. . . . He was a patriot to the core.''

Morse makes the following remarkable statement:' ''Greeley and Seward and Wendell Phillips, representative men, were little better than Secessionists. The statement sounds ridiculous, yet the proof against each comes from his own mouth. The *Tribune* had retracted none of those disunion sentiments of which examples have been given.'' A. K. McClure shows that Greeley was not alone in these views. He says (*Lincoln and Men of War Time*, p. 292, *et seq.*), ''Not only the Democratic party, with few exceptions, but a very large proportion of the Republican party, including some of its ablest

---

[2] We have a letter of July, 1861, from Seward to Minister Adams, in Rhodes' *History of the United States*, Vol. IV., p. 304, of like dispassionate tone. It blames alike ''the extreme advocates of African slavery and its most vehement opponents,'' as seeming ''to act together to precipitate a servile war.''

[3] *Lincoln*, Vol. I., p. 231. He quotes from Greeley's editorials repeated bitter censures of forcing seceded States back into the Union.

and most trusted leaders, believed that peaceable secession might reasonably result in early reconstruction."

Would Jefferson Davis, would Robert E. Lee, have asked more than McClure here says the two great parties of the North and West agreed in believing ought to be done?

Even so late as April 10, 1861, Seward wrote officially to Charles Francis Adams, Minister to England, "Only an imperial and despotic government could subjugate thoroughly disaffected and insurrectionary members of the States." On April 9th the rumor of a fight at Sumter being spread abroad, Wendell Phillips said, "Here are a series of States girding the Gulf who think that their peculiar institutions require that they should have a separate government; they have a right to decide that question without appealing to you and to me.
. . . Standing with the principles of '76 behind us, who can deny them the right? . . . Abraham Lincoln has no right to a soldier in Fort Sumter.
. . . You cannot go through Massachusetts and recruit men to bombard Charleston and New Orleans." Morse is comprehensive in his statement (*Lincoln*, Vol. I, p. 233) of the position taken by the Republicans, saying of Lincoln's early days in Washington, . . . "None of the distinguished men, leaders of his own party whom Lincoln found about him at Washington, were in a frame of mind to assist him efficiently." Dr. E. Benjamin Andrews deplores (*History of the United States*, Vol. II, p. 95) the fact that "coolness and absurd prejudice

against coercing largely possessed even the loyal masses,'' and that (Vol. II, p. 95) ''throughout the North the feeling was strong against all efforts at coercion.'' A. K. McClure says,[4] ''Even in Philadelphia . . . nearly the whole commerical and financial interests were arrayed against Lincoln at first.''

For months after the secession of South Carolina, while the other States were sucessively passing ordinances of secession and seizing the forts, arsenals, etc., within their boundaries, the Government at Washington, President, Cabinet, Supreme Court, and Congress, took not one step toward coercion, nor did either house of Congress listen to a suggestion of emancipation. These Senators and Representatives were almost all from the North and the West, and we may surely conclude that, at so critical a period, they ascertained and carried out the will of their constituents. See the testimony of General B. F. Butler (*Butler's Book,* Boston, 1892, p. 1009) as to how the Supreme Court of the United States stood. He says that ''during the whole war of the rebellion the Government was rarely ever aided, but usually impeded, by the decisions of the Supreme Court, so that the President was obliged to suspend the writ of *habeas corpus* in order to relieve himself from the rulings of the court.'' This is stated by General Butler quite seriously and not, as might possibly be supposed, in any satirical mood. Of the Supreme Court's Dred Scott decision, Woodrow

[4] *Our Presidents and How We Make Them,* p. 177. See also Morse's *Lincoln,* Vol. I., p. 4, and p. 22.

Wilson says (*Division and Reunion,* p. 198), "The opinion of the court sustained the whole Southern claim."

Ropes says (*Story of the Civil War,* Part 1, p. 19), "It is true that during the winter of 1860 Congress took no action whatever looking toward preparation for the conquest of the outgoing States." . . . From page 355 to 553 of the first volume of Greeley's *American Conflict* there is little but a record of the opposition to coercion of the South in the "loyal" States. Pages 357 *et seq.* and 354 *et seq.* show the action of the Legislatures of New Jersey and Illinois, both nearly unanimous, in the same direction. See, also (Vol. I, p. 380, *et seq.*), the very strong support given to the amendment of the Constitution proposed by one whom Greeley called "the venerable and Union-loving Crittenden, of Kentucky," which amendment guaranteed ample protection to slavery, and it could have been passed in Congress, but for the fact that they knew the South thought the time for compromise was past.

Greeley describes (*American Conflict,* p. 387, *et seq.*) a tremendous demonstration against the threatened war made in New York State in February, 1861, in which her leaders promised about all the South could ask. In this, as in the New York State Democratic Convention, which he describes (p. 392) as "probably the strongest and most imposing assembly of delegates ever convened in the State," Greeley records expressions of the purpose not only not to coerce, but to aid the South in case of war, which expressions were heard with applause; and in a speech of James S. Thayer, it was alleged that these views had been asserted in the last election by 333,000 votes in New York. Greeley further makes the following very remarkable statement: "That throughout the Free States eminent and eager advocates of adhesion to the new Confederacy by those States were widely heard and heeded." Vice-President Hamlin said (*Life of Hannibal Hamlin,* by his son, p. 459), "If we had had a common union in the North and a common loyalty to the government, we could have ended this civil war months ago, but this aid and comfort the rebels had received from the Northern allies." . . .

Morse (*Abraham Lincoln,* Vol. I, p. 76) copies from a speech made by Lincoln in Congress, January 12, 1848, "Any people anywhere, being inclined and having the power, have the right to rise up and shake off the existing government, and form a new one that suits them better. This is a most valuable, a most sacred right—a right which we hope and believe is to liberate the world. Nor is this right confined to cases in which the whole people of an existing government may choose to exercise it. Any portion of such people, *that can,* may revolutionize, and make their *own* of so much of the territory as they inhabit." On this Morse comments as follows: "This doctrine, so comfortably applied to Texas in 1848, seemed unsuitable to the Confederate States in 1861."

Woodrow Wilson (*Division and Reunion,* p. 165) says some of the Northern Whigs had not hesitated to join John Quincy Adams, early in 1843, in declaring to their constituents that in their opinion the annexation of Texas would bring about and fully justify a dissolution of the Union; while later, in 1845, Wm. Lloyd Garrison had won hearty bursts of applause from an anti-annexation convention held in Boston by the proposal that Massachusetts should lead in a movement to withdraw from the Union.''

And Woodrow Wilson sets forth the mind of the Government and the people of the United States in 1860 as follows (*Division and Reunion,* p. 214) : That President Buchanan. . . . . "agreed with his Attorney-Generál that there was no constitutional means or warrant for coercing a State to do her duty under the law. Such, indeed, for the time seemed to be the general opinion of the country.''

Colonel Roosevelt says in his *Oliver Cromwell,* p. 193: "Of course if the Constitution''—of 1789— "had made such a declaration''—of the abolition of slavery in all the States—"it would never have been adopted, while if the Republican platform of 1860 had taken such a position, Lincoln would not have been elected, no war for the Union would have been waged.'' And Edward Everett Hale says,[5] "The reader of today forgets that in the same years in which South Carolina was defying the North, Massachusetts gave directions that the national flag should not float over her State-House.'' It is interesting to observe *what* the Rev. Mr. Hale thinks South Carolina was defying.

[5] *James Russell Lowell and His Friends,* p. 105, *et seq.*

Schouler (*History of the United States,* p. 214, *et seq.*) records that General B. F. Butler offered his Massachusetts brigade to put down any negro insurrection, and that "few, North or South, during the first year of the war, sought or approved emancipation." General B. F. Butler says (*Butler's Book,* Boston, 1892, p. 293), "If we had beaten at Bull Run, I have no doubt the whole contest would have been patched up by concessions to slavery, as no one in power then was ready for its abolition." Lincoln himself said in his famous letter to Greeley in the *Tribune* "If I could save the Union without freeing any slave, I would do it."

General B. F. Butler says (*Butler's Book,* p. 168, *et seq.*), "Mr. Lincoln's Inaugural Address, under advice of Seward, left it wholly uncertain whether he would attempt to retake Forts Pickens and Moultrie."

Bancroft (*Life of Seward,* Vol. I, p. 93) describes Lincoln's first message as meaning either war or peace, and says, "It is now plain that no definite course of action had been determined;" and (p. 104) "Seward's method of dealing with secession was remarkably like Buchanan's."

Nicolay and Hay record (*Abraham Lincoln,* Vol. III, p. 247, *et seq.*) that Lincoln called using force "the ugly point."

Ropes says (*Story of the Civil War,* Part II, p. 70, *et seq.*) of the policy urged by Governor Pickens, but not adopted by the Confederate Government at Montgomery—to seize Sumter before Buchanan's term should end—"It is very improbable that Mr.

Buchanan would have thought himself authorized
to call the North to arms if Sumter had been attacked while he was President, and it is almost certain that Mr. Lincoln would never have taken the
risk involved in beginning an aggressive war
against the South in retaliation for any past act, no
matter how flagrant.''

What impression as to his intentions Lincoln
meant to produce is plain from the following: Greeley quotes (*American Conflict,* Vol. I, p. 422) assurances given by Lincoln in his Inaugural Address that
he would not "interfere with the institution of slavery where it exists in the States." Ida Tarbell
quotes the same,[6] and both say the assurances were
so strong that they should have removed the ap-
prehensions of the South. Burgess sums up the
light on history given by that Inaugural as follows:[7]
"This language was certainly a little confusing to
the minds of Union men, and by so much encouraging to the Secessionists. . . . Mr. . Lincoln
should never have used the word invasion to describe the presence of the National Government in
any State of the Union, or the entrance, so to speak,
of the National Government into any State of the
Union. . . . The idea rests upon the most radical misconception of the distinction between in-
ternational and constitutional law. . . . Mr.
Lincoln also made a mistake in announcing that he
would not, for the time being, fill the United States

[6] *McClure's Magazine* for January, 1899, p. 261.
[7] *The Civil War and the Constitution,* Vol. I., p. 141, very recently published.

offices, and cause the execution of the United States laws, in the interior of hostile communities. This encouraged still further the hope and belief among the masses of the Southern States that peaceable disunion was even probable. . . . Taken altogether the address shows that even Mr. Lincoln's mind was not altogether clear as to the national character of our political system, but it also shows that it was clearer than that of any of his contemporaries. The whole country, North and South, was more or less tainted with the doctrine of States' Rights. The difference between all the public men of that day was a difference of degree more than of kind. It is wonderful that Mr. Lincoln should have been, in the midst of such surroundings, so clear as he was.''

Is it not shown above that Lincoln's use of military force was contrary to views which he had deliberately formulated twelve years earlier—contrary to the right that John Quincy Adams and William Lloyd Garrison had claimed for New England in Boston with applause sixteen years earlier —contrary to the mind of the Government and people of the United States on the day when he called for 75,000 soldiers? Is it not shown, besides, that he betrayed or professed in his Inaugural such hesitation as encouraged secession, and that this hesitation was in the mind of all the public men of that day who were not decided in denial of all right to use force?

Burgess says (*The Civil War and the Constitution*, p. 174), ''The Governors of Virginia, North Carolina, Kentucky, Tennessee, Missouri, and Arkansas flatly and insolently refused to obey the President's call for troops from those Common-wealths, and the Governors of Maryland and Dela-ware did not obey it. No ordinance of secession had yet been passed by any of these Commonwealths, and no one of them claimed to be out of the Union. . . . These men made themselves, by their mili-tary insubordination, subject to a United States court-martial. They ought to have been arrested, tried, and condemned by a military tribunal for one of the most grievous offenses known to public juris-prudence. It was the physical power to carry out such a procedure that was lacking. . . . At this day such an attitude on the part of State Governors would be regarded very differently from what it was then, and might be dealt with very differently." But, he says, on p. 198 of same Vol., "It is doubtful if Mr. Lincoln himself and his chief advisers real-ized the enormity of the offense which these 'Border-State' Governors had committed in refusing to send forward the troops."

See below testimony from very numerous and distinguished witnesses contrasting the unanimity of the people of the South and the hesitation about the war everywhere in the North, and the wide and bitter opposition to it in many places in the North and West.

Russell[8] writes from the South: "I have now been in North Carolina, South Carolina, Georgia, Alabama, and in none of these great States have I found the least indication of the Union sentiment

[8] *My Diary North and South*, p. 976, May 12, 1860.

which Mr. Seward always insists to exist in the South.''

Schouler describes (*History of the United States,* Vol. VI, p. 37) the effect in the South of the news of the fall of Fort Sumter. ''National allegiance raised scarcely a whisper, but in the whole insurgent area volunteers rallied for defense, and at sight of the waving stars and bars, as trains crowded with soldiers went by, the population of the hamlets, and the workers in the field, black and white, cheered for Jeff Davis and the Confederate States.''

Greeley, too, describes the time (*American Conflict,* Vol. I, p. 362): ''For the great mails, during the last few weeks of 1860, sped southward, burdened with letters of sympathy and encouragement to the engineers of secession. . . . As trade fell off and work in the cities and manufacturing villages was withered at the breath of the Southern sirocco, the heart of the North seemed to sink within her; and the charter elections at Boston, Lowell, Roxbury, Charlestown, Worcester, etc., in Massachusetts, and at Hudson, etc., in New York, which took place early in December, 1860, showed a striking and general reduction of Republican strength.''

The Appendix shows that Greeley was an ardent Abolitionist and the most honored and respected and influential Republican of his day, yet see what George William Curtis tells of him (*Orations and Addresses,* Vol. II, p. 429, *et seq.*), as follows: ''For the right of secession, as Greeley maintained, was bottomed on the Declaration of Independence.'' . . . Such a political philosophy as this, proclaimed by a leading organ of the Republican party, created difficulties for a President situated as Mr. Buchanan was which posterity cannot overlook.

James Russell Lowell wrote[9] of the day when Lincoln's Administration began, "Even in that half of the Union which acknowledged him as President there was a large and at that time dangerous minority that hardly admitted his claim to office, and even in the party that elected him there was also a large minority that suspected him of being secretly a communicant with the church of Laodicea."

Russell quotes (*My Diary, North and South*, p. 13) Bancroft, the historian, afterwards Minister to England, for the opinion in 1860 that the United States had no authority to coerce the people of the South, and Bancroft told Russell that this opinion was widely entertained among men of all classes in the North. And Russell reports that he found the same opinion prevailing in Washington in March, 1861. Russell reprobates with contempt such a view for people or government, which makes his evidence the more valuable. He quotes (p. 14) a gentleman as saying that "the majority of the people of New York, and all of the respectable people, were disgusted at the election of such a fellow as Lincoln to be President, and would back the Southern people if it came to a split." And Russell goes on (p. 15), in March, 1860, "I was astonished to find little sympathy and no respect for the newly-installed Government." Dining with a banker in New York city, March 18, 1860, he met Hon. Horatio Seymour, Mr.

[9] *North American Magazine* for January, 1864.

Tilden, and Mr. Bancroft. He says (p. 16), "There was not a man who maintained that the Government had any power to coerce a State, or force a State to remain in the Union." Mr. Seymour held that though secession would produce revolution, it was, nevertheless, "a right." Russell adds, "In fact, the Federal Government is groping in the dark;" and again (p. 18), it "appears to be drifting with the current of events." He found (p. 28) Senator Sumner and Secretary Chase disposed to let the South "go out with their slavery." Elsewhere (p. 211) he says of Chase, "He has never disguised his belief that the South might have been left to go at first, with a certainty of their returning to the Union. . . . Nay (p. 134), more, when I arrived in Washington"—which was in March, 1861—"some members of the Cabinet were perfectly ready to let the South go. One of the first questions put to me by Mr. Chase, in my first interview with him, was whether I thought a very injurious effect would be produced to the *prestige* of the Federal Government in Europe if the Northern States let the South have its own way, and told them to go in peace." "For my own part," said he, "I should not be adverse to let them try it, for I believe they would soon find out their mistake." Again Russell (p. 30), describing a conference with Secretary Seward, April 4, 1861, says that Seward "admitted that it would not become the spirit of the American Government, or of the Federal system, to use armed force in subjugating the Southern States against the will of the majority of the people. Therefore, if the majority desire secession, Mr. Seward would let them have it.'' Russell reports (p. 34) a similar conference with Seward in Seward's house, as follows: . . . ''The Secretary is quite confident in what he calls 'reaction.' '' ''When the Southern States,'' he says, ''see that we mean them no wrong—that we intend no violence to persons, rights, or things— . . . they will see their mistake, and one after another they will come back into the Union.''

See another entry in Russell's Diary for July 5, 1861 (p. 143), about Lincoln's message just delivered: ''After dinner I made a round of visits, and heard the diplomatists speak of the message; few, if any, of them, in its favor. With the exception of Baron Gerolt, the Prussian Minister, there is not one member of the Legations who justifies the attempt of the Northern States to assert the supremacy of the Federal Government by force of arms.'' And again Russell records (September 3, 1861) that, when there was an alarm in Washington, ''the Ministers were in high spirit at the prospect of an attack on Washington. Such agreeable people are the governing party of the United States at present, that there is only one representative of a foreign power here who would not like to see them flying before Southern bayonets.''

General Horace Porter records[10] that during a visit of Stanton to Grant, near Richmond, Stanton gave a graphic description of the anxieties that had been experienced for some months at Washington

[10] *Century Magazine* for June, 1897, p. 201.

on account of the boldness of the disloyal element in the North.

General W. T. Sherman says (*Memoir,* Vol. I, p. 167) that in March, 1861, "it certainly looked as though the people of the North would tamely submit to a disruption of the Union." And of Washington city he says, "Even in the War Department and about the public offices there was open, unconcealed talk amounting to high treason."

Channing says (*Short History of the United States,* p. 303, *et seq.*), "At first it seemed as if Jeff Davis was right when he said that the Northerners would not fight." And Keifer says (*Slavery and Four Years of War,* p. 172), "Of course there was a troublesome minority North who, either through political perversity, cowardice, or disloyalty, never did support the war, at least willingly. . . . . And there were those also, even in New England, who had never had an opportunity to be tainted with slavery, who opposed the coercion of the seceding States, and who would rather have seen the Union destroyed than saved by war. . . . . Though patriotism was the rule with persons of all parties in the North, there were yet many who professed that true loyalty lay along lines other than the preservation of the Union by war."

Leland says (*Lincoln,* p. 111), "Yet . . . the Democratic press of the North and the rebel organs of the South continued to storm at the President for irritating the secessionists, declaring that *coercion* or resistance of the Federal Government to single States was illegal." And (p. 103): . . . "The

Anti-War party was so powerful in the North that it now appears almost certain that, if President Lincoln had proceeded at once to put down the rebellion with a strong hand, there would have been a counter-rebellion in the North. For not doing this he was bitterly blamed, but time has justified him. By his forbearance, Maryland, Kentucky, and Missouri were undoubtedly kept in the Federal Union."
. . . "Hitherto (p. 105) the press had railed at Lincoln for wanting a policy; and yet if he had made one step towards suppressing the rebels "a thousand Northern newspapers would have pounced upon him as one provoking war." . . . "It is certain (p. 168) that by this humane and wise policy"—not sending more soldiers through Baltimore —which many attributed to cowardice, President Lincoln not only prevented much bloodshed and devastation, but also preserved the State of Maryland. In such a crisis harshly aggressive measures in Maryland would have irritated millions on the border, and perhaps have promptly brought the war further North."

CHAPTER X

LINCOLN, knowing the opposition to abolition and coercion and the readiness to resist both that has been shown in the last two chapters to exist in the North and West, disclaimed, as he had so often done before, any purpose of emancipation, and disguised even in his Inaugural whatever purpose he had of forcing back the seceded States, and astutely used the firing on Fort Sumter *to rouse the war spirit*. The word "astutely" is aptly applied, for the flag had been fired on in the same place two months earlier—an exceedingly important fact which has been very strangely ignored, but cannot be denied. The steamer Star of the West had been [1] sent two months earlier, January 9, 1861, with food and two hundred recruits [2] to relieve the United States garrison in Fort Sumter, and while flying the great flag of a garrison was fired on, was struck twice, and driven away—"retired a little ignominiously," Morse reports it (*Lincoln*, Vol. I, p. 141); and he adds that Senator Wigfall jeered insolently: "Your flag has been insulted; redress it if you

---

[1] Nicolay and Hay's *Abraham Lincoln*, Vol. VIII., p. 96, *et seq.*

[2] It has been represented that the only purpose of the Star of the West was to *feed* the soldiers of the garrison, but, like Nicolay and Hay above, Channing in his *History of the United States*, p. 313, says she carried "supplies and soldiers," and Greeley says, in his *American Conflict*, Vol. I., p. 412, "with two hundred men and ample provisions."

dare." John A. Logan (*Great Conspiracy,* p. 143) adds further words of Senator Wigfall, "You have submitted to it for two months." George William Curtis (*Orations and Addresses,* Vol. I, p. 141) deplores it as follows: "We were unable or unwilling to avenge a mortal insult to our own flag in our own waters upon the Star of the West." Ropes and Channing[3] give a like description of the occurrence. Every particular above given about the Star of the West is confirmed[4] by letters of J. Holt, Secretary of War; of L. Thomas, Assistant Adjutant-General, and of Lieutenant Charles R. Wood, who conducted the expedition. Thomas instructed Wood to expect to be fired on by "the batteries on James' or Sullivan's Island," and Holt wrote Major Anderson, commandant of Fort Sumter, "Your forbearance to return the fire is fully appreciated by the President."[5]

Dr. E. Benjamin Andrews says (*History of the United States,* Vol. II, p. 50) that Major Robert Anderson, commanding Fort Sumter, "was expressly forbidden," by the Government in Washington, "to interfere with the erection and progress of the works that were being built . . . for use against his fort."

Russell wrote to the *London Times* from America (*My Diary, North and South,* p. 72, *et seq.,* and p. 131 *et seq.*): "It is absurd to assert . . . that

[3] Ropes' *Story of the Civil War,* Part I., p. 45; Channing's *Short History of the United States,* p. 313.

[4] *War of the Rebellion; Official Records of the Union and Confederate Armies,* Series I., Vol. I., pp. 9, 10, 131-2, 137, 140.

[5] For Major Anderson's own opinion and feeling about using force to restrain secession, see page 38 of the same volume.

the sudden outburst when Fort Sumter was fired upon was caused by the insult to the flag. Why, the flag had been fired on long before Sumter was attacked; . . . it had been torn down from the United States arsenals and forts all over the South and fired upon when the Federal flag was flying from the Star of the West." He says, too, "Secession was an accomplished fact months before Lincoln came into office, but we heard no talk of rebels and pirates till Sumter had fallen. . . . The North was perfectly quiescent. . . . What would not the value of 'the glorious burst' of patriotism have been, had it taken place before the Charleston batteries had opened on Sumter—when the Federal flag, for example, was fired on flying from the Star of the West, or when Beauregard cut off supplies, or Bragg threatened Pickens, or the first shovelful of earth was thrown up in hostile battery. But, no. New York was then engaged in discussing States' Rights and in reading articles to prove that the new Government would be traitors if they endeavored to reinforce the Federal forts." Gen. Wm. T. Sherman says (*Memoir,* Vol. II, p. 382): "After the election of Mr. Lincoln in 1860, there was no concealment of the declaration and preparation for war in the South. In Louisiana, as I have related, men were openly enlisted, officers were appointed, and war was actually begun, in January, 1861. The forts at the mouth of the Mississippi were seized, and occupied by garrisons that hauled down the United States flag and hoisted that of the State. The United States arsenal at Baton Rouge was

captured by New Orleans militia, its garrison ignominiously sent off, and the contents of the arsenal
distributed. These were as much acts of war as was
the subsequent firing on Fort Sumter, yet no public
notice was taken thereof." . . . This "firing on
the flag" on the Star of the West produced no sensa-
tion at all, but was accepted by the whole country as
an accompaniment of the secession of the States.

Burgess says (*The Civil War and the Constitution,* Vol. I, p. 106) "the firing upon the Star of the
West was really the beginning of the war of the
rebellion— . . . (p. 107) the Administration
simply chose not so to regard it; . . . Congress
was not prepared for it, and it is not certain that
the people of the North would then have rallied to
the President's support."

If there is still any need of apology for the action of
the Confederate Government in forcibly seizing Fort
Sumter, as it had for many weeks been seizing other
forts within its territory, we have the defense of it
formulated by Greeley and recorded without objection or comment by Burgess, who quotes (*The Civil
War and the Constitution,* p. 167) Greeley's words,
that "the Confederacy had no alternative to an attack upon Fort Sumter except its own dissolution."

We have learned afresh of late the meaning of
the words used above, *"to arouse the war spirit."*
A very respectable part of the wisdom and virtue
of this country deplored and reprobated the war
lately waged by the United States in the Philippines, and yet did make, and could make, no opposition, but supported the war just as those did who

approved it most warmly. We know now that a war, once begun, sweeps into its suport, not only the regular army, the navy, and the treasury, but volunteer organizations and the youth of the country, who think they must respond to any national call for arms. That this "war spirit" sent large armies to the field is well known. But Rhodes says (*History of the United States,* Vol. III, p. 404), "Had the North thoroughly understood the problem; had it known that the people of the Cotton States were practically unanimous; that the action of Virginia, North Carolina, and Tennessee was backed by a large and generous majority, it might have refused to undertake the seemingly unachievable task. . . . (p. 405). It is impossible to escape the conviction that the action of the North was largely based on a misconception of the strength of the disunion sentiment in the Confederate States. The Northern people accepted the gage of war and came to the support of the President of the United States on the theory that a majority of all the Southern States except South Carolina were at heart for the Union, and that if these loyal men were encouraged and protected they would make themselves felt in a movement looking towards allegiance to the National Government."

Rhodes is an historian who speaks with very high authority. May not the concession that he makes above be called an apology for a great wrong done the South. And does it not suggest the question who it was that led the North into the "misconception" that he describes?

CHAPTER XI

THE attitude of Congress towards coercion and emancipation is our best guide as to the attitude of their constituents—the people of the States called "loyal." Horace Greeley comments as follows on the concession made in President Buchanan's last message that he had no authority to use force against secession (*American Conflict*, Vol. I, p. 272): . . . "This assertion of the radical impotence of the Government . . . on the part of the President was received in Congress with general and concerted taciturnity." . . . Greeley (Vol. I, p. 370) commends ardently the long and distinguished career of John J. Crittenden, and outlines the *Crittenden Compromise* proposed by him as follows: "It allows slavery in the Territories south of 36° 31′, and says that States from south of that line may come in as Slave States. It protects slavery and its owners in the District, so long as it exists in Virginia and Maryland, or either. The United States shall pay the owners of slaves, where they are obstructed by the people of a county in using the law for recovery of a fugitive slave. It gives assurance that no amendment in the future shall give Congress the power to interfere with slavery in the States. It pronounces the Personal Liberty Laws null and void." Greeley is hotly indignant that such should have been the feeling of Congress, but he goes on (Vol. I, p. 380): "The *Conservatives,* so called, were still able to establish this *Crittenden Compromise* by their own proper strength, had they been disposed to do so. The President was theirs; the Senate strongly theirs; in the House they had a small majority, as was evinced by their defeat of John Sherman for Speaker."

As conclusive proof that the North and West had no such purpose as emancipation, Schouler (*History of the United States,* Vol. V, p. 507) says of the action of Congress, after Lincoln's inauguration, as follows: "One proposed amendment, and only one, was sent out with the constitutional assent of the two Houses;[1] not as a compromise, but as a pledge. It provided that no amendment should be made to the Constitution authorizing Congress to abolish or interfere within any State with the domestic institution of slavery. . . . Republicans, Democrats, and the great mass of the loyal citizens at the North were willing to be bound by such an assurance, hand and foot, if need be, in proof that they meant no aggression." Is it necessary to suppose they made any sacrifice in giving assurance that they would not interfere, in view of the vast amount of evidence that they did not think they ought to interfere and had no inclination to interfere?

Dr. E. Benjamin Andrews confirms the above accounts of the *Crittenden Compromise* that was proposed and the amendment that was passed in

---

[1] In a note Schouler gives the vote on it in the House as 133 to 65, and in the Senate as 24 to 12.

Congress (*History of the United States*, Vol. II,
p. 97), as follows: "Both Houses, each by more
than two-thirds majority, recommended a constitutional amendment depriving Congress forever of
the power to touch slavery in any State without the
consent of all the States." And he says of the *Crittenden Compromise* above described, "This measure, before Congress all winter, was finally lost for
lack of Southern votes."

How far Congress was from approving the Emancipation Proclamation may be judged by the following words of Rhodes (Vol. IV, p. 215) about
Lincoln's recommendation of emancipation in his
Message of December, 1862: "Owing to distrust of
him and his waning popularity, his recommendations in this message were not considered by Congress, nor had they, so far as I have been able to
ascertain, any notable influence on public sentiment."

Boutwell describes (*Lincoln, Tributes from His
Associates*, p. 87) Lincoln's dealings with one of the
amendments and the reluctance of Congress, as follows: "Slavery existed in States that had not engaged in the rebellion, and the legality of the
Emancipation Proclamation might be drawn in
question in the courts. One thing more was wanted
—an amendment to the Constitution abolishing
slavery everywhere within the jurisdiction of the
United States.

The preliminary resolution was secured after a
protracted struggle in Congress, and the result was
due, in a pre-eminent degree, to the personal and

official influence of Mr. Lincoln. In one phrase it may be said that every power of his office was exerted to secure in the Thirty-eighth Congress the passage of the resolution by which the proposed amendment was submitted to the States."[2]

Nicolay and Hay say (*Abraham Lincoln,* Vol. IV, p. 38) that even when his most subservient Congress subsequently "legalized" his usurpations, "there was about the action a certain hesitation which robbed it of the grace of spontaneous generosity." How persistent the opposition continued to be may be judged by the fact that Mr. Lincoln's Emancipation Proclamation failed, as late as June, 1864, to get in Congress the two-thirds vote necessary to fix it in the Constitution, and had to go over to the next session, when the war was practically ended.

[2] In connection with Boutwell's account of the way the "preliminary resolution" was passed in Congress for this amendment, it will be interesting to see, in the chapter headed Fictitious States, how enough States were voted to pass the amendment.

CHAPTER XII

OPPOSITION IN THE REGULAR ARMY

COL. A. K. McCLURE says (*Lincoln and Men of the War Time,* p. 56), "When Lincoln turned to the military arm of the Government, he was appalled by the treachery of the men to whom the nation should look for its preservation." Scarcely any were so devoted to the flag, none knew so well the seriousness of the step, as the officers of the regular army, but, notwithstanding, Ida Tarbell says,[1] three hundred and thirteen, nearly one-third, resigned. General Keifer says (*Slavery and Four Years of War,* p. 171) that about March, 1861, "disloyalty among prominent officers was for a while the rule." General Butler says that General Scott, commander of the army, recommended to the President (*Butler's Book,* p. 99 and p. 142) "that the wayward sisters be allowed to depart in peace," meaning the seceded States, and Butler's story is confirmed by Channing (*Short History of the United States,* p. 380, *et seq.*). George Ticknor Curtis gives (*Life of James Buchanan,* Vol. II, p. 297) the particulars of General Scott's "views," submitted to President Buchanan, dated October 9, 1860, which provided for a division of the Union into four separate confederacies. Ida Tarbell shows [2] that General

---

[1] *McClure's Magazine* for February, 1899.
[2] *McClure's Magazine* for April, 1899, p. 263.

Scott recommended to the President the withdrawal of the United States troops from Fort Sumter and from Fort Pickens in Pensacola harbor. Much pity has been spent on Major Anderson, cut off from supplies and bombarded in Fort Sumter, but one of Lincoln's eulogists has to rejoice now that he was spared the pain of reading the reproaches contained in a letter written him by Major Anderson, censuring him for proposing to use force. The letter miscarried. We have other letters of Major Anderson's showing that he, like Scott and Seward, and the rest, thought coercion out of the question. He wrote,[3] signing officially, to Thomas, United States Adjutant-General, earnestly deprecating the expedition proposed to bring him reinforcements in Fort Sumter, saying, "I frankly say that my heart is not in the war that I see is to be commenced. That God will still avert it, and cause us to revert to pacific measures to maintain our rights, is my ardent prayer." Nicolay, too,[4] tells of a reproachful letter that Anderson wrote Lincoln about using force at Fort Sumter. Major-General Abner Doubleday gives (*Battles and Leaders of the Civil War,* Vol. I, p. 40, *et seq.*) a very full account, as eyewitness of Anderson's whole course, in accord with the above. Rhodes (*History of the United States,* Vol. IV, p. 72) quotes from a letter of Senator Sumner to John Bright, that Lincoln had answered Bright, who urged him to issue an edict of emanci-

---

[3] *War of the Rebellion; Official Records of the Union and Confederate Armies,* Series I., Vol. I., p. 294.

[4] In the earlier book that he wrote, *The Outbreak of the Rebellion,* at page 55.

pation, "I would do it if I were not afraid that half
the officers would fling down their arms and three
more States would rise." Hamlin says (*Life and
Times of Hannibal Hamlin,* p. 430), "Yet many a
gallant Union officer . . . declared disdainfully
that he would not fight for the Abolitionists."
. . . Schouler says (*History of the United
States,* Vol. VI, p. 218), that in 1861 "Sherman and
Buell in Kentucky, Dix in Maryland, and Halleck
in Missouri, slave regions less positively disloyal,
took a more conservative attitude, and ordered
slaves to be kept out of their lines," instead of encouraging them to leave their masters. Rhodes
says (Vol. IV, p. 182) that Governor O. P. Morton,
of Indiana, charged, in his official communications
to Washington, General Rosecrans with being a
rebel sympathizer, which Rhodes records, though he
does not believe it true, Rosecrans being the predecessor of Buell, Grant's predecessor in the chief
command in the West. Rhodes says (*History of the
United States,* Vol. IV, p. 335), "The attitude of all
but three of Grant's corps commanders on the 19th
of April, 1862, may be inferred from the following
letter of Grant to Halleck of that date: 'At best
three of my army corps commanders take hold of
the new policy of arming the negroes and using them
against the enemy with a will. They, at least, are
so much of soldiers as to feel themselves under obligation to carry out a policy which they would not
inaugurate, in the same good faith and with the
same zeal as if it was of their own choosing.'

Rhodes quotes (*History of the United States,*

Vol. IV, p. 73) from Greeley's "prayer of twenty million," elsewhere described in this book, the following: . . . "A large portion of our regular officers, with many of the volunteers, evidence far more solicitude to uphold slavery than to put down the rebellion."

CHAPTER XIII

OPPOSITION IN THE VOLUNTEER ARMY

IT WOULD be supposed that however many, as above shown, of the people of the North and West opposed or disapproved the war, it had the ardent support of all the soldiers at least who volunteered "to defend the flag" on Lincoln's first call for seventy-five thousand men. About this we get a strange enlightenment in the account given by Russell (*My Diary, North and South*, p. 155, *et seq.*) of his meeting the Fourth Pennsylvania Regiment going home from the Bull Run battlefield to the sound of the cannon that opened the battle. A note on page 553 of Greeley's *American Conflict* describes the same from General McDowell's official report of the battle of Bull Run,[1] how on the eve of battle the Fourth Pennsylvania Regiment of Volunteers and the battery of artillery of the Eighth New York Militia, whose term of service had expired, insisted on their discharge, though the General and the Secretary of War, both on the spot, tried hard to make them stay five more days; . . . "and the next morning, when the army moved into battle, these troops moved to the rear to the sound of the enemy's guns, every moment becoming more dis-

---

[1] See the account of it in General McDowell's report of the battle, in the *War of the Rebellion; Official Records of the Union and Confederate Armies*, Series I., Vol. II., p. 325.

tinct and more heavy." And Greeley goes on to say, "It should here be added that a member of the New York battery aforesaid, who was most earnest and active in opposing General McDowell's request and insisting on an immediate discharge, was at the next election, in full view of all the facts, chosen sheriff of the city of New York—probably the most lucrative office filled by popular election in the country." [2]

In the *Outlook* of September 6, 1902, the Rev. Edward Everett Hale quotes as of unchallenged historic value a letter written three weeks after the battle of Bull Run by a gentleman in an important political position in Washington, which attributes like shameful desertion in the face of the enemy to "various batteries," and their welcome home. He goes on, "How does the country behave? . . . The poltroons, ... have you hung any of them yet in Boston? . . . . And the people of New York let these people return to their business?"

Russell gives as the reason why General Patterson did not bring his army from the upper Potomac to help General McDowell at Bull Run,[3] that "out of twenty-three regiments composing his force, nineteen refused to stay an hour after their time." Can any explanation be suggested but that these soldiers and their friends at home reprobated the

[2] If it was possible to conceive of any of the soldiers on the Southern side so deserting the field that day, where would they have found kinsman or friend to give them shelter, food, or water, from that day forward?

[3] *My Diary, North and South*, p. 179; see, too, Channing's *Short History of the United States*, p. 308, *et seq.*

task to which they were ordered? We have General Patterson's report to General Scott ˙ of his repeated unsuccessful appeals to his men not to leave the army with the enemy in their very presence. He furthermore complained (p. 175) that his own zeal and loyalty to the cause was publicly impeached, and General Scott's contemptuous answer (p. 178) gives no sort of contradiction to the charges. Russell says (*My Diary, North and South,* p. 179), "The outcry against Patterson has not yet subsided, though" . . . nineteen out of twenty-three of his regiments refused to stay in the field, as shown above. Gen. W. T. Sherman says (his *Memoir,* Vol. I, p. 188), four days after the first battle of Manassas, or Bull Run, . . . "I had my brigade about as well governed as any in that army, although most of the ninety-day men, especially the Sixty-ninth, had become exceedingly tired of the war and wanted to go home. Some of them were so mutinous, at one time, that I had Ayre's battery to unlimber threatening if any dared leave camp without orders, I would open fire on them." Pages 188 to 191 describe a mutiny with Lincoln present, and end with, "This spirit of mutiny was common to the whole army, and was not subdued till several regiments, or parts of regiments, had been ordered to Fort Jefferson, Florida, as punishment."

The above is hard to reconcile with the popular belief that the early campaigns were pushed with enthusiasm by the volunteers. Later, at the time when

---

˙ *War of the Rebellion; Official Records of the Union and Confederate Armies,* Series I., Vol. II., pp. 166–170.

General Hooker took command of the Army of the Potomac, we have Hooker's testimony, quoted from the Report of the Congressional Committee on the Conduct of the War, by Col. Henderson, of the English Army (*Life of Stonewall Jackson*, Vol. II, p. 505), "At the time the army was turned over to me, desertions were at the rate of about two hundred a day." Then, after describing, in his words elsewhere quoted, the efforts of great numbers of the people at home to induce the soldiers to desert, he goes on as follows: "At that time perhaps a majority of the officers, especially those high in rank, were hostile to the policy of the Government in the conduct of the war. The Emancipation Proclamation had been published a short time before, and a large element of the army had taken sides antagonistic to it, declaring they would never have embarked in the war had they anticipated the action of the Government."

Major-General John E. Wool wrote Secretary Stanton, September 3, 1862,[5] "We have now more treason in the army than we can well get along with."

Ida Tarbell says,[6] "Nothing could have been devised which would have created a louder uproar in the North than the suggestion of a draft. All through the winter of 1862-63 Congress wrangled over the bill ordering it, much of the press denouncing it meantime as despotic and contrary to American institutions." General Grant says (*Memoir,* Vol. II, p. 23) that during August, 1864, "right in the midst

[5] *War of the Rebellion; Official Records of the Union and Confederate Armies*, Series III., Vol. II., p. 509.

[6] *McClure's Magazine*, Vol. XIII., for June, 1899, p. 156.

of these embarrassments, Halleck informed me that there was an organized scheme on foot to resist the draft, and suggested that it might become necessary to withdraw troops from the field to put it down.'' Nicolay and Hay (Vol. VI, p. 3) tell of violent resistance to the draft in Pennsylvania.

About the volunteer soldiers' attitude toward emancipation we find the following:

Schouler says of General B. F. Butler (*History of the United States*, Vol. VI, p. 216), When he reached Maryland, under the first call to arms, ''he offered the use of his regiment, as a Massachusetts Brigadier, to put down any slave uprising that might occur there.'' Nicolay and Hay say (*Abraham Lincoln*, Vol. I, p. 185) that the Union army showed the strongest sympathy with its always immensely popular general, McClellan, in his bold protests against emancipation, and that there was actual danger of revolt in the army against the Emancipation Proclamation when General Burnside turned over the command of his army of one hundred and twenty thousand men to General Hooker in Virginia. In Warden's *Life of Chase* (p. 485, *et seq.*) a letter of September, 1862, from Chase to John Sherman, says: ''I hear from all sources that nearly all the officers in Buell's army, and that Buell himself, are proslavery in the last degree.'' From Hilton Head, South Carolina, General O. M. Mitchell reported to Secretary Stanton,[7] September 20, 1862, ''I find a feeling prevailing among the officers and soldiers of

---

[7] *War of the Rebellion; Official Records of the Union and Confederate Armies*, Series II., Vol. XIV., p. 438.

prejudice against the blacks; . . . am entirely certain that under existing organization there is little hope of allaying or destroying a feeling widely prevalent and fraught with the most injurious consequences.'' Page 431 shows the same General, writing to Halleck, General in Chief at Washington, in March, 1863, ''I was thus saddled with pro-slavery generals in whom I had not the least confidence.''

CHAPTER XIV

OPPOSITION TO THE EMANCIPATION PROCLAMATION

CHANNING says (*Short History of the United States*, p. 329) of freeing the slaves as a war measure, that though he knew he had a perfect right to do it, Lincoln knew that public opinion in the North would not approve this action.

A. K. McClure, discussing the question whether to emancipate, speaks of . . . "the shivering hesitation of even Republicans throughout the North." . .

The same says,[1] "The Emancipation Proclamation had been issued that caused a cold chill throughout the Republican ranks, and there was little prospect of filling up the broken ranks of our army." And the same McClure refers (p. 228) to the "blatant disloyalty that was heard in many places throughout the North."

Rhodes says (*History of the United States*, Vol. IV, p. 162), "But Lincoln himself, with his delicate touch on the pulse of public opinion, detected that there was a lack of heartiness in the response of the Northern people." In his "strictly private" letter to Hamlin, the Vice-President, he manifested his keen disappointment. "While I hope something from the proclamation," he wrote, "my expectations are not as sanguine as those of some friends. The time for

---

[1] *Recollections of Half a Century*, copyright, 1902, p. 220.

97

its effect southward has not come; but northward the effect should be instantaneous. It is six days old, and while commendation in the newspapers and by distinguished men is all that a vain man could wish, the stocks have declined and troops come forward more slowly than ever. This, looked soberly in the face, is not very satisfactory."

Henderson (*Life of Stonewall Jackson*, Vol. II, p. 355, *et seq.*), though he commends with ardor Lincoln's issue of the Emancipation Proclamation, says that by it "the Constitution was deliberately violated," and that "the armies of the Union were called upon to fight for the freedom of the negro;" . . . that "the measure was daring. It was not approved by the Democrats—and many of the soldiers were Democrats—or by those—and they were not a few—who believed that compromise was the surest means of restoring peace; . . . who thought the dissolution of the Union a smaller evil than the continuance of the war. The opposition was very strong." . . .

A. B. Hart says (*Life of Salmon P. Chase*, p. 309), . . . "But one of the effects . . . of the first Proclamation of Emancipation was an increase of the Democratic vote in Ohio and in Indiana, and the consequent election of many Democratic members of Congress."

In the *Life and Times of Hannibal Hamlin*, by Chas. Eugene Hamlin, Cambridge, 1899, pp. 436, 437, we find the following: "The generally accepted explanation of the Republican reverses in the election of 1862 is that they were primarily due to the

Emancipation Proclamation, which was issued in September.''

Dr. Holland says (*Abraham Lincoln*, 1866, p. 408) ''Either through the failure of McClellan's campaign, or the effect of the emancipation, or the influence of both together, the Administration had received a rebuke through the autumn elections of 1862.'' Rhodes says (*History of the United States*, Vol. IV, p. 163), ''In October and November elections took place in the principal States, with the results that New York, New Jersey, Pennsylvania, Ohio, Indiana, Illinois, and Wisconsin, all of which except New Jersey had cast their electoral votes for Lincoln, declared against the party in power. A new House of Representatives was chosen, the Democrats making conspicuous gains in the States mentioned. The same ratio of gain extended to the other States would have given them the control of the next House—a disaster from which the Administration was saved by New England, Michigan, Iowa, and the Border Slave States. The elections came near being what the steadfast Republican journal, the *New York Times*, declared them to be, 'A vote of want of confidence in the President.' Since the elections followed so closely upon the Proclamation of Emancipation, it is little wonder that the Democrats declared that the people protested against Lincoln's surrender [2] to the radicals, which was their construction of the change of policy from a war for the Union to a war for the Negro. Many writers have since agreed with them in this interpretation of the result.

[2] Observe the significant word used by Rhodes.

No one can doubt that it was a contributing force operating with these other influences: the corruption in the War Department before Stanton became Secretary, the suppression of free speech and freedom of the press, arbitrary arrests which had continued to be made by military orders of the Secretary of War.''

Nicolay and Hay record (*Abraham Lincoln,* Vol. II, p. 261) great losses in the elections in consequence of the Emancipation Proclamation. General B. F. Butler says (*Butler's Book,* p. 536): ''November came, and with it the elections in the various States. The returns were ominous and disheartening enough. Everywhere there was reaction of feeling adverse to the Administration. In the strong Republican States majorities were reduced. In all others the opposition was triumphant and the Administration party defeated. . . . Among the causes of the defeat was opposition to the Government's anti-slavery policy.'' And Butler quotes from a letter of Seward to his wife that ''the returns were ominous;'' that in all but strong Republican States ''the opposition was triumphant and the Administration party defeated.'' Ida Tarbell, in *McClure's Magazine* for January, 1899 (p. 165), says: ''Many and many a man deserted in the winter of 1862–1863 because of the Emancipation Proclamation. He did not believe the President had the right to issue it, and he refused to fight. Lincoln knew, too, that the Copperhead agitation had reached the army, and that hundreds of them were being urged by parents and friends hostile to the Administration to desert.'' Page 162 shows that Lincoln, himself ''comprehended the failure to respond to the emancipation or to support the war;'' that (p. 163) ''New York, Pennsylvania, Ohio, Indiana, Illinois, and Wisconsin reversed their vote, and the House showed great Democratic gains.'' A. K. McClure's (*Lincoln and Men of the War Times*, p. 112, *et seq.*) says: ''There was no period from January, 1864, until 3d of September, when McClellan would not have defeated Lincoln for President.''

Charles A. Dana, in his *Recollections of the Civil War* (p. 180, *et seq.*) says: ''The people of the North might themselves have become half rebels if this proclamation had been issued too soon,'' and that ''two years before, perhaps, the consequences of it might have been our entire defeat.''

The Emancipation Proclamation has been described in song and story, on canvas and in marble, as a joyous and exultant announcement of freedom to the slaves. See how differently Ida Tarbell describes it and its author, and she is almost a worshipper of Lincoln. She says: ''At last (p. 525, *et seq.*) the Emancipation Proclamation was a fact, but there was little rejoicing in his heart, . . . no exultation; . . . indeed, there was almost a groan in the words in which, the night after he had given it out, he addressed a party of serenaders.'' . . . Rhodes says (*History of the United States*, Vol. IV, p. 72, *et seq.*) that on the 22nd of July, 1862, Seward objected in Cabinet meeting to giving out the threat of his purpose to emancipate that Lincoln issued ''as likely to seem at this juncture the last measure of an exhausted government; . . . our last shriek in retreat." And Miss Tarbell records that Lincoln himself said a few months later: "Hope and fear contended over the new policy in uncertain conflict." And she goes on: "As he had foreseen, dark days followed. There were mutinies in the army; . . . the events of the fall brought him little encouragement. Indeed, the promise of emancipation seemed to effect nothing but disappointment and uneasiness; stocks went down; troops fell off. In five great States—Indiana, Illinois, Ohio, Pennsylvania, and New York—the elections went against him."

CHAPTER XV

IF ALL this testimony suggests a desire to know in what proportion the people of the North and West were divided between those who approved Lincoln's great achievements and those who disapproved them, answers more or less specific—some of them estimating the numerical ratio—are furnished by the witnesses whose testimony we have been considering. Burgess says (*The Civil War and the Constitution,* Vol. I, p. 134) of the Democratic party in 1860, . . . "There was another great party at the North, numbering almost as many adherents as the Republican party itself, which was ready to yield to almost any demand, as the price of the Union, that the Secessionists might make." . . . A letter of General Wm. T. Sherman to General Halleck, of September 17, 1863, says (*Memoir,* Vol. I, p. 339) : "The people of even small and unimportant localities, North as well as South, had reasoned themselves into the belief that their opinions were superior to the aggregated interests of the whole nation. Half our territorial nation rebelled, on a doctrine of secession which they themselves now scout; and a real numerical majority actually believed that a little State was endowed with such sovereignty that it would defeat the policy of the great whole." Leland, after stating (*Lincoln,*

p. 94) that when the Confederate Government was organized at Montgomery "no one had threatened the new Southern Government, and at this stage the North would have suffered it to withdraw in peace from the Union," . . . says (p. 96) specifically that "the number of men in the North who were willing to grant them everything very nearly equalled that of the Republican party." Again Leland says (p. 95, *et seq.*), "But the strict truth shows that the Union party, what with the Copperheads, or sympathizers with the South, at home, and with the open foes in the field, was never at any time much more than equal to either branch of the enemy, and that, far from being the strongest in numbers, it was as one to two. Those in its ranks who secretly aided the enemy were numerous and powerful. The Union armies were sometimes led by generals whose hearts were with the foe." And Leland goes on (p. 96), "President Lincoln found himself in command of a beleaguered fortress, . . . a powerful enemy storming without, and nearly half his men doing their utmost to aid the enemy from within." So quite consistently Leland explains (p. 170) the attitude of England as follows: "To those who did not understand American politics in detail, the spectacle of about one-third of the population, even though backed by constitutional law, opposing the majority, seemed to call for little sympathy." And Dr. Holland says (*Abraham Lincoln,* p. 291), "All these labors Lincoln performed with the knowledge . . . that seven States were in open revolt and that a majority throughout the

Union had not the slightest sympathy with him." [1]

Henderson says,[2] "The majority of the Northern people held the Federal Government paramount, but, at the same time, they held that it had no power either to punish or coerce the individual States. This had been the attitude of the founders of the Republic, and it is perfectly clear that their interpretation of the Constitution was this: Although the several States were morally bound to maintain the compact into which they had voluntarily entered, the obligation, if any one State chose to repudiate it, could not be legally enforced. Their idea was a Union based upon fraternal affection.

"Mr. Lincoln's predecessor in the presidential chair had publicly proclaimed that coercion was both illegal and inexpedient, and for the three months which intervened between the secession of South Carolina and the inauguration of the Republican President, made not the slightest attempt to interfere with the peaceable establishment of the new Confederacy. Not a single soldier reinforced the garrisons of the military forts in the South. Not a single regiment was recalled from the western frontiers; and the seceded States, without a word of protest, were permitted to take possession, with few exceptions, of the forts, arsenals, navy-yards, and custom-houses which stood on their own territory.

---

[1] Dr. Holland is one of Lincoln's most ardent eulogists. Perhaps he did not know that Lincoln had said, in a published letter, which Rhodes says, Vol. IV., p. 409, may be called "a stump speech" as follows: "I freely acknowledge myself the servant of the people, according to the bond of service —the United States Constitution—and that, as such, I am responsible to them."

[2] *Life of General Thomas J. Jackson—Stonewall Jackson—*p. 116, *et seq.*

It seemed that the Federal Government was only waiting until an amicable adjustment could be arrived at as to the terms of separation.'' Morse, in like manner, goes back to tell how President Buchanan and the leaders and the press regarded and dealt with the actual secession of States which began and grew to maturity in President Buchanan's administration. Referring to Buchanan's last message, in which he pronounced coercion to be quite out of the question, Morse says (his *Lincoln,* Vol. I, p. 190, *et seq.*): ''But while this message of Mr. Buchanan has been bitterly denounced, and with entire justice, . . . yet a palliating consideration ought to be noted. He had little reason to believe that, if he asserted the right and duty of forcible coercion, he would find at his back the indispensable force, moral and physical of the people. Demoralization at the North was widespread. After the lapse of a few months this condition passed, and then those who had been beneath its influence desired to forget the humiliating fact, and hoped that others might either forget, or never know the measure of their weakness. In order that they might save their good names, it was natural that they should seek to suppress all evidence which had not already found its way upon the public record; but enough remains to show how grievously for a while the knees were weakened under many who enjoy—and rightfully, by reason of the rest of their lives—the reputation of stalwart patriots.[3]

[3] Morse might have quoted Governor Hicks, of Maryland, as a notable example. General Butler, at page 208 of *Butler's Book,* says, in describing his moving his Massachusetts troops to Washington by way of Annapolis, ''Gov-

For example, late in October General Scott suggested to the President a division of the country into four separate confederacies, roughly outlining their boundaries. Scott was a dull man, but he was at the head of the army and enjoyed a certain prestige, so that it was impossible to say that his notions, however foolish in themselves, were of no consequence. But if the blunders of General Scott could not fatally wound the Union cause, the blunders of Horace Greeley might conceivably do so. Republicans everywhere throughout the land had been educated by his teaching and had become accustomed to take a large part of their knowledge and their opinions in matters political from his writings. Then follows (p. 191) Greeley's full acknowledgment of the right of secession which appears above.[4] And it was this man—an authoritative though unofficial *power in the land*—who dared to say in his great *open letter* addressed to Lincoln through his *Tribune* as quoted above, "Nine-tenths of the whole American people, North and South, are anxious for peace—peace on almost any terms;" a ratio of opposition greatly above Leland's computation above quoted. That Greeley said this advisedly, with the fullest

ernor Hicks had protested to me against the landing of my troops, and he had also protested to the President, to whom he had made the amazing proposition that the national controversy should be referred to Lord Lyons, the British Minister." Nicolay's *Outbreak of the Rebellion* quotes Hicks, at page 88, as assuring the Baltimoreans gathered on Monument Square, after their bloody collision with the Massachusetts soldiers, on the 19th of April, that he would wish his "right arm might wither" should he fail in such an emergency. And Lamon's *Lincoln*, at page 517, quotes the words from a letter of Governor Hicks about the same time which expresses his wish that the guns he is issuing may be used "to kill Lincoln." This Morse, too, quotes in his *Lincoln*, p. 197, *et seq.*

[4] Pages 62 and 72 of this book.

knowledge, and honestly, cannot be questioned.

Nor was the *New York Herald* behind the *New York Tribune* in like protests. Morse says (*Lincoln,* Vol. I, p. 193), "On November 9, 1860, the Democratic *New York Herald,* discussing the election of Lincoln, said: "For far less than this our fathers seceded from Great Britain;" it also declared coercion to be "out of the question," and laid down the principle that each State possesses the "right to break the tie of the confederacy as a nation might break a treaty, and to repel coercion as a nation might repel invasion." Greeley, too, quotes (*American Conflict,* Vol. I, p. 358, *et seq.*) the *New York Herald* of 9th of November, 1860: . . . "And if the Cotton States shall decide that they can do better out of the Union than in it, we insist on letting them go in peace. The right to secede may be a revolutionary one, but it exists nevertheless; and we do not see how one party can have a right to do what another party has a right to prevent. We must ever resist the asserted right of any State to remain in the Union and nullify or annul the laws thereof. To withdraw from the Union is quite another matter. And whenever a considerable section of our Union shall deliberately resolve to go out we shall resist all coercive measures to keep it in. We hope never to live in a Republic whereof one section is pinned to the residue by bayonets."

See also *Butler's Book,* p. 141, *et seq.,* for editorials of Greeley's *Tribune,* avowing that States might properly secede.

Hugh McCulloch says (*Men and Measures of Half*

a Century, p. 15), "Still, as I have said, it is by no means certain that secession would have been crushed in its incipient stages if a more resolute man than Mr. Buchanan had been in his place." Again he says (p. 154) that the leaders in secession, "did not, however, anticipate a general uprising of the people of the Middle and Western States in defense of the Union. They confidently expected that Missouri, Kentucky, and Maryland would unite with other States in which slavery existed, and that Indiana, Illinois, and Ohio would give reluctant and partial aid to the Federal Government, if coercive measures should be resorted to for its support. For these expectations there were apparently good reasons.[5] The most prominent men in Missouri, Kentucky, and Maryland, if not Disunionists, were more attached to slavery than the Union, while their people generally were bound to the people of the Southern States by family or commercial ties. What might be called the civilization of those Central States was widely different from that of the Northern States, and they would undoubtedly have joined the South if they had not been prevented by the prompt and energetic measures of the Government. The disposition of the people of Maryland was indicated by the treatment which a Massachusetts regiment received as it passed through Baltimore. At the commencement of the war Mis-

[5] Besides the "good reasons" given by McCulloch, other very strong reasons are given in this book for the failure in every one of the States he names to meet the expectations of the Southern leaders. For these "strong reasons" see chapters 19 to 25, inclusive, of this book.

souri was in open revolt, and desperate battles were fought upon her soil before she could be prevented from casting in her lot with the South. The same influences which were at work in Missouri and Maryland were potent also in Kentucky.'' He then gives his personal observations in Kentucky, showing that it was with the South. He says (p. 155) of Missouri and Kentucky, ''Both would have united with the South if they could have had their own way. Nor was the expectation unreasonable that the Western free States and some of the leading Republicans also were opposed to coercion.'' McCulloch goes on (p. 158): ''In traveling through Southern Indiana in the autumn of 1860 and the following winter, I was amazed and disheartened by the general prevalence of the non-coercive sentiment. . . . As far as I could learn, the same opposition to coercion prevailed to a considerable extent in the other free States bordering upon the Ohio and Mississippi rivers, and I could not help feeling that the Union . . . had no deep hold on the affection of the people. My duties as President of the Bank of the State required my presence at Indianapolis when the Legislature of 1860–61 was in session, and I was astonished at some of the speeches of some of its most prominent members against what they called coercion—the coercion of sovereign States. In their opinion, the Union was not worth preserving, if it could only be preserved by force. Indiana, they said, would furnish no soldiers, nor would she permit soldiers from other States to pass through her territory, to subjugate the South. . . . The sentiment of southern Illinois was in sympathy with that of the people of southern Indiana.''

If any higher and more conclusive authority than those above quoted about the question in hand can be imagined, it is Secretary Stanton, speaking as Secretary of War for Lincoln. In defense of the President's usurpation of despotic powers, he issued February 14, 1861, a paper which contains the following: ''Every department of the Government was paralyzed by treason. Defections appeared in the Senate, in the House of Representatives, in the Cabinet, in the Federal Courts. Ministers and Consuls returned from foreign countries to enter the insurrectionary councils. Commanding or other officers of the army and in the navy betrayed our councils or deserted their posts for commands in the insurgent forces. Treason was flagrant in the revenue and in the post-office service, as well as in the Territorial governments and in the judicial reserves.

''Not only governors, judges, legislators, and ministerial officers in the States, but whole States, rushed out one after another with apparent unanimity into rebellion. . . . Even in the portions of the country which were most loyal political combinations and secret societies were formed furthering the work of disunion. . . . Armies, ships, fortifications, navy-yards, arsenals, military posts and garrisons, one after another, were betrayed or abandoned to the insurgents.''

CHAPTER XVI

THE fact that the great number of people in the North and West who opposed coercion had the sympathy of England will not be without interest. Rhodes says (*History of the United States,* Vol. III, p. 503): "John Stuart Mill speaks of the 'rush of nearly the whole of the upper and middle classes of my own country, even those who pass for liberals, into a furious pro-Southern partisanship, the working classes and some of the literary and scientific men being almost the sole exceptions to the general frenzy.' *Autobiography,* p. 268." Mill's tone shows that he is an unwilling witness to the state of feeling in England. And on the next page to the above, Rhodes quotes the *London Times* of the 7th of November, 1861, as follows: "The contest is really for empire on the side of the North and for independence on that of the South, and in that respect we recognize an exact analogy between the North and the government of George III, and the South and the thirteen revolted provinces. These opinions may be wrong, but they are the general opinion of the English nation." On page 509 Rhodes again quotes the *London Times* of October 9, 1861: "The people of the South may be wrong, but they are ten million." Elsewhere (Vol. IV, p. 358) Rhodes says "Four-fifths of the House of Lords were 'no well-

112

wishers of anything American,' and most of the
House of Commons desired the success of the
South.'' And Rhodes shows (Vol. IV, p. 337) such
an attitude of the premier and of Earl Russell that
Mr. Adams, United States Minister to England,
wrote, September 2, 1862, ''Unless the course of the
war should soon change, it seems to me my mission
must come to an end by February.'' Again he reports (p. 339) that ''Gladstone, October 7, 1862, at
a banquet at New Castle said, 'We may anticipate
with certainty the success of the Southern States so
far as their separation from the North is con-
cerned.' '' Rhodes quotes (p. 392, *et seq.*) Gladstone
writing to Senator Sumner, November, 1863, ''In
England I think nearly all consider war against
slavery unjustifiable,'' and complains (p. 80) that
Gladstone said to the men of Manchester, April 14th,
''We have no faith in the propagation of free institutions at the point of the sword.'' Rhodes quotes,
too (note on p. 85), from a letter from the Duke of
Argyle to Sumner, ''I cannot believe in there being
any Union party in the South, and, if not, can the
continuance of the war be justified?''

Not the war only upon the South, but its being
forced on the people of the North and West met
heavy censure from England. Rhodes says (*History
of the United States,* Vol. III, p. 514) of the *London
Times* and the *Saturday Review,* Their ''criticisms
of the arbitrary measures of our Government . . .
were galling,'' and quotes from the *Saturday Review* of the 19th of October, 1861, ''The arrest of
the newly-elected members of the legislative assem-

bly of Maryland before they had had any time to meet, without any form of law or prospect of trial, merely because President Lincoln conceived that they might in their legislative capacity do acts at variance with his interpretation of the American Constitution, was as perfect an act of despotism as can be conceived. . . . It was a *coup d'état* in every essential feature," and the paper goes on, November 23, 1861, "The land of the free is a land in which electors may not vote, for fear of arrest, and judges may not execute the law, for fear of dismissal—in which unsubmissive advocates are threatened with imprisonment and hostile newspapers are suppressed." No wonder, then, that, as Rhodes tells us (Vol. II, p. 27), "James Russell Lowell took grievously to heart the comments of the English press and the actions of the English Government."

If to any one it seems that England's course needs apology or defense, we have it, published lately, and by a very able writer, and one with no sort of leaning towards the South or tolerance of slavery. The *Literary Digest* for March 29, 1902, at page 417, quotes from the *Atlantic Monthly,* Goldwin Smith, as follows: "The sympathy of the people of England in general could be challenged by the North only on the ground that the North was fighting against slavery. But when we, friends of the North, urged this plea, we had the misfortune to be met by a direct disclaimer of our advocacy on the part of our clients. President Lincoln repudiated the intention of attacking slavery. Seward repudiated it in still more emphatic terms. Congress had tried to bring back the Slave States to the fold by promises of increased securities for slavery, including a sharpening of the Fugitive-Slave Law. What had we to say? . . . Had the issue been, as Lincoln, Seward, and Congress represented, merely political and territorial, we might have had to decide against the North. Few who have looked into the history can doubt that the Union originally was, and was generally taken by the parties to be, a compact dissoluble, perhaps most of them would have said at pleasure, dissoluble certainly on breach of the articles of the Union. Among these articles, unquestionably, were the recognition and protection of slavery, which the Constitution guaranteed by means of a fugitive-slave law. It was not less certain that the existence of slavery was threatened by the abolition movement at the North, and practically attacked by the election of Lincoln, who had declared that the continent must be all slave or all free; meaning, of course, that it must be all free." He quotes Lincoln's formal declaration of the right of secession in his speech beginning "any people anywhere," etc., recorded at page 66 of this book, and goes on as follows: "A stronger ground for separation there could not possibly be than the radical antagonism between the social organizations of the two groups of States, which made it impossible that they should live in harmony under the same political roof, and had rendered their enforced union a source of ever increasing bitterness and strife. . . .

"If England was divided in opinion, so was the

North itself. There was all the time in the North a
strong Democratic party opposed to the war. The
autumn elections of 1862 went greatly against the
Government. It was in expectation of calling forth
Northern support that Lee invaded Pennsylvania,
and had he conquered at Gettysburg, his expectation
would probably have been fulfilled. It actually was
fulfilled, after a fashion, by the draft riot in New
York." The *Independent,* too, (for April 10, 1902,
p. 850), quotes Goldwin Smith: "In justice to the
British people it must always be borne in mind that
the American Government had distinctly proclaimed
that the abolition of slavery was not the object of
the war."

The sympathy of the Continental powers of
Europe concerns us less than that of England, exhibited above, but it is interesting to notice how the
sympathy of one of them lay, as exhibited in the
following extract:

Munsey's Magazine (for May, 1902) quotes from
George Bancroft's Eulogy of Lincoln, delivered
12th February, 1866, in the Hall of Representatives,
a reference to the Pope, who "alone among the tem-
poral sovereigns recognized the Chief of the Confederate states as a President, and his supporters
as a people, and gave counsels for peace at a time
when peace meant the victory of secession."

CHAPTER XVII

DESPOTISM CONCEDED

IF ANY are scandalized or startled at seeing Lincoln called usurper or despot, they are invited to observe that he was denounced as both by many great Republican leaders of his own day. The words in which Frémont, Wendell Phillips, Fred Douglass, and Horace Greeley, all stanchest of Republicans and Abolitionists, issued their call for the convention of Republicans that met at Cleveland, Ohio, May 31, 1864, for the sole purpose of defeating Mr. Lincoln's second election, were as follows: "The public liberty was in danger:" that its object was to arouse the people "and bring them to realize that while we are saturating Southern soil with the best blood of the country in the name of liberty, we have really parted with it at home."[1]

Capt. C. C. Chesney, of the Royal Engineers, says,[2] the garrison of Washington was being drained, not

[1] It is interesting to compare these words with those in which John Paul Jones gave a warning to the great Constitutional Convention in Philadelphia, when Jefferson asked and obtained from him an elaborate memorandum of his views of the merits of the constitution when it was finished. His words in the memorandum are as follows: . . . "Though General Washington might be safely trusted with such tempting power as the chief command of the fleet and the army, yet, depend on it, in some other hands it could not fail to overset the liberties of America. . . . Deprive the President of the power or the right to draw his sword and lead the fleet and the army, under some plausible pretext or under any circumstances whatever, to cut the throats of part of his fellow citizens in order to make himself tyrant over the rest."

[2] Vol. II., p. 131. Just after Gettysburg.

so much for Mead's re-enforcement as to check the insurrection in New York. And when Lee had retired to the Rapidan, Chesney says of Meade in his front, ''Large detachments were at this time made from his strength to increase the garrison which was to aid General Dix in enforcing the obnoxious conscription in New York.'' Again he speaks (p. 149) of Lincoln and his Cabinet as reducing the Army of the Potomac largely in order to carry out the conscription, which they had been obliged to postpone in New York. Thirty thousand troops under General Dix occupied that rebellious city in August, 1863, and the obnoxious ballot was enforced without further resistance, in spite of ''the strenuous opposition of Governor Seymour.''

Rhodes tells (*History of the United States,* Vol. IV, p. 164, *et seq.*) of . . . ''open dissatisfaction which in Pennsylvania and Wisconsin broke out into positive violence over the draft necessary under the call for 300,000 militia.''

Among many records of the suppression of newspapers we have the following, in a letter of Gen. John A. Dix[3] to Secretary Stanton, February 18, 1862, ''Samuel Sands Mills, publisher and proprietor, and Thomas H. Piggott, editor, of *The South,* were arrested last evening, kept in the station-house during the night, and sent to Fort McHenry this morning. The office of *The South* was seized last evening, and is in possession of the police. John M. Mills, a partner in the concern, has also

---

[3] *War of the Rebellion; Official Records of the Union and Confederate Armies,* Series II., Vol. II., p. 788.

been arrested, and will be sent to Fort McHenry immediately.''

The same (page 791) has in a note, ''For the full proceedings of the House on July 18, 1861, concerning the charges against May, the attack by a Baltimore man on the Federal troops, and Chief of Police Kane's connection therewith, see *Congressional Globe* for July 20, 1861, p. 196, *et seq.*''

The same volume (page 795) gives Pinkerton's report of the arrest, about midnight, 12th September, 1861, of Messrs. Scott, Wallis, F. Key Howard, Hall, May and Warfield.

The same volume (pp. 938 to 956) tells of the arrest of Messrs. Flanders Brothers, editors of the *Gazette,* Franklin county, N. Y., for complete opposition to the war—and of exclusion of the *Gazette* from the mails.

Rhodes describes (*History of the United States,* Vol. IV, p. 175, *et seq.*) the suppression of a ''disloyal'' paper in Cincinnati, and (p. 253) the exclusion from the mails of the *New York World* and the suppression of the *Chicago Times* by General Burnside, and says of Burnside's orders, ''Strange pronunciamentos were these to apply to the States of Ohio, Indiana, and Illinois, where there was no war; where the courts were open and the people were living under the American Constitution and English law.'' Could there be more conclusive evidence of the attitude of Chicago and the great States he names, for which Chicago is a great commercial centre, than Rhodes' record, as follows: ''The *Times* had gone beyond any print, North or South, in its opposition to the war and its devotion to the interests of the rebellion.'' Rhodes goes on to say (p. 254) that "the President yielded, . . . but he deserves no credit, . . . for he simply responded to the outburst of sentiment" in Chicago, manifested by action of the city government and the State government, "which sentiment," he adds, "was beginning to spread over the whole North." Rhodes' note on page 253, quoted from the *Chicago Tribune* of June 5, 1863, gives more light on the matter and fixes the date of the events.

We have Lincoln's own order to General Dix of May 18, 1864,[4] to "arrest and imprison in any fort or military prison in your command the editors, proprietors and publishers of the *New York World* and the *New York Journal of Commerce*." The two journals were the very embodiment of all that was most respected, so that General Dix hesitated (p. 388), and was compelled to obey by peremptory letters from Secretary Stanton. Rhodes mentions (*History of the United States,* Vol. III, p. 555) "the arrest of a crippled newsboy for selling the *New York Daily News* in Connecticut."

It would be difficult to characterize the above described usurpations in language stronger than was applied at the time. Rhodes quotes (p. 555) from a lecture of Wendell Phillips delivered in New York and Boston, December, 1861, as follows: "Lieber says that *habeas corpus*, free meetings like this, and a free press, are the three elements which distin-

---

[4] *Record of the Rebellion; Official Records of the Union and Confederate Armies,* Serial Number 125, p. 388.

guish liberty from despotism. All that Saxon blood
has gained in the battles and toils of two hundred
years are these three things. But today, Mr. Chairman, every one of them—*habeas corpus*, the right of
free meeting, and a free press—is annihilated in
every square mile of the Republic. We live today,
every one of us, under martial law. The Secretary
of State puts into his bastile, with a warrant as irresponsible as that of Louis XIV, any man whom he
pleases. And you know that neither press nor lips
may venture to arraign the Government without
being silenced. At this very moment one thousand
men at least are 'bastiled' by an authority as despotic as that of Louis. . . . For the first time
in our history government spies frequent our great
cities." And Rhodes quotes (p. 534) protests of
Robert C. Winthrop, in a speech of November 2,
1864—almost three years later—of "newspapers
silenced and suppressed at the tinkling of an executive bell a thousand miles away from the scene of
hostilities." And Rhodes goes on (p. 556), "Yet
the matter did not go unquestioned. Senator Trumbull introduced a resolution asking information from
the Secretary of State in regard to these arrests,
and, in his remarks supporting it, pointed out the
injustice and needlessness of such procedure.
"What are we coming to," he asked, "if arrests may
be made at the whim or the caprice of a Cabinet
Minister?" and, when Senator Hale asked, "Have
not arrests been made in violation of the great
principles of our Constitution?" no one could gain-
say it; and Rhodes says (p. 557), "In truth, the

apprehension of men in Maine, Vermont, Connecticut, and northern New York on suspicion that they were traitors, instead of leaving them to be dealt with by the public sentiment of their thoroughly loyal communities, savored rather of an absolute monarch than of a desire to govern in a constitutional way."[5]

Rhodes quotes from a letter from Schleinden to Sumner (p. 442), "One of the most interesting features of the present state of things is the unlimited power exercised by the Government. Mr. Lincoln is in that respect the equal, if not the superior, of Louis Napoleon, and Rhodes refers, too, (p. 514) to "the comparison constantly made in England between the *coup d'état* of Louis Napoleon and the *coup d'état* of Abraham Lincoln," and, excusing the use of such power, adds, "The county attorney of Illinois had assumed the power of a dictator;" and this as early as July, 1861.

Rhodes' *History of the United States* is one of the latest records in this matter. While he eulogizes Lincoln as ardently as any other, as is shown in the Appendix, he speaks (Vol. IV, p. 234, *et seq.*) of "the enormity of the acts done under his authority," and says "he stands responsible for the casting into prison of citizens of the United States to be counted by thousands (p. 230) on orders as arbitrary as the *Lettres de Cachet* of Louis XIV," when the mode

[5] Lincoln has been accused by no one else of "capriciousness." Does not this book show that the States Rhodes names, and all the rest where these despotic methods were used, were *not* "thoroughly loyal," and that at least four of them would have joined the Confederacy if Lincoln had not restrained them by these methods and other similar defiance of all constitutional restraint?

of procedure might have been, "as in Great Britain in her crises between 1793 and 1802, on legal warrants," and he pronounces Lincoln's conduct "inexpedient, unnecessary, and wrong."[6]   And Rhodes says more specifically on the same page, "After careful consideration, . . . I do not hesitate to condemn the arbitrary arrests and the arbitrary interference with the freedom of the press in States which were not in the theatre of the war and where the courts were open; . . . that the offenders should have been prosecuted according to law, or, if their offenses were not indictable, permitted to go free." Besides all this, Rhodes gives (Vol. IV, p. 169 to p. 172) unqualified commendation to Governor Seymour for a patriotic spirit and proper jealousy for his country's liberty shown in his bitter opposition to Lincoln's usurpations, and shows how very far Seymour's resentment towards Lincoln went. Rhodes even calls Lincoln a "tyrant." Of a proclamation issued two days after the edict of Emancipation (Sept. 24, 1862) he says (p. 169, *et seq.*), after giving particulars of it, that it "applied to the whole country, . . . and was the assumption of the authority exercised by an absolute monarch." And he quotes Joel Parker, Professor of Law in Harvard, as follows: "Do you not perceive that the President is not only an absolute monarch, but that his is an absolutely uncontrollable government, a perfect military despotism?" And Rhodes

---

[6] "Wrong" it was, doubtless; but was it inexpedient or unnecessary? Without it would the people of the States called "loyal" have continued the war or re-elected Lincoln?

says (p. 170) of Curtis, a Justice of the Supreme Court, that "he now published a pamphlet, entitled *Executive Power*, which called Lincoln, "a usurper" and his power "a military despotism." And Rhodes adds, . . . "Indeed it is not surprising that it gave currency to an opinion that he intended to suppress free discussion of political events."

Appleton's Annual Cyclopaedia for 1864 (page 307) calls the Wade-Davis Manifesto, which will be described below, "a bitter attack on the President, remarkable as coming from the leaders of his own party," and this Rhodes quotes (p. 487) without dissent and even gives the following commendation of Wade and Davis (p. 229) : "Their criticism of the Executive for suspending the privilege of the writ of *habeas corpus* for arbitrary arrests, for the abridgment of the freedom of speech and of writing, was justly taken and undoubtedly had influence for good on the legislation of the session." This commendation, like what he gives Seymour and others for bitter opposition to Lincoln and denunciation of him, sounds strange, coming from Rhodes.

Rhodes twice concedes (Vol. IV, p. 169, *et seq.*, and p. 556, *et seq.*) Lincoln's full responsibility for the despotic acts of his ministers, Stanton and Seward, but appends to the latter the following—a feeble defense indeed: "It is not probable that Lincoln of his own motion would have ordered them, for although at times he acted without warrant of the Constitution, he had a profound preference for it. . . . It was undoubtedly disagreeable to him to be called by Vallandigham 'the Caesar of the

American Republic,' and by Wendell Phillips 'a more unlimited despot than the world knows this side of China,' and to be aware that Senator Grimes described a call at the White House, for the purpose of seeing the President, as 'an attempt to approach the footstool of the power enthroned at the other end of the Avenue.' ''

The above follows his account of very notable arrests (p. 555 to p. 557) arbitrarily made in Northern States.

William A. Dunning, President of Columbia University, says in his *Essays on the Civil War*, dated 1898 (p. 39, *et seq.*), that President Lincoln's Proclamation of September 24, 1862, was "a perfect plot for a military despotism," and that "the very demonstrative resistance of the people to the Government only made the military arrests more frequent;" . . . that (p. 24, *et seq.*) "Mr. Lincoln asserted the existence of martial law . . . throughout the United States." He says "thousands were so dealt with," . . . and that (p. 46) "the records of the War Department contain the reports of hundreds of trials by military commissions with punishments varying from light fines to banishment and death." Lalor's Encyclopedia says the records of the Provost Marshal's office in Washington show thirty-eight thousand political prisoners, but Rhodes (Vol. IV, p. 230, *et seq.*) says the number is exaggerated. Holland's *Lincoln* shows (p. 476, *et seq.*) that when Lincoln killed, by "pocketing" it, a bill for the reconstruction of the Union which Congress had just passed, Ben Wade and Winter Davis, aided by Greeley, published in Greeley's *Tribune*, of August 5th "a bitter manifesto." It is charged that the President, by preventing this bill from becoming a law *"holds the electoral vote of the rebel States at the discretion of his personal ambition,"* and that "a more studied outrage on the authority of the people has never been perpetrated." A. K. McClure's *Lincoln and Men of the War Time* gives the same account. See, too, Schouler's *History of the United States*, p. 469. Channing says (*Short History of the United States*, p. 331, *et seq.*): "Many persons in the North thought that the Southerners had a perfect right to secede if they wished. Some of these persons sympathized so thoroughly with the Southerners that they gave them important information and did all they could to hinder Lincoln in conquering the South. It was hard to prove anything against these Southern sympathizers, but it was dangerous to leave them at liberty. So Lincoln ordered many of them to be arrested and locked up. Lincoln now suspended the operation of the writ of *habeas corpus*. This action angered many persons who were quite willing that the Southerners should be compelled to obey the law, but did not like to have their neighbors arrested and locked up without trial." And Channing goes on (p. 332), "The draft was bitterly resisted in some parts of the North, especially in New York city."

CHAPTER XVIII

THE opposition to coercion and to emancipation that has been shown so strong in the people of the States called "loyal," in their Congress, in their regular army, and in their volunteer army, was all included under one charge of "disloyalty" and suppressed by the usurpation of despotic power.

How fully Lincoln used every method of a military despot in suppressing it is shown by examination of a single chapter of Bancroft's *Life of William H. Seward.* The following extracts from it need little comment. Lest any reader should suppose that Bancroft means to expose or arraign Lincoln or his agent, Seward, for the arbitrary arrests and imprisonments that he describes, be it understood that he does no more than mildly concede that Seward's zeal in a good cause betrayed him into undue severities in the "loyal" States. He says expressly (Vol. II, p. 276, *et seq.*): "For the general policy as practiced in the Border States there is no . . . occasion to apologize. . . . But there were some serious abuses of this arbitrary power in the far Northern States." Again he says (Vol. III, p. 254) of Seward, "Probably the detection of political offenders and the control of political prisoners were the most distracting of all his cares." His mode of arrest and confinement of the prisoners is described as follows (Vol. II, p. 259): ''Some of the features bore a striking resemblance to the most odious institutions of the ancient regime in France —the *Bastile* and the *Lettres de Cachet*.'' ''The person 'suspected' of disloyalty was often seized at night, borne off to the nearest fort, deprived of his valuables, locked up in a casemate, . . . generally crowded with men who had similar experiences. . . If he wished to send for friends or an attorney, he was informed that the rules forbade visitors, that attorneys were entirely excluded, and that the prisoner who sought their aid would greatly prejudice his case.[1] An appeal to Seward was the only recourse—a second, third, and fourth, all alike useless. The Secretary was calm in the belief that the man was a plotter and would do no harm while he remained in custody.'' It was found best (Vol. II, p. 262) ''to take prominent men far from their homes and sympathizers. . . . The suspected men, notably Marylanders, were carried to Fort Warren or other remote places. . . . In most cases from one to three months elapsed before definite action was taken by the department. . . . If the arrest had been made without due cause, no oaths or conditions of release were required.'' . . . So, too, ''if the alleged offence had been too

---

[1] Secretary Seward wrote to Keys, U. S. Marshal, ''you will therefore please inform all the prisoners at Fort Warren . . . that if the fact comes to the knowledge of this department that any prisoner has agreed to pay to any attorney a sum of money, or to give him anything of value as a consideration for interceding for the release of such prisoner, that fact will be held as an additional reason for continuing the confinement of such persons. *War of the Rebellion; Official Records of the Union and Confederate Armies*, Series II., Vol. I., p. 614.

highly colored by a revengeful enemy."² See particulars of several cases (Vol. II, pp. 264 to 276) given by Bancroft, and especially one where the action was aimed at Ex-President Pierce, "who believed," Bancroft records, "the South to be the aggrieved party." Bancroft winds up this with the comprehensive statement that "not one of the political prisoners³ was brought to trial. As a rule they were not even told why they were arrested. When the pressure for judicial procedure or for a candid discussion of the case became too strong to be resisted on plausible grounds, the alleged offender was released."⁴

Bancroft says further (Vol. II, p. 276, *et seq.*), "The least excusable feature was the treatment of the prisoners. Month after month many of them were crowded together in gloomy and damp casemates, where even the dangerous 'pirates' captured on privateers and soldiers taken in battle ought not to have remained long. Many had committed no overt act. There were among them editors and political leaders of character and honor, but whose

² In the *War of the Rebellion; Official Records of the Union and Confederate Armies*, Series I., Vol. I., p. 599, Gen. John A. Dix cautions Secretary Seward as follows: "I arrested in an interior county and brought to this city two men charged with open acts of hostility to the government on testimony vouched by the United States Marshal, yet they turned out to be two of the most consistent and active Union men in the neighborhood."

³ Vol. II., p. 276. He means of those confined by Seward.

⁴ It is notable that Bancroft, a man of our own day—he lectured to the students of the Hopkins University in 1901—records with complacency, or at least without apology, such despotic treatment of American citizens. It is however, consistent with his calling the ships of war and the officers of the Confederate Navy "privateers" and "pirates," as elsewhere quoted. Semmes and Arthur Sinclair have told how this navy swept from the face of the waters the whole merchant marine of the United States with the sympathy of nearly all Christendom.

freedom would be prejudicial to the prosecution of the war. (Vol. II, p. 278.) It was inevitable that innocent men should be caught in the dangerous machinery. It afforded rare opportunities for the gratification of personal enmities and the display of power on the part of United States marshals and military officers. . . . It happened more than once that men languished in prisons for weeks before any one at the department even heard their names.''

Justice to the great States that were reduced to submission makes it necessary to give a few of the cruelties—the barbarities—suffered by many of the imprisoned. The Hon. Charles James Faulkner, who enjoyed very high honors from Virginia before and after the war, came back from his duties as Minister to Paris, was arrested on landing in New York and imprisoned in Fort Lafayette, whence he wrote the Secretary of State,[5] September 13, 1861, ''A small casemate of this frontier and isolated fortification accommodates eight persons including myself. Through three small apertures a dim and imperfect light is admitted—not sufficient to enable the occupants to read or write unless when the door is open, which can only be when allowed by the state of the weather and the regulations of the fort. . . . In another casemate near me are twenty-four prisoners in chains.''

This would have been extraordinary cruelty if the prisoners had been under conviction of crimes, but the same volume, at pp. 411 to 413, describes far

[5] *War of the Rebellion; Official Records of the Union and Confederate Armies*, Series II., Vol. II., p. 470.

more barbarous treatment of the gallant Colonel Thomas—known as *Zarvona* Thomas.

Godkin, of the New York *Nation* (Jan. 12, 1899), might well say, as he did in one of his later editorials, "The first real breach in the Constitution was made by the invention of the *war power* to enable President Lincoln to abolish slavery. No one would now say that this was not at that time necessary, but it made it possible for any President practically to suspend the Constitution by getting up a war anywhere." . . . Bancroft gives various examples (p. 235, note) of the method of arrest —simple telegrams, signed "Seward," "Stanton," or "Richard H. Dana"—one was, "Send Wm. Paine to Fort Lafayette. F. W. Seward;" for even a deputy, son of the Secretary, exercised tremendous power. Republicans were arrested, too, (p. 235). Most notable of the protests against the arrests was one in a special message of Gov. Curtin, of Pennsylvania, one of the great "war-governors," attached to Lincoln, and from the first a zealous supporter of the Emancipation Proclamation. A. K. McClure describes (*Lincoln and Men of the War Time*, p. 164) how he got a man named Jere McKibben released from quite causeless imprisonment by Stanton, and adds, "I had quite frequently been to Washington before when arbitrary and quite unjustifiable arrests of civilians had been made in Pennsylvania." Rhodes says (*History of the United States*, Vol. IV, p. 413), "Seward and Stanton had caused many arrests with no more formality than a telegraphic dispatch."

The sacred right to trial, without which all other rights are vain, was almost always denied, as elsewhere shown, but release was sometimes granted on singular conditions, as when⁶ James G. Berdet, Mayor of Washington city, "was required as a condition of his discharge from Fort Delaware to resign the office of Mayor." The same volume tells of the arrest and imprisonment of the editor of the *Republican Watchman*, of Greenport, Long Island, and (p. 670) shows that his family were supported by subscriptions of sympathizing neighbors.

The story is well known that when the English Minister, Lord Lyons, called the attention of the Secretary of State, Seward, to the bitter opposition to the war that was showing itself everywhere, Seward answered that with his little bell he could imprison any citizen in any State, and that no one but the President could release him. Bancroft says (Vol. II, p. 280) : "If he made this remark, it is of no special importance; it was a fact that he was almost as free from restraint as a dictator or a sultan."

The methods of the State Department that are described above did not surpass in any respect those of the War Department. The latter even *created new offenses*, ending a list of them with,⁷ "any other disloyal practice," and it authorized and directed "arrest and imprisonment in the discretion of even chiefs of police of any town or district."

⁶ *War of the Rebellion; Official Records of the Union and Confederate Armies*, Series II., Vol. II., pp. 596 to 599.

⁷ *War of the Rebellion; Official Records of the Union and Confederate Armies*, Series III., Vol. II., p. 321.

CHAPTER XIX

GENERAL OPPOSITION AND RESISTANCE TO COERCION AND EMANCIPATION

THE advocacy of views strongly opposed to the war and to emancipation did not cease in the North and the West when the war began, dangerous as it soon became to advocate them. Imprisonment without trial, trials by court-martial, sentences to confinement in prisons or fortresses remote from home and friends, did reduce at last to silence all but the boldest—even Missourians, Kentuckians, and Marylanders; and similar methods of repression were used in States remotest from the scenes of the war. In this chapter an account will be given of the general resistance throughout the North and West, and succeeding chapters will describe the resistance in the separate States and groups of States, and the methods by which resistance was suppressed.

Nicolay and Hay give (Vol. VIII, p. 29, *et seq.*) a full account of the "disloyalty" in the North and West, and say, too (Vol. IV, p. 234), that "in the Western States the words Democrat and Copperhead became after January, 1863, practically synonymous, and a cognomen applied as a reproach was assumed with pride." Professor Channing, of Harvard, says,[1] "In the Mississippi Valley hundreds of

[1] Channing's *Short History of the United States*, p. 314.

thousands of men either sympathized with the slave-holders or cared nothing about the slavery dispute.'' George S. Boutwell says,[2] ''With varying degrees of intensity the Democratic party of the North sympathized with the South, and arraigned Lincoln and the Republican party for all that the country was called to endure. During the entire period of the war New York, Ohio, and Illinois were doubtful States, and Indiana was kept in line only by the active and desperate fidelity of Oliver P. Morton.'' Secretary Welles, of Lincoln's Cabinet, says (*Atlantic Monthly,* Vol. XVI, p. 266): ''The Democrats were in sympathy with the rebels, . . . and opposed to the war itself.''

Ridpath says,[3] ''During this year (1863) the Administration of President Lincoln was beset with many difficulties. . . . The Anti-War party of the North had grown more bold, and openly denounced the measures of the Government. . . . In many places the draft officers were forcibly resisted. . . . The anti-war spirit in some parts of the North ran so high that on the 19th of August President Lincoln issued a proclamation suspending the privileges of the writ of *habeas corpus* throughout the Union.''

Everywhere there were men who made more or less bitter protest or resistance against such subversion, by methods known only to the Sultan or the Czar, of what Americans had been taught to call the conditions of freedom—a free press, free speech,

---

[2] *Abraham Lincoln, Tributes from His Associates,* p. 85, *et seq.*

[3] *Popular History of the United States,* published in 1883, p. 522.

the writ of *habeas corpus*, and trial by jury. In Cincinnati, in Chicago, in Boston, and elsewhere, demonstrations toward violent resistance very alarming to the Administration at Washington were suppressed with the strong hand before coming to a head. Gilmore (*Personal Recollections of Lincoln*, p. 199) speaks of "the wide Western conspiracy so opportunely strangled in Chicago," and devotes a chapter to it.

When the storm was rising there came from the Democratic leaders in the "loyal" States as distinct asseverations of the wrongs the South was enduring, as full assurances that the South had the right to withdraw from the partnership, as full denial of any possible right in the Federal Government to use coercion, as any Southern leader ever set forth; with further assurances that the Democrats of the North and West would fight on the Southern side in any appeal to arms.

The extreme Abolitionists also bitterly opposed the war. President Theodore Roosevelt's *Cromwell* says (p. 103) that at the close of the war "the Garrison . . . or disunion Abolitionists . . . had seen their cause triumph, not through, but in spite of, their efforts." And Gorham's *Life of Stanton* (Vol. I, p. 163, *et seq.*) says, "The Republicans . . . were divided into two classes, one, which desired separation, etc.," . . . and (Vol. I, p. 193) tells of "a new element, headed by prominent Republican leaders like Greeley and Chase, who thought that a union of non-slaveholding States would be preferable to any attempt to maintain by force the Union with the slaveholding States.'' Observe how exactly these conclusions agreed with the conclusions to which the Southern leaders had come.

A letter of Chase quoted in his *Life* by Warden (p. 363, *et seq.*) says: ''It is precisely because they anticipate abolition as the result that the Garrison Abolitionists desire disunion.'' Schouler says of Garrison, Phillips and their immediate followers (*History of the United States,* Vol. VI, p. 225), ''They were the avowed Disunionists on the Northern side.'' . . . Burgess says (*The Civil War and the Constitution,* Vol. I, p. 148), ''The Abolitionist wing of the Republican party was never noted for strong unionism,'' and (p. 227) ''down to our civil war the Abolitionist preached destruction of the Union.'' Leland says (*Lincoln,* p. 199) about the election of 1864: ''The ultra abolition adherents of General Frémont were willing to see a proslavery President—McClellan—elected rather than Mr. Lincoln, so great was their hatred of him and emancipation. . . . As the election drew on, threats and rumors of revolution in the North were rife.'' Keifer says (his *Slavery and Four Years of War,* p. 172, *et seq.*), ''There was also, though strangely inconsistent, a very considerable class of the early Abolitionists of the Garrison-Smith-Phillips school who did not support the war for the Union, but preferred the slaveholding States should secede.'' Channing says (*Short History of the United States*), ''The Abolitionists welcomed the secession of the Slave States.''

In spite of the support of the war forced on the Democracy, as above described, they made a steady struggle in the courts, in Congress, and in the State governments, to keep down the war to something like constitutional limits as far as possible, and to such conditions as might leave room for reconciliation in the future. Vallandigham's and Seymour's conduct, of which particulars will be given below, furnish examples, and General McClellan's is another example. For years no pains were spared to cry down General McClellan in vindication of Lincoln's dealings with him, but evidence of the truth has been too strong. Even Nicolay and Hay have to concede to McClellan the very highest praise for pure patriotism, and the concessions have grown greater with each succeeding historian till Rhodes, one of the ablest, deplores [4] the fact that Lincoln could not see McClellan as we see him, and that Lincoln deferred the capture of Richmond and the downfall of the Confederacy for two years by removing McClellan from command of the army. Ropes passes hardly less severe censure on Lincoln [5] for his dealings with McClellan, and Rhodes and Ropes are very hostile critics of McClellan. [6]

In this connection there are some unconscious betrayals of the real estimate of Lincoln that was entertained by a number of his eminent eulogists.

[4] *History of the United States*, Vol. IV., p. 109 and p. 106, *et seq.*

[5] *Story of the Civil War*, Part II., p. 132, *et seq.*, p. 442, *et seq.*, p. 473, *et seq.*

[6] See John Fiske's *Mississippi Valley in the Civil War*, p. 148, *et seq.*, and his quotation of censure of Lincoln to the same effect from the Count of Paris. See Ida Tarbell in *McClure's Magazine* for May, 1899, pp. 192 to 199, *et seq.*, and see Henderson's *Life of Stonewall Jackson*, Vol. I., p. 307.

Eight of them [7] have thought it worth while, if not necessary, to declare very expressly their belief that Lincoln did not purposely betray General McClellan and his army in the Seven-Days' battles before Richmond. McClellan, in his celebrated dispatch after his retreat, reproached Stanton with this atrocious crime, and so worded the dispatch that he imputed the same guilt to Lincoln.

A. K. McClure [8] and Nicolay and Hay (*Abraham Lincoln,* p. 441, *et seq.,* and p. 451) deplore that McClellan should have believed Lincoln capable of it, both conceding to McClellan the most exalted character, ability, and patriotism.

Of Lincoln's dealings with McClellan, A. K. Mc-Clure says [9] "Many charged, as did McClellan, that he had been with his army, deliberately betrayed by the Secretary of War, if not by Lincoln." A gentleman who commanded a division in the Union army in one of the great battles said to the author of this book, "If McClellan had taken Richmond, it would have been an end of the Republican party."

Dr. Burgess, Professor of Political Science in the Columbia University, closes the treatment of

---

[7] The eight are the following: A. K. McClure, see *Lincoln and Men of the War Time,* p. 102, p. 207, *et seq.;* Dr. Holland, see *Abraham Lincoln,* p. 753, *et seq.;* John Coddman Ropes, see *Story of the Civil War,* Part II., p. 116, p. 171, p. 230, p. 442, *et seq.,* and p. 473, *et seq.;* Rhodes, see *History of the United States,* Vol. IV., p. 50, *et seq.;* Hon. George S. Boutwell, see *Tributes from His Associates,* p. 69; Schouler, see *History of the United States,* p. 193, *et seq.;* Henderson, see *Life of Stonewall Jackson,* Vol. I., p. 499; Nicolay and Hay, see *Abraham Lincoln,* Vol. VI., p. 189, *et seq.,* p. 441, *et seq.,* and p. 451.

[8] *Lincoln and Men of the War Time,* p. 102.

[9] *Lincoln and Men of the War Time,* pp. 208, 248; see too, Nicolay and Hay's *Abraham Lincoln,* Vol. VI., p. 189, *et seq.*

the subject of General McClellan's military career with the following very curious and very suggestive words: [10] "Whether a crushing victory over the Confederates, ending at once the rebellion before slavery was destroyed, was wanted by all of those who composed the Washington Government, may well be suspected. And it is very nearly certain that there were some who would have preferred defeat to such a victory with McClellan in command. It was a dark, mysterious, uncanny thing, which the historian does not need to touch and prefers not to touch."

Those who have labored most to discredit McClellan as a general have been obliged to concede to him some of the noblest qualities and highest gifts—perfect purity, honor and patriotism, unsurpassed skill in army organization, and the power to win and to keep, even when consigned by the President to disgrace, the ardent love and admiration of his soldiers. It is full time that some one who loves his good name, or some one who loves justice, should "touch" and reveal to the world "the dark, mysterious, uncanny thing" that Dr. Burgess points at.

When Lincoln refused to hear at all, or to see the Southern Commissioners—Clement Clay and James P. Holcombe—unless they could show "written authority from Jefferson Davis" to make unconditional surrender, Greeley, who had procured their coming to negotiate a cessation of the war, protested against Lincoln's action as follows in a letter written him and published in the *Tribune* in July 1864

---

[10] *The Civil War and the Constitution*, published lately.

(Holland's *Abraham Lincoln,* p. 478): "Our bleeding, bankrupt, almost dying country longs for peace, shudders at the prospect of fresh conscriptions, of further wholesale devastation, and new rivers of human blood; and there is a widespread conviction that the Government and its supporters are not anxious for peace and do not improve proffered opportunities to achieve it." Greeley further intimates (p. 482) the possibility of a Northern insurrection. Charles A. Dana, Lincoln's Secretary of War, says, in his *Recollections of the Civil War,* that in April, 1862, Greeley "was for peace." Nicolay and Hay (*Abraham Lincoln,* Vol. I, pp. 184 to 200) describe the transaction above as "Horace Greeley's Peace Mission." The *Life of Hamlin,* p. 437, says Greeley called the above letter "the prayer of twenty millions of people."

Gilmore (*Personal Recollections of Lincoln,* p. 231) shows the bitterest reprobation on his own part of the South and of its cause, but he records the following as "the almost unanimous feeling of the Northern people—of Radical Republicans as well as honest Democrats—during the winter of 1863 and the spring of 1864:" "There must be some way to end this wretched business. Tell us what it is, and be it armistice, concession, compromise, anything whatever, we will welcome it, so long as it terminates this suicidal war."

Rhodes quotes (*History of the United States*) General Hooker's testimony to a committee of the House, as follows: "So anxious were parents, wives, brothers, and sisters to relieve their kindred.

that they filled the express trains to the army with packages of citizen's clothing to assist them in escaping from the service." Hooker was testifying as Commander in Chief of the Army of the Potomac.

General U. S. Grant complains [11] "that General Lee's praise was sounded through the entire North after every action;" . . . that he was "extolled by the entire press of the South after every engagement and by a portion of the press of the North with equal vehemence; . . . that there were good and true officers who believed now that the Army of Northern Virginia was superior to the Army of the Potomac, man to man." James Russell Lowell wrote Motley, July 18, 1864, "The apathy and discouragement throughout the country took the shape of a yearning for peace." General Ben. F. Butler pictures the public mind (*Butler's Book,* p. 576, *et seq.*) in such words as follow: . . . "There being several parties who wanted a dictator, . . . the property men of the country, who thought that the expenses of the war were so enormous that it should be immediately ended by negotiation, . . . the *New York Times,* in an elaborate editorial, proposed that George Law, an extensive manufacturer of New York, should be made dictator." . . .

Rhodes says (*History of the United States,* Vol. IV, p. 222) that "Greeley in his great journal (*New York Tribune*) advocated the mediation of a European power between the North and the South;" that

[11] *Personal Memoirs of U. S. Grant,* New York, 1886, pp. 291, 292.

he corresponded with Vallandigham and the French Minister, Mercier, "setting forth that the people would welcome a foreign mediation that terminated the war;" and Rhodes adds, in a note, the following, from *John Sherman's Letters,* that Greeley said to Raymond, editor of *New York Times:* "I mean to·carry out this policy and bring the war to a close. You'll see that I'll drive Lincoln to it;" which shows his opinion as to Lincoln's purposes.

Rhodes says (*History of the United States,* Vol. IV, p. 492), "When Lincoln visited Grant's army, June 21, 1864, . . . gloom had settled down on the Army of the Potomac and was soon spread over the country. . . . The entire army seemed demoralized." And Rhodes quotes Joseph Medill's letter to Colfax, "Sometimes I think nothing is left now but to fight for a boundary." Again Rhodes says (*History of the United States,* Vol. IV, p. 506), "July 19, 1864, Halleck wrote Grant: 'We are now receiving one-half as many as we are discharging. Volunteering has virtually ceased;'" and he says that about the middle of June, 1864, after Grant crossed the James river and was attacking Petersburg (p. 490, *et seq.*), "Reinforcements were constantly sent to Grant, but they were for the most part mercenaries, many of whom were diseased, immoral, or cowardly. Such men were now in too large a proportion to insure efficient work."

Rhodes says (*History of the United States,* Vol. IV, p. 236, *et seq.*), to justify the conscription act of Congress that was approved March 3, 1863, "volunteering had practically ceased," and he uses just the same words on p. 330, adding ''Only a pretty vigorous conscription could furnish the soldiers needed.''

Rhodes quotes (Vol. III, p. 486, *et seq.*) a letter to Chase from Richard Smith, editor of the *Cincinnati Gazette,* which tells of 'sober citizens . . . trampling under foot the portrait of the President; . . . burning the President in effigy; . . . low murmurings favorable to a Western Confederacy; . . . sudden check to enlistments; . . . rejection of treasury notes by German citizens. . . .''

Bancroft (*Life of Seward,* Vol. II, p. 407) says of the fall of Atlanta, that it was as unwelcome to the Democrats as an earthquake.

The attitude of the Protestant Episcopal Church towards coercion and emancipation is illustrated by the following: Allen's *Life of Phillips Brooks,* says (Vol. I, p. 425), . . . ''Its membership was to a large extent in the Democratic party, with whom the question of States' Rights was the chief political issue involved in the war.'' The Convention of Western New York, seeking exemption from draft for its clergy, found no better evidence of the Church's ''loyalty'' to urge than is in the following words:[12] ''Appealing to our liturgy and practice in proof of our loyalty to our Government on the broad principle of Christian truth, praying constantly in our public worship for yourself''—they were addressing the President—''and all in authority, and

[12] *War of the Rebellion; Official Records of the Union and Confederate Armies,* Serial Number 125, p. 694.

deprecating all sedition, privy conspiracy and rebellion.'' Resolutions known as the ''Brunot resolutions'' were adopted by the General Convention of
the Protestant Episcopal Church in 1862. The New
York *Nation,* of April 11, 1891, says of them ''Mild
as the resolutions were, they reached the highest
point of loyalty that the Episcopal Church attained.''

CHAPTER XX

DESPOTISM IN MARYLAND

FAMILIARITY has made our ears very dull to facts that once would have set the country's heart aflame with patriotic wrath—of newspapers suppressed, a censored press, the Great Writ suspended. It may profit our old men to recall and our young men to learn accurately how such things worked when applied in Baltimore and Maryland. Dr. Holland says (*Abraham Lincoln,* p. 296) that in Maryland, "out of 92,000 votes cast at the presidential election of 1860, only a little more than 2,000 had been cast for Mr. Lincoln. . . . The sympathies of four persons in every five were with the rebellion."

General Butler sets forth that with the force organized already at Charleston, South Carolina, and the welcome that awaited them in Virginia and Maryland, success would have been easy for the Confederate Government at Montgomery, Alabama, and that (*Butler's Book,* p. 220) "the capture and occupation of Washington would have almost insured the Confederacy at once a place by recognition as a power among the nations of the earth;" and that (pp. 19–22) Maryland undoubtedly would have hastened to join the Confederacy in such a contingency. That would have transferred the line of battle from the Potomac to the Susquehanna.

Very probably Delaware would have in that event joined the Confederacy, or at least have remained neutral, as her leading statesman, Senator Bayard, said that if the war could not be averted, and if his State preferred war to the peaceful separation of the States, he would cheerfully and gladly resign his seat in the Senate."

Schouler (*History of the United States*, Vol. VI, p. 47, *et seq.*) describes how Gen. B. F. Butler, 13th May, 1861, "made a sudden entry into Baltimore" with his troops—proceeded to make "vindictive civil arrests," and was replaced by General Scott— how Scott deputed "the high and delicate trust of suspending *habeas corpus*" to Cadwalader, a Pennsylvania General of Militia. He says, "In vain did Chief Justice Taney record his protest against such suspension," and tells how General Banks, successor to Cadwalader, "pursued by orders from Washington, the same stern military course." He broke up the Baltimore Police Board, whose designs were believed disloyal. He prevented the Legislature from meeting once more in September, by boldly arresting its disunion members and preventing a quorum.[1]

The War of the Rebellion, Series 1, Vol. V, pp. 193–'7, gives as follows orders of Cameron, Secretary of War, to Gen. N. P. Banks, September 11, 1861: "The passage of any act of secession by the Legislature of Maryland must be prevented. If necessary all or any part of the members must be

---

[1] Russell's *My Diary* (p. 198) mentions the news that twenty-two "members of the Maryland Legislature have been seized by the Federal authorities." This is of date September 11, 1861. See Dunning's *Essays on the Civil War, &c.*, pp. 19, 21, *et seq.*

arrested.'' Letters of Allen Pinkerton and of Generals John E. Wool, John A. Dix, and N. P. Banks, report with enthusiasm the arrest, by use of soldiers from New York, and the close confinement of members of Congress, officers of the Baltimore city government, and members of the Legislature, among whom are named Henry May, Mayor George William Brown, S. Teakle Wallis, Henry M. Warfield, Charles H. Pitts, Ross Winans, John Hanson, Thomas, R. C. McCubbin, and F. Key Howard.

Rhodes says (*History of the United States,* Vol. III, p. 553, *et seq.*) of these same occurrences, ''Under this order General Dix apprehended ten members-elect of the Legislature, the Mayor of Baltimore, a congressman, and two editors; and at Frederick City, the meeting-place of the Legislature, General Banks laid hold of nine secession members. These men were subsequently confined in Fort Lafayette, New York, and in Fort Warren, Boston, where other state-prisoners, arrested in Kentucky and Missouri, were also incarcerated. Rhodes concedes that these were ''infractions of the Constitution,'' but tries to justify it all. Leland is more frank, both in clearly conceding it was Lincoln's doing and in justifying it, as follows (*Abraham Lincoln,* p. 132): ''But he could be bold enough to sail closely enough to the law when justice demanded it. In September, 1861, the rebels in Maryland came near procuring the passage of an act of secession in the Legislature of that State. General McClellan was promptly ordered to prevent this by the arrest of the treasonable legislators, and the State was saved from civil war. Raymond also tells (*Life and State Papers of Abraham Lincoln,* p. 4) of the arrest of nine members of the Maryland Legislature, and gives (p. 5) the President's statement about arrests and (pp. 7, 8, and 10) his suspension of the writ and his system of provost marshals that enabled him to reach every part of the country.

Schouler, after presenting the facts in like manner as the rest, makes the following remarkable presentation of the consequences: "But the secession spirit of Maryland waned speedily, as the popular vote for Congress on the 13th June first indicated, and the Star-Spangled-Banner State could not be seduced by lyric or artful flattery from her national allegiance. . . . In November there was a newly-chosen Legislature, "loyal in its composition," and Governor Hicks, "no longer wavering, announced with emphasis that Maryland had no sympathy with rebellion, but desired to do her full share in the duty of suppressing it." Schouler might have found a rhetorical designation for Maryland better suited to the occasion than the "Star-Spangled-Banner State." The grandson of the author of the Star-Spangled Banner, Francis Key Howard, editor of the *Exchange* Newspaper of Baltimore, had been arrested on the morning of the 13th of September, 1861, about 1 o'clock, by order of General Banks, and taken to Fort McHenry. He says (*Fourteen Months in American Bastile,* p. 9): "When I looked out in the morning, I could not help being struck by an odd and not pleasant coincidence. On that day forty-seven years before my grandfather,

Mr. F. S. Key, then prisoner on a British ship, had witnessed the bombardment of Fort McHenry. When on the following morning the hostile fleet drew off, defeated, he wrote the song so long popular throughout the country, the Star-Spangled Banner. As I stood upon the very scene of that conflict, I could not but contrast my position with his, forty-seven years before. The flag which he had then so proudly hailed, I saw waving at the same place over the victims of as vulgar and brutal a despotism as modern times have witnessed."[2]

Bancroft (*Life of Wm. H. Seward,* Vol. II, p. 276, *et seq.*) says, "It is extremely doubtful if Maryland could have been saved from secession and Washington from consequent seizure if the Mayor and Police Commissioners of Baltimore, several members of the Legislature, and many prominent citizens of both Maryland and Virginia, had not been deprived of their power to do harm." An earlier statement (p. 254) shows how they were deprived of it, as follows: After the suspension of the writ of *habeas corpus,* "the Baltimore Marshal of Police, the Police Commissioners, and other men of prominence were seized and sent to the United States fort. Several members of the Legislature that were expecting to push through an ordinance of secession the next day were arrested in September, 1861, and treated like other political prisoners." The list would be long of the men most honored and trusted in Maryland

---

[2] For his imprisonment in Fort Monroe and that of twenty-three members of the Maryland Legislature and others see "Life of Senator J. M. Mason" by his daughter, Miss Virginia Mason, pp. 205–207 and p. 209.

who were kept in close, painful, and often fatal confinement until the next election-day was past.   A
special proclamation of the War Department was
addressed to Marylanders, deploring the necessity
of keeping in prison so large a number of prominent
citizens of the State, and expressing regret that
"public policy" did not permit the charges on which
they were arrested to be revealed to themselves or
to their friends, with assurances that no private
grudges have been allowed to have influence in the
arrests.   Mr. Charles A. Dana records,[3] with evident
complacency, the arrest in one day of ninety-seven
of the first people in Baltimore and their imprisonment in Washington, mostly in solitary confinement.

General John A. Dix writes Mr. Montgomery
Blair, August 31, 1861,[4] that he hesitates to suppress
the *Exchange* newspaper without authority from
the commanding general, McClellan, and Blair forwards the letter to McClellan, with the endorsement:
"I believe the *Exchange,* the *Republican* and the
South should be suppressed.   They are open disunionists.   The *Sun* is in sympathy, but less diaboli-
cal."

In October, 1861, General Dix writes the Secretary of War, Stanton, that he has "some doubt
about the expediency of allowing Dr. A. C. Robin-
son to return to Baltimore until after the fall election," though he concedes that Dr. R. is "not a
dangerous man like Wallis."   He is "confident that

---

[3] In his lately published *Recollections of the Civil War*, p. 236, *et seq.*

[4] *War of the Rebellion; Official Records of the Union and Confederate Armies*, Series II., Vol. I., p. 590.

Maryland will be a Union State in November,'' and he might well be confident, for between pages 536 and 738 of the volume above indicated are scores of letters of Generals Dix, N. P. Banks, John E. Wool, and Winfield Scott, and of Secretary Seward, which show that a very great number of the most honored men in Maryland including a large part of the officials of the State government and the Baltimore city government, were in prison and that every man of the least importance who had left it in doubt whether he meant to support Mr. Lincoln had good reason to expect imprisonment. And these same officials concede, on pages 596, 648, 603, and 682, that the prisons were loathsome and dangerous to life, and so crowded that the prisoners had to be sent to Forts Delaware and Warren and Columbus and Monroe, and that these distant points were selected for the plainly avowed purpose of placing the prisoners where their captors would be less annoyed by the solicitations for their release by their friends. On page 586 of the same volume, General Banks formulates the policy very plainly: "While I confidently assure the Government that their detention is yet necessary, I do not think that a trial for any positive crime can result in their conviction." He recommends, however, on page 627, that Mr. Charles D. Hinks be released because he is dying, and "his death in prison would make an unpleasant impression." The need to keep confined even those under slightest suspicion is frequently urged, based on the fact that they cannot safely be allowed to reach home before the State election.

It is curious to read, at page 622, the official report that as many as nine companies of Massachusetts soldiers were sent to arrest Mr. Charles Howard, and four companies of Pennsylvania soldiers to arrest William H. Gatchell, and seven companies of the same to arrest Messrs. John W. Davis and Charles D. Hinks. Marshal Kane was arrested by a like force in his bed at 3 o'clock in the morning, and "the police in the route were taken into custody to prevent an alarm." His imprisonment lasted seventeen months.

Even to the most "loyal" Marylanders it must have been more or less trying to have these despotic functions executed in their midst by men from Vermont, Massachusetts, and Pennsylvania, and the absolute control of property and life in Maryland committed to men from a distance, like Generals Scott, Butler, Schenck, Banks, Wool, and McClellan, to ex-Governors of other States, like Seward and Chase. General Dix refused to furnish arms asked by Mr. J. Crawford Neilson for protection of himself and neighbors in Hartford county, expressing a doubt on which side the arms would be used, and adding: "Until a better feeling prevails the preservation of Maryland to the Union (and without her the Union could not exist) cannot safely be left to herself. I trust the time is not far distant when it may, and when it comes my occupation will be gone." See Series I, Vol. V, pp. 632–633.

The satraps themselves sometimes gagged at the nauseous doses prescribed for them to swallow, as when General Wool explained to Secretary Stanton why he declined to furnish troops called for by the Governor of Maryland to enforce the draft (Series III, Vol. 2, p. 509): "If a State cannot enforce its own laws without United States soldiers, we may as well give up at once. . . . I do not want men who are forced into the service. We have now more treason in the army than we can well get along with." And he rather strangely adds: "This is no fiction."

In a memorandum (Series II, Vol. I, p. 713) sent Secretary Seward for his guidance, by General Dix, it is set against the names of some of the prisoners that they "voted wrong" or "voted treasonably." Pendleton, Vallandigham, Voorhees, and many others were "voting treasonably" in Congress at this very time; but when the Administration could spare time from Maryland to attend to Ohio and Indiana, these gentlemen were gotten out of the way by banishment and other methods new in America.

On page 712 of Series II, Vol. I, I find that General Dix, still providing against election-day, writes: "Dr. A. A. Lynch, Senator, might, I think, be released, on condition that he should resign his place in the Senate and take the oath. The Union men have a majority in the Senate, but it is now considered desirable to have three more." But he writes, on page 727, to Secretary Seward: "I do not think Mr. T. Parkin Scott should be released, even if he should agree to take the oath of allegiance. His presence here (in Baltimore) would be very distasteful to the friends of the Union, whose feelings should be respected." This tender consideration

for the feelings of certain persons is further illustrated by a letter (p. 682) of Simon Cameron, then
Secretary of War: "My Dear Seward,—In order
to gratify Johnson, I say that the release of Ross
Winans will not pain me." No humble subordinates are acting. We find the order of Simon
Cameron himself, as Secretary of War, to General
Banks (p. 678): "The passage of any act of secession by the Legislature of Maryland must be
prevented. If necessary, all or any part of the
members must be arrested." And the commander-
in-chief, General McClellan, orders General Banks,
page 605, "to send detachments of a sufficient number of men to the different points in your vicinity
where the elections are to be held."

After we have learned that the State election was
beyond question held under certain conditions as
above described, it is curious to read in a "draft of
a proclamation by the President of the United
States found among the files of the State Department" (Series II, Vol. I, p. 617) that the reason
assigned in it by Mr. Lincoln for releasing all the
political prisoners is the recent declaration of the
people of Maryland of their adhesion to the Union
so distinctly made in their recent election."[*]

The minute scale of the supervision over Mary-
land thought necessary by men so conspicuous as
Montgomery Blair and the general commanding,
McClellan, is indicated by the following letter of

[*] See Lincoln's message to Congress in 1861 in Raymond's "Life of Lincoln." The election was a farce.

Blair to McClellan September, 1861,[5] "No secession
flag has to the knowledge of the police been exhibited
in Baltimore for many weeks, except a small paper
flag displayed by a child at an upper window. It
was immediately removed by them." The large
scale, too, on which Maryland was thought to need
restraint as late as June 16, 1862, is indicated[6] when
General Wool gives to the Secretary of War as one
of the reasons why "a reserve corps, if practicable,
of 50,000 men should be stationed between Washington and Baltimore, that they would give protection and confidence to the loyal men of both these
cities," and the same is urged again on the same
by the same on page 424. Burgess shows (*The Civil
War and the Constitution,* Vol. I, p. 204) his bitter
partisanship for North against South and his blind
injustice to Maryland, as follows: Maryland "had
played a disgraceful part, but it had served the
national interest by rousing the anger of the North
to the fighting point."

[5] *War of the Rebellion; Official Records of the Union and Confederate
Armies,* Series II., Vol. I., p. 591, or 511.
[6] Series I., Vol. XII., Part II., p. 397.

CHAPTER XXI

DESPOTISM IN KENTUCKY

BURGESS says (*The Civil War and the Constitution,* Vol. I, p. 191), "It was the attitude of Kentucky, however, which, next to that of Maryland, gave Mr. Lincoln the greatest concern."

Ida Tarbell says: "Moreover, he feared that the least interference with slavery would drive from him those States lying between the North and the South." Hapgood quotes (*Lincoln,* p. 245) from a confidential letter of Lincoln's to his old friend, Browning, dated September 22, 1862, his words to this point. He says about his forbidding the execution of Frémont's emancipation proclamation, "The Kentucky Legislature would not budge—would be turned against us. I think to lose Kentucky is nearly the same as to lose the whole game. Kentucky gone, we cannot hold Missouri, nor, I think, Maryland. These all gone, and the job on our hands is too large for us." Ropes says (*Story of the Civil War,* Part II, p. 41), "The people of Kentucky were, as we know, very evenly divided in sentiment," and Rhodes says (*History of the United States,* Vol. III, p. 391): "The course of public opinion was very like that of Virginia up to the parting of their ways; and as most of the leaders of ability were with the South, it is easy to see that a little change of circumstances, a little alteration of the direction of feeling, might in the end have impelled Kentucky to take up arms for the Confederacy instead of for the Union. Lincoln's own knowledge of the division of mind in Kentucky is shown even better than above by the following: Leslie F. Perry, late of the War Record's Board of Publication, Washington, D. C., shows[1] that Lincoln, July 9, 1861, referred the question whether Jesse Bagley should be allowed to raise a Kentucky regiment by a letter addressed to "Gentlemen of the Kentucky Delegation who are for the Union." Fowlke says (*Life of Morton*, Vol. I, p. 133, *et seq.*) that Governor Bramlette replied in response to Lincoln's call for soldiers, "Kentucky will furnish no troops for the wicked purpose of subduing her Southern Sisters," that he convened the Legislature and got their approval of his answer by a vote of eighty-nine to four." The following document pictures vividly the state of things in Kentucky. Major Sidell, Acting Assistant Provost Marshal-General, writes[2] on 13th March, 1864, from Louisville, Kentucky, to Col. Fry, Provost Marshal-General in Washington, reporting that Colonel Walford, of the First Kentucky Cavalry, has, in speeches at Lexington and Danville, "denounced the President and his Administration, and even went so far as to counsel forcible resistance to the enrollment of negroes under the present act of Congress. Governor Bramlette was on the stage at the time and gave no evidence of dissent then or subsequently.

[1] *Lippincott's Magazine* for February, 1902, pp. 205, 209.
[2] *War of the Rebellion; Official Records of the Union and Confederate Armies*, Serial Number 125, p. 174, p. 175.

. . . Public opinion grows very fast. Unfortunately there is no really loyal paper in the State,[3] so that no means exists to set forth loyal views.'' On pp. 288–9, the same reports to the same, ''The presence of guerillas and a sympathizing population and absence of mounted force create difficulty in the First District. In four counties negroes cannot be enrolled, and their enrollment in other counties is incomplete. The seven counties west of the Tennessee river . . . are the worst.'' Kentucky must have been disloyal indeed when the approach of General Morgan's little force could cause such a report as the following, found in the above-named:[4] Brigadier-General J. T. Boyle writes Secretary Stanton, July 19, 1862, from his headquarters at Louisville, Kentucky, ''The State is in imminent danger of being overrun by Morgan and those joining him. If he should succeed in a fight with our forces there is danger of the uprising of the traitors in our midst. . . . There is a concerted plan between the traitors at home and the rebels in arms. Morgan's force has increased. It is estimated at from 2,500 to 3,500. I do not believe it is so large.'' A letter from the same to the same, on the next page, says, ''His whole force does not exceed 1,200, if that. . . . There are bands of guerillas in Henderson, Davis, and Webster counties.'' And yet another, on page 749 says ''They have bands in many parts of this State. Many of the best men in the State believe there is preparation for a general

---

[3] What evidence could be more conclusive of the attitude of Kentucky.
[4] Series I., Vol. XVI., p. 747.

uprising.   I believe there is such purpose and plans.''

John Brough, Governor of Ohio, wrote, June 9, 1864, to Secretary Stanton,[5] ''External raids and internal trouble in Indiana and Illinois promise a warm summer's work.'' The same wrote the same,[6] ''You must change policy in Kentucky. . . . Nothing but a vigorous application of Maryland policy will do in Kentucky.''

[5] *War of the Rebellion; Official Records of the Union and Confederate Armies*, Serial Number 125.

[6] Same volume, p. 429, June 11, 1864.

CHAPTER XXII

FOWLKE says (*Life of Morton,* Vol. I, p. 35), "The feelings of the people of Indiana were not unfriendly to the South, nor to her 'peculiar institution.' The State was considered 'one of the outlying provinces of the empire of slavery.' In 1851 a new Constitution had been submitted to the people, forbidding negroes to come into the State and punishing those who employed them. It was ratified by a popular majority of nearly ninety thousand. Morton had voted for it. Moreover he had always been opposed to Abolitionists."

Fowlke quotes (p. 297) Harrison H. Dodd, Grand Commander of the Sons of Liberty in Indiana, addressing a Democratic meeting in Hendricks county and saying that "the real cause of the war was the breach of faith by the North in not adhering to the original compact of the States;" . . . that "in twenty-three States we had governments assisting the tyrants and usurpers at Washington to carry on a military depotism." At page 179 Fowlke says, "When the news came that Fort Sumter had been fired on and the North was one blaze of patriotism, there were several centres of disaffection in Indiana where sentiments favorable to the South were freely spoken." Page 381 shows that the order of

the Golden Circle [1] had been introduced into the
Federal camps at Indianapolis. At p. 98, *et seq.*, of
Vol. I, Fowlke says, "A meeting of citizens in Cannelton, in Perry county, on the Ohio, resolved that,
. . . if a line was to be drawn between the sections, it must be drawn north of Cannelton."
Fowlke quotes (Vol. I, p. 262, *et seq.*) the following
denunciation of Governor Morton, published in the
Sentinel newspaper by John C. Walker, a prominent
official just elected for special duties by the Legislature: "The disposition manifested by the party
in power to fasten a despotism upon this county by
the destruction of the ballot-box may yet compel a
people naturally forbearing and tolerant to rise in
their might and teach our modern Neros and Calig-
ulas that they cannot be sustained." Fowlke goes
on (Vol. I, p. 175), "But Democratic County Con-
ventions still criticised the Administration and opposed the war. The convention at Rushville, on
December 28, 1861, . . . declared that the Union could not be preserved by the exercise of coercive power." And Fowlke shows (Vol. I, p. 175,
et seq.) that the action of the Democratic State
Convention was *dead against* the Administration,
the war, and emancipation, and quotes (Vol. I, p.
208) a letter of Governor Morton to Lincoln, of
October 27, 1862, as follows: "The Democratic politicians of Ohio, Indiana, and Illinois assume that
the rebellion will not be crushed." And the letter
goes on to say that they urge (p. 209) that "their
interests are antagonistic to New England's and

[1] An organization of which see more hereafter.

in harmony with those of the South, . . . that reasonable terms of settlement offered by the South and refused had brought on the war'' Governor Morton wrote Lincoln, October 7, 1862 (Vol. I, p. 197), ''Another three months like the last six and we are lost—lost.'' . . . Fowlke says (p. 199), ''The draft was conducted without disturbance, except at Hartford City, in Blackford county, where the draft-box was destroyed and the draft was stopped, but on the third day after it was completed.'' Fowlke does not say by what force, but goes on (Vol. I, p. 205, *et seq.*): ''The outcome of the election was the choice of Democratic State officers and of a Democratic Legislature. In a Democratic jubilee at Cambridge City, November 15th, where Vallandigham, Hendricks, Jason B. Brown, H. H. Dodd, Geo. H. Pendleton, and others spoke, . . . cheers for Jeff Davis and curses for Abolitionists were heard.'' And he says (p. 382), ''After the election of 1862, the Democratic majorities in both Houses of the General Assembly were bitterly hostile to the Administration and to the further prosecution of the war.''

A note on p. 382 tells of sixteen meetings held within two months to advocate peace. The men who thus boldly led this opposition to Lincoln and all his aims, like Governor Seymour, in New York, were not turned down or blamed for it by their constituency when the war was over, for Morton said in a speech in the Senate, 20th June, 1866 (Vol. I, p. 270), ''The leaders who are now managing the Democratic party in the State are the men who, at

the regular session of the Legislature in 1861, declared that if an army went from Indiana to assist
in putting down the then approaching rebellion, it
must first pass over their dead bodies." Fowlke
goes on (Vol. I, p. 213) to describe what he calls
"The Peace Legislature" of Indiana, as follows:
"The political outlook was gloomy. . . . Peace
at any price, recognition of Southern independence,
the formation of a Northwestern Confederacy, had
their advocacy." And he describes (Vol. I, p. 220)
a demonstration held January 14th, in Shelby
county, at which "resolutions were adopted recommending a cessation of hostilities, opposing the conscription act, and declaring that soldiers had been
induced to enter the army by the false representation
that the war was waged solely to maintain the Constitution and restore the Union." Fowlke quotes
(Vol. I, p. 243, *et seq.*) from a speech of Governor
Morton in January his statement that General
Grant had disbanded the 109th Illinois regiment for
disloyalty, its officers being sworn members of a
disloyal society, one of the purposes of which was
to encourage desertion and demoralize the army.
Morton says that the 1st, 2nd, 3rd, and 5th regiments had been similarly demoralized, and an artillery company had been destroyed, by this agency.
He records (p. 250) that Vallandigham, who had
been required to leave the country on account of
his disloyal utterances, had become the idol of the
peace Democrats, and quotes (p. 302) from a speech
of D. H. Corrick, to the Democratic Convention, received with applause, "Nine hundred and ninety-

nine men out of every thousand whom I represent breathe no other prayer than to have an end of this hellish war. When news of our victories come, there is no rejoicing. When news of our defeat comes, there is no sorrow.'' Fowlke says plainly (Vol. I, p. 99) that the action of the State Convention of the Democratic party ''looked like revolution in the bosom of the North.'' Most significantly the meetings held for such purposes were called ''Union meetings.'' To quote Fowlke's words (p. 99), ''Union meetings, as they were called, were held everywhere throughout the State, the object being to propose some concessions which should bring the South back to the Union.'' And Morton telegraphed (p. 183) to the President, October 21st, ''In the Northwest, distrust and despair are seizing on the hearts of the people.'' At what Fowlke calls, as above explained, ''a Union meeting,'' of 18th June, Morton said that ''the traitors . . . would array the Northwest against New England. . . . There were many persons in Indiana who still cherished this wild and wicked dream.''

Rhodes quotes (*History of the United States,* Vol. IV, p. 223) the following telegram from Governor Morton to the Secretary of War, ''I am advised that it is contemplated when the Legislature meets in this State to pass a joint resolution acknowledging the Southern Confederacy, and urging the States of the Northwest to dissolve all constitutional relations with the New England States. The same thing is on foot in Illinois.''

In Illinois resolutions praying for an armistice,

and recommending a convention of all the States
to agree upon some adjustment of the trouble between them, passed the House, but failed by a few
votes to obtain consideration in the Senate. Then
Rhodes gives a letter of Morton to Stanton, taken,
he says, "from the War Department archives," as
follows, dated January 4th, 1863: "It has been discovered within the past two weeks that the treasonable political secret organization having for its
object the withdrawal of the Northwestern States
from the Union, which exists in every part of this
State, has obtained a foothold in the military camps
in this city." The *War of the Rebellion; Official
Records of Union and Confederate Armies,* Serial
No. 124, p. 19, gives the following letter of Colonel
Carrington, of the 18th U. S. Infantry to General
Thomas, Adjutant-General United States army,
Washington, from Headquarters Mustering and
Disbursing Service, State of Indiana, Indianapolis,
January 24, 1863: "Nearly 2,600 deserters and
stragglers have been arrested within a very few
weeks; generally it requires an armed detail. Most
of the deserters, true to the oath of the order
(Knights of the Golden Circle), desert with their
arms, and in one case seventeen fortified themselves
in a log cabin with outside paling and ditch for
protection, and were maintained by their neighbors." On p. 75 the same writes to the same, March
19, 1863: "Matters assume grave import. Two
hundred mounted armed men in Rush county have
today resisted arrest of deserters. Have sent one
hundred infantry by special train to arrest desert-

ers and ringleaders. Southern Indiana is ripe for revolution.''

The *War of the Rebellion,* Serial No. 125, p. 529, gives a letter from R. W. Thompson, Captain and Provost Marshal at Terre Haute, Indiana, July 20th, 1864, to Provost-Marshal-General Fry that reports fighting in Sullivan county between ''butternuts'' and soldiers, with one killed and one wounded. ''The result is that there are large numbers of men riding about over the country armed and some of them shouting for Vallandigham and Jeff Davis, and professing to be in search of soldiers. There have been more than two hundred together at one time . . . We have a terrible state of things; such as excites a reasonable apprehension of resistance to the draft.'' . . .

Fowlke's claim for Morton is that (p. 254, *et seq.*) he kept Indiana from becoming ''an ally of the Confederacy;'' that he acted (p. 259) despite the decisions of the Supreme Court. He says that when Morton told Stanton that Lincoln said he could find no law for supporting him with money, Stanton answered, ''By God, I will find a law.''

Fowlke (*Life of Morton,* Vol. I, p. 115) concedes that even in the ebullition on the call to arms only fear kept down the feeling for the South in Indiana, and that the Legislature of the 13th January (p. 99) . . . ''repeated in its small way the follies and weaknesses of Congress.'' Their follies and weaknesses, seem to mean the resistance of each to the Executive, for finally, Fowlke says (Vol. I, p. 98), ''public opinion in Indiana was an epitome of public sentiment in the Nation at large"—a very comprehensive concession.

Fowlke writes as late as 1899, and in eulogy, not censure of Morton. He heads a chapter (*Life of Governor Morton,* Chapter XXII): "I am the State," and begins, "Morton accomplished what had never before been attempted in American history. For two years he carried on the government of a great State solely by his own personal energy, raising money without taxation on his own responsibility, and distributing it through bureaus organized by himself." French says (*Life of Morton,* p. 423) that at the commencement of the year 1863 . . . the secret enemies of the Government . . . had succeeded in the election of an Indiana Legislature which "was principally composed of men sworn to oppose to the bitter end the prosecution of the war, with the purpose of encouraging the enemies of American liberty in their work of rebellion and destruction." Nicolay and Hay (*Abraham Lincoln,* Vol. VIII, p. 8, *et seq.*) confirm the above account of Indiana, and say that but for Governor Morton the Indiana Legislature would have recognized the Confederacy and "dissolved the federal relation with the United States."

In *"Life and Services of O. P. Morton,"* on p. 43 —published by the Indiana Republican Committee —we find the following: "During the winter of 1862 and the summer of 1863 the disloyal sentiment (in Indiana) was very active. County and local meetings were held in many parts of the State, which declared the war cruel and unnecessary, denounced President Lincoln as a tyrant and usurper, Union soldiers as Lincoln's hirelings, etc.'' . . . In the fall of 1862 the Democrats carried the State, electing a Democratic Legislature. It was thoroughly disloyal, the Democrats having a majority of six in the Senate and twenty-four in the House. The first thing they did was to decline to receive Governor Morton's message and to pass a joint resolution tendering thanks to Governor Seymour of New York for the exalted and patriotic sentiments contained in his recent message. . . . They adopted resolutions denouncing arbitrary arrests, and declared that Indiana would not voluntarily contribute another man or another dollar to be used for such wicked, inhuman, and unholy purposes as the prosecution of the war. They instructed the Senators and requested the Representatives in Congress from Indiana to take measures to suspend hostilities, etc.

CHAPTER XXIII

VALLANDIGHAM'S career gives much light on the attitude of Ohio. Rhodes gives (*History of the United States,* Vol. IV, p. 226, *et seq.*) extracts from his speech in Congress, 14th January, 1863, with bitter censure of it, as follows: "The war for the Union is on your hands, a most bloody and costly failure. The President confessed it on the 22nd September. . . . War for the Union was abandoned; war for the Negro openly began. . . . I trust I am not 'discouraging enlistments.' If I am, then first arrest Lincoln and Stanton and Halleck. . . . But can you draft again? . . . Ask Massachusetts. . . . Ask not Ohio, nor the Northwest. She thought you were in earnest and gave you all, all—more than you demanded. . . . But ought this war to continue? I answer, No—not a day, not an hour. What then? Shall we separate? Again I answer, No, no, no! What then? . . . Stop fighting. Make an armistice. Accept at once the friendly foreign mediation and begin the work of reunion, we shall yet escape." . . . After this daring defiance of Lincoln in his capital city, Vallandigham returned to meet in his home the acclaim of his party.

John A. Logan records (*The Great Conspiracy,* p. 557) a gathering at Springfield, Illinois (Lincoln's home), of nearly one hundred thousand *Vallandigham, Anti-War, Peace, Democrats,* which utterly repudiated the war. See also, page 559, *et seq.*

General Burnside was in command of the three States, Ohio, Indiana, and Illinois, excluding from circulation such papers as the *New York Herald;* suppressing the *Chicago Times,* and this in a region—as Rhodes describes it (Vol. IV, p. 252) —"where there was no war—where the courts were open—where the people were living under the American Constitution and English law." Rhodes says (p. 246, *et seq.*) that Burnside began "literally to breathe out threatenings, . . . denouncing the penalty of death for certain offenses."

The story is too long as Rhodes tells it (Vol. IV, p. 247): Two of Burnside's captains, in citizen's clothes,[1] were sent to hear Vallandigham's speech at Mount Vernon, Ohio. The officers broke into his house at 2 A. M., and took him before a military commission for trial. The whole mode of procedure and the sentence to "close confinement during the continuance of the war" provoked such wide and bitter criticism and resentment that Lincoln commuted the sentence to banishment—a penalty not before known to the country, and "not for deeds done, but for words spoken," to use the language in which it was denounced by John Sherman, and these were words that had been spoken in public

[1] Officers in the service of the United States very rarely laid aside their uniform as is so constantly done now.

debate and received with wild applause by thousands of his constituents.[2]

Dr. Holland tells, too, of the bitter reprobation this provoked in New York. Nicolay and Hay tell (*Abraham Lincoln,* Vol. VII, p. 328) very nearly the same story about Vallandigham and the resentment in New York (p. 341) at Lincoln's treatment of Vallandigham. Rhodes labors to defend the banishment and two long papers issued by Lincoln in defense of his course, but is reduced to the strait of reciting as one argument in justification of the conviction that "it was known no jury would convict." But at last he has to say (p. 248, *et seq.*), "From the beginning to the end of these proceedings law and justice were set at naught;" . . . that the "President should have rescinded the sentence and released Vallandigham;" . . . that "we may wish that the occasion had not arisen;" . . . that (p. 251) "a large portion of the Republican press of the East condemned Vallandigham's arrest and the tribunal before which he was arraigned." He quotes heavy censure of it by Justice David Davis, Lincoln's intimate friend, recorded in the Milligan case, ending his warning of the danger of such a precedent with the words, "The dangers to human liberty are frightful to contemplate."[3]

[2] John Sherman's *Recollections,* Vol. I., p. 323, and Holland's *Abraham Lincoln,* p. 471, *et seq.*

[3] N. B.—What a political opponent, Col. A. K. McClure, says of Vallandigham in his *Recollections of Half a Century,* copyright, 1902, p. 231; "There was not a single blemish on his public or private life until he became involved—insensibly involved—in violent hostility to the Government."

Rhodes says (Vol. IV, p. 252) that "the nomination for Governor now came to Vallandigham spontaneously and with almost the unanimous voice of an earnest and enthusiastic convention;" . . . that "the issue had come to be Vallandigham or Lincoln," and Rhodes quotes John Sherman as follows: "The canvass in Ohio is substantially between the Government and the Rebellion." Rhodes says (p. 412), "Lincoln was termed a usurper and a despot;" . . . and (p. 414) . . . the Vallandigham meetings were such impressive outpourings of the people," . . . while . . . "the Republican meetings fell short probably in numbers of those who gathered out of warm sympathy with the cause of Vallandigham."

To many it is a new and strange idea that there was any strong leaning to the South in Ohio, but a book notice in the *New York World* of June 15, 1901, refers, as to a familiar theme, to "the story of Cincinnati in the time of those September days when the city was the centre of a Confederate plot, participated in by outsiders and insiders; . . . that by the dividing line of the causes brother is set against brother." The evidence of a loyal Governor seems conclusive.

In *The War of the Rebellion,* Serial No. 125, p. 599, John Brough, Governor of Ohio, writes Secretary Stanton, August 9, 1864, "Recruiting progresses slowly. There will be a heavy draft, and strong organizations are making to resist its enforcement. There is no sensational alarm in this. Force, and a good deal of it, will be required to overawe the resistance party. . . . What is your view in regard to it? There must be not less than 10,000 to 15,000 men under arms in Ohio in September if the draft is to be enforced.'' We have, besides, the testimony of General Grant (*Personal Memoir,* p. 24 and p. 35): "Georgetown, . . . county seat of Brown county, . . . is, and has been from its earliest existence a Democratic town. There was probably no time during the rebellion when, if the opportunity could have been afforded, it would not have voted for Jefferson Davis for President of the United States over Mr. Lincoln or any other representative of his party, unless it was just after Morgan's raid. . . . There were (p. 36) churches in that part of Ohio where treason was regularly preached, and where, to secure membership, hostility to the Government, to the war, and to the liberation of slaves was far more essential than a belief in the authenticity or credibility of the Bible.''

Part of what has been shown about the attitude of Indiana and Ohio was shown to be true about Illinois, too. Dr. Holland says (*Abraham Lincoln,* p. 67) that in 1830 the "prevailing sentiment" of Illinois was "in favor of slavery." Nicolay and Hay quote (*Abraham Lincoln,* Vol. I, pp. 140 and 141) pro-slavery action of the Legislature of Illinois, 3rd March, 1837, saying that Congress had no power to interfere with slavery except in the District, and not there unless at the request of the people of the District. Nicolay and Hay show at some length (Vol. I, p. 143, *et seq.*) a very nearly successful effort made by the Illinois Legislature in 1822–3 "to open the State to slavery," and say that "the apologists of slavery, beaten in the canvass, were more successful in the field of public opinion. In the reaction which succeeded the triumph of the anti-slavery party it seemed as if there had never been any anti-slavery sentiment."

Fowlke gives (*Life of Oliver P. Morton,* Vol. I, p. 229 and p. 230) numerous resolutions offered and some resolutions passed, in the Illinois General Assembly, in January, 1863, against emancipation . . . and against the conscription. Ida Tarbell says [4] that "among the things that told Lincoln the seriousness of the situation, before he took his seat, . . . was the averted faces of his townsmen of Southern sympathies."

It has been shown how Chicago resented and successfully resisted the suppression of the *Chicago Times,* a paper about which Rhodes quotes (Vol. IV, p. 253, note) from a Provost Marshal's report, "It would not have needed to change its course an atom if its place of publication had been Richmond or Charleston instead of Chicago."

Governor Yates, of Illinois, wrote Secretary Stanton,[5] "I have the best reasons for believing that a draft if made will be resisted in this State," and asks arms for 10,000 infantry and five batteries of artillery to put it down. And again the same wrote the same (Serial No. 125, p. 558), "I must have a district commander for this State. A large portion

---

[4] *McClure's Magazine* for 1899, p. 167.
[5] *War of the Rebellion,* Serial No. 124, p. 627, August 5, 1863.

of my time is consumed by appeals to put down disloyal desperadoes, against whom the courts have no protection. Numbers of men are now here driven from their homes by an armed force of 150 men in Fayette county.'' And a third time the same wires the same, March 2nd, 1864 (Serial No. 148), ''Insurrection in Edgar county, Illinois. Union men on one side, Copperheads on the other. They have had two battles; several killed. Please order . . . two companies . . . to put down the disturbance.'' . . .

D. L. Phillips, United States Marshal, writes Secretary Seward, February 22, 1862 (Series II, Vol. II, p. 241): . . . ''I think that the disloyal in our State feel that they are completely at my mercy unless;'' . . . and again, . . . ''It is now well understood that nothing but the restraining fear of the marshal's office has kept from deeds of violence a great many men in the Ohio and Wabash river counties of Illinois.''

CHAPTER XXIV

JOHN A. LOGAN (*The Great Conspiracy,* p. 108, note) describes "in Philadelphia, December 13, 1860, a great meeting held at the call of the Mayor in Independence Square," . . . which offered the most complete submission to the demands of the South. Greeley quotes (*American Conflict,* Vol I, p. 428) from the Philadelphia *Pennsylvanian,* commenting on Lincoln's Inaugural, as follows: "Let the Border States submit ignominiously to the abolition rule of this Lincoln Administration if they like, but don't let the miserable submissionists pretend to be deceived. Make any cowardly excuse but this." Allen's *Life, &c., of Phillips Brooks* tells (Vol. I, p. 448) of Philadelphia's . . . "avowed hostility towards the Government in its prosecution of the war. That such sentiments towards Lincoln and his Administration did exist in Philadelphia is evident, but it should also be said that the same apathy or hostility might be found in the Northern cities, in New York and in Boston." On the same page Brooks writes, in a letter, deploring that he found in Jersey an opposition that "made the State disgraceful." A deliberate refusal of a large mass of organized soldiers to advance, in the midst of the war, is as conclusive proof of their "disloyalty"

as can be conceived, yet four thousand Pennsylvanians took that desperate stand, as the following
shows: A letter [1] of September 18, 1862, from Hag-
erstown to Major-General H. W. Halleck, General
in Chief, signed by I. Vogdes, Major, says, "A large
portion of the Pennsylvania Militia, now here, have
declined to move forward as requested by General
McClellan. . . . About 2,500 have gone, but the
10th, 11th, 12th, 13th, and 15th, numbering about
800 each, declined to proceed. The 14th has not
finally decided whether to go or not. Governor
Curtin has just arrived, and may induce the troops
to advance." In the same volume, p. 629, is shown
the daring resistance of the Pennsylvanians to the
draft. Major-General D. N. Couch writes Provost-
Marshal-General J. B. Fry, August 5th, 1863, "I
have two regiments and a battery at East Potts-
ville and Scranton and vicinity. My idea is that
the enrollment can be completed with present force.
I think it should be increased when the drafted men
are taken." In the same volume, at pp. 321, 324,
and 325, are reports of Provost Marshals to their
Chief in Washington of forcible resistance to the
draft, . . . and of all refusing to be enrollers,
in the year 1863. In the same great Record (Series
III, Vol. II, p. 735) the Adjutant-General of Pennsylvania wrote Secretary Stanton: "Of the draft
in this State about one-fourth has not been delivered,
and the State is powerless to deliver them. . . .
Of those delivered . . . very many are totally

---

[1] *War of the Rebellion; Official Records of the Union and Confederate
Armies,* Series I., Vol. XIX., Part II., p. 329, of September 18, 1862.

unfit for service." The Adjutant-General would seem final authority in the matter, and it must have been the will of the people of the State that made the State "powerless." But see further confirmation. Capt. Richard I. Dodge, Acting Assistant Provost-Marshal-General, writes (Serial No. 125) to General Fry, Provost-Marshal-General, August 10, 1864: "In several counties of the Western Division of Pennsylvania, particularly in Columbia and Cambria, I am credibly informed that there are large bands of deserters and delinquent drafted men banded together, armed and organized for resistance to the United States authorities. The organization in Columbia county alone numbers about 500 men; in Cambria it is said to be larger. These men are encouraged in their course and assisted by every means by the political opponents of the Administration. . . . The Union men are overawed by the organized power of the malcontents, while many who have heretofore been supporters of the policy of the Goverment, preferring their comfort to their principles, are going over to its enemies. Several deputations and committees have called upon me, representing these facts in the strongest light." General Whipple reports,[2] August 9, 1863, the need of more soldiers for the draft in Schuylkill county, Pennsylvania, and describes how a force of about 3,000 was intimidated from attacking the 47th Pennsylvania Militia at Minersville "by the opportune arrival of a re-enforcement

---

[2] *War of the Rebellion, &c.,* Serial No. 124. For the later volumes the serial number suffices.

of a battery of field artillery and four companies of infantry.''

These are no irresponsible sources of information. See next the evidence of the Governor of Pennsylvania. He wrote[3] to Stanton, Secretary of War, October 23, 1862, that ''the organization to resist the draft in Schuylkill, Luzerne, and Carbon counties is very formidable. There are several thousand in arms and the people who will not join have been driven from the county. They will not permit the drafted men, who are willing, to leave, and yesterday forced them to get out of the cars. I wish to crush the resistance so effectually that the like will not occur again. One thousand regulars would be most efficient.'' His need for ''regulars'' is explained on the next page by the answer of Gen. Jno. E. Wool to General Halleck's order to help Governor Curtin, that the 108th New York Volunteers have killed an engineer and are threatening ''other injuries to passing trains,'' so that he had removed it from the Relay House to Washington, ''where it would do no harm.''

As to New York city, it has ever since been made a reproach to it by Republicans that Mayor Wood proposed, before the war began, that the city of New York should announce herself an independent republic, rather than side with the President. Even soldiers of New York State who had volunteered were ''disloyal.'' Gen. B. F. Butler's farewell to his command at Fort Monroe, Virginia, of August

[3] *War of the Rebellion, &c.*, Series I., Vol. XIX., Part II., p. 493.

18, 1861, gives[4] curiously qualified commendation "to the men and a large portion of the officers of the 20th New York Volunteers, and to the officers and true men of the 1st New York Volunteers, who have withstood the misrepresentation of newspapers, the appeals of partisans and politicians, and the ill-judged advice of friends at home, . . . and remained loyal to the flag of their country. Very great credit is due them."

Dr. E. Benjamin Andrews tells us (*History of the United States*, Vol. II, p. 65, *et seq.*), "A Democratic Convention met at Albany in January, 1861, to protest against forcible measures. The sentiment that if force were to be used it should be 'inaugurated at home,' here evoked hearty response. There were signs of even a deeper disaffection." . . .

Governor Horatio Seymour had been among the foremost to avow when the first States seceded that the South had suffered wrongs that justified her secession, and to protest that States should not be pinned to the Union with bayonets. He had enormous backing, as is shown above and will be further shown, in his opposition as Governor to the war and to emancipation, persisted in to the end so far as was at all possible.

General Dix showed himself well informed about New York city, whence he wrote Secretary Stanton[5] in words that proved minutely prophetic: "Neither

---

[4] *War of the Rebellion; Official Records of the Union and Confederate Armies,* Series I., Vol. V., p. 601.

[5] *War of the Rebellion; Official Records of the Union and Confederate Armies,* Serial No. 125, p. 625.

the State nor the city authorities can be counted on for any aid in enforcing the draft, and, while I impute no such designs to them, there are men in constant communication with them who, I am satisfied, desire nothing so much as a collision between the State and General Governments and an insurrection in the North in aid of the Southern rebellion.'' Again General Dix wrote, for himself, General Canby, and the Mayor (Serial No. 124, p. 671), ''We are of opinion that the draft can be safely commenced in New York on Monday with a sufficient force, but there ought to be 10,000 troops in the city and harbor. There is little doubt that Governor Seymour will do all in his power to defeat the draft short of forcible resistance to it.''

Schouler makes the comprehensive concession (*History of the United States,* Vol. VI, p. 417, *et seq.*) that the State of New York was ''obstructive to the President's wishes''—a mode of expression which is significant—and records that Seymour said in his Inaugural as Governor that ''the conscription act was believed by one-half the people of the loyal States a violation of the supreme constitutional law.'' For Seymour's view of the *purpose* for which that act was procured, see Nicolay and Hay, who record (*Abraham Lincoln,* Vol. VII, p. 22 and p. 25) that both Governor Seymour and Archbishop Hughes not only made friendly addresses to the mob that was forcibly stopping the draft in New York city, but manifested a measure of sympathy with its purpose; that Seymour in his address called the war (p. 16, *et seq.*) ''the ungodly conflict that is distracting the land,'' and said that the *purpose* of the draft was ''to stuff ballot-boxes with bogus soldier votes.'' Yet they concede that, in spite of all this, Seymour was (pp. 9 to 26) ''then and to his death the most honored Democratic politician in the State.'' And this is shown beyond all question by the fact that after the war was over he was selected by the National Democratic party as its candidate for the presidency. They also attest unstintedly (Vol. VII, p. 13) Seymour's integrity and patriotism.

It was just at the time when the great fight came on at Gettysburg that the people of the city of New York rose and defied the Federal Government— keeping control for four days. It was a mob, but they had evidence, as shown above, of sympathy from the Governor and the Catholic Archbishop, and they accomplished their purpose of stopping the draft, until a month later veterans were brought from the Army of the Potomac and New York was made ''tranquil.'' Gorham, the latest biographer of Secretary Stanton, says that had Gettysburg resulted differently New York would have made no submission.

Rhodes (*History of the United States*, Vol. IV, p. 320 to p. 328) gives particulars of the struggle, ''with a loss in killed and wounded of one thousand, most of whom were of the mob.'' He says (p. 327) that the Provost Marshal ''in charge of the draft in New York,'' Robert Nugent, wrote ''a notice over his own name,'' saying ''The draft has been suspended in New York city and Brooklyn,'' that this notice "appeared in nearly all the newspapers, and undoubtedly was the cause of the rioters returning to their homes and employments. The militia regiments which had been sent to Pennsylvania began to arrive and used harsh measures to repress the mobs, who still with rash boldness confronted the lawful powers. Cannon and howitzers raked the streets. . . . More regiments . . . reached the city and continued without abatement the stern work. . . . The draft was only temporarily suspended. Strenuous precautions were taken to insure order during its continuance. Ten thousand infantry and three batteries of artillery—'picked troops, including the regulars'—were sent to New York city from the Army of the Potomac." Of course the example made of New York told elsewhere. Rhodes says (*History of the United States,* Vol. IV, p. 328, note), "Riots in resistance to the draft broke out in Boston and in Troy, but were speedily suppressed." The temper of the people of the interior of the State and the methods used for repressing it are shown in the following: W. A. Dart,[•] after procuring from the Postmaster-General the exclusion from the mails of the *Gazette* of Franklin county, New York, got the two editors, the Franklin brothers, imprisoned in Fort Lafayette by Secretary Seward. One of them had been a judge and member of the Constitutional Convention. They had found readers and listeners in their work, "proving to the people of Franklin county, through the columns of the *Gazette* by letter and in

[•] *War of the Rebellion, &c.,* Series II., Vol. II., p. 941.

public speeches at meetings called for that purpose, that the Southern States had a right to secede and that the prosecution of the war on the part of the North was aggressive and wrong, and that the South was really occupying the position now that the original States did in the war of the Revolution," Dart further writes Seward "that whole county has raised but one company of volunteers for the war, and in several of the towns nearly as many persons could be enlisted for the Southern Confederacy as could be for the United States."

CHAPTER XXV

THE case of Wm. H. Hill[1] gives evidence of the feeling of the people of Iowa between December, 1861, and April, 1862, as to the guilt of Southern sympathizers, and as to the Government's mode of repressing such sympathy, as follows: United States Marshal Hoxie and Governor Kirkwood report (p. 1322–1324) to Secretary Seward clear proof of Hill's guilt, but say that he will be cleared by the jury, who are "in sympathy with the rebels." Seward (p. 1325) has him arrested and confined in Fort Lafayette "as soon as he is discharged from civil custody." Hoxie complains to Seward (p. 1327) that the Davenport *Democrat* and *News* is reporting to its Iowa readers "the movement of the scoundrel Hoxie and his kidnapped prisoner, Hill." The whole Iowa delegation, Senate (p. 1331) and House (1337), urge Hill's release, and he is released, but on condition (p. 1339) that he withdraw his prosecution of Hoxie, which would have to be tried before an Iowa jury. General Halleck, commanding in Iowa, writes Hoxie (p. 1334): "I permit the newspapers to abuse me to their heart's content, and I advise you to do the same."

H. M. Hoxie, United States Marshal of the Dis-

---

[1] *War of the Rebellion; Official Records of the Union and Confederate Armies,* Series II., Vol. II., p. 1321 to p. 1339.

trict of Iowa, writes Secretary Seward in December, 1861 (Series II, Vol. II, p. 1322), "The accused will not be found guilty, though of his guilt there can be no question. There is a large secession element in the jury selected to try him. . . . It would be better for the government to enter a *nolle* and have him committed to military custody by order of the State Department." About the same man, Wm. M. Hill, the Governor of Iowa, Kirkwood, writes Secretary Seward (p. 1324) that "a conviction would be at least doubtful" and that he "would suggest that Hill be removed from the State by your order and imprisoned elsewhere under military authority."

From Fairfield, Iowa, July 28, 1862, James F. Wilson, as inspector, reports to Secretary Stanton[2] that "Men in this and surrounding counties are daily in the habit of denouncing the Government, the war, and all engaged in it, and are doing all they can to prevent enlistments;" and gives as an instance an account of how a wounded officer was driven out of Rome, in Henry county, from his business of recruiting, by threats of hanging. A year later the Governor of Iowa, Kirkwood, forwards to the Secretary of War a complaint of J. B. Grinnell, who calls himself "a war candidate for Congress" that "secret societies are being organized to defy the draft and the collection of taxes. The traitors are armed. Our soldiers are defenseless. We want arms." And Governor Stone, of Iowa, says,[3] as

---

[2] *War of the Rebellion; Official Records of the Union and Confederate Armies*, Series III., Vol. II., p. 265 and p. 403.
[3] *War of the Rebellion, &c.*, Serial No. 125.

late as May 11, 1864, of several counties and townships that they are "Copperheads."

The Governor of Wisconsin forwards and endorses a letter[4] dated August, 1864, showing scandalous fleeing from the draft in Wisconsin and Minnesota, and military preparation to resist the draft in Wisconsin. At p. 1010 of the same, he asks from Washington aid to stop the escape of his people from the draft, and says to Secretary Stanton in January, 1865, that "The Government must depend mainly upon recruiting for its soldiers. Out of 17,000 drafted in this State during the last year, I am informed that but about 3,000 are in the service."

Major General Pope, assigned to the control of Wisconsin after his terrible failure as Commander of the Army of the Potomac, wrote August, 1863,[5] to Washington in much detail, about the resistance to the draft in Wisconsin, and (p. 639 of same volume) Secretary Stanton gives him "six companies of the Seventh Cavalry, temporarily to preserve the peace within your State."

Even in Connecticut, D. D. Perkins, Acting Assisting Provost Marshal reports[6] from Hartford, May 18, 1863, that Governor Buckingham "hoped there would be no difficulty in completing the draft, but that if there was to be any difficulty at all, it might as well be here as anywhere." And Fred H. Thompson, Deputy Collector, writes Secretary Seward[7] from Bridgeport, Connecticut, in January,

---

[4] Same volume last quoted, p. 683.

[5] *War of the Rebellion, &c.*, Serial No. 124, p. 637 and p. 638.

[6] *War of the Rebellion, &c.*, Serial No. 124.

[7] *War of the Rebellion, &c.*, Series II., Vol. II., p. 1934.

1862, "This city is the focus and centre of the secession sympathizers in this portion of Connecticut," and that it has "a lodge of the Knights of the Golden Circle." The *New York Churchman* said [8] August 5, 1899: "At the breaking out of our late civil war there was in the Western part of Connecticut, and extending into the adjoining counties of New York, an ugly feeling of discontent against what seemed to be the policy of Mr. Lincoln towards the rebelling States."

General John A. Dix reported to Provost-Marshal-General Fry,[9] his sending soldiers to Oswego and Oneida, and two hundred to Schenectady, and that there was no resistance. He goes on, "In the river districts, troops will be needed. . . . In Albany and Ulster districts, I think artillery as well as infantry will be needed . . ."

Nicolay and Hay (*Abraham Lincoln,* Vol. VI, p. 217) record "deep seated disaffection" in New Jersey, shown by legislation and elsewise. Major Hill, 2nd Artillery, Acting Provost Marshal, asks [10] from the Provost-Marshal-General at Washington, in August, 1863, for soldiers to execute the draft in Detroit, Michigan. Captain Conner of 17th United States Infantry, reports [11] using soldiers to put down resistance to the draft at Rutland, Vermont, August 3rd, 1863.

Governor Gilmore, of New Hampshire wrote Secretary Stanton [12] January 13th, 1864, of a clamor

[8] In a letter signed Henry Chauncy, New York, headed *Bishop Williams.*
[9] *War of the Rebellion, &c.,* Serial No. 124, p. 665.
[10] *War of the Rebellion, &c.,* Serial No. 124, p. 639.
[11] Same book as last reference, p. 624 and p. 625.
[12] *War of the Rebellion, &c.,* Serial No. 125.

against the Government and that "the Copperheads are jubilant." In the same volume, p. 1188, the same wrote the same, February 20, 1865, what gives light on the means used to fill the drafts: "The war news is glorious. Let us have $200,000, and I will see that our whole quota of 2,072 men is filled by the 20th March. We want the money to pay bounties with to fill our quota."

Ropes says, "and though Maryland, Kentucky, and Missouri remained in the Union,[13] yet the feeling of a considerable part of the people in those States in favor of the new movement was so strong —aided as it was by the conviction that their States would have seceded, but for the active interference of the United States Government—that the Southern cause received substantial aid from each of them."

The War of the Rebellion, Series III, Vol. IV, Serial No. 125, pp. 1173–5, gives a memorial address to President Lincoln, January 31, 1865, by the Constitutional Convention of Missouri, at St. Louis. Among reasons why the draft presses too hard on Missouri, they say (p. 1174), "You will bear in mind that at the beginning of the second year of this war almost, if not quite, half our people were disloyal."

Schouler says (*History of the United States,* Vol. V, p. 508), " . . . And not without internal bitterness and fratricide were Delaware, Kentucky, Tennessee and Missouri rescued from the perilous brink" of secession. It may surprise us to find

[13] But Missouri did secede October 1, 1861, and Kentucky November 20, 1861.

Delaware first in Schouler's list above, but the Appendix shows how very far he was from any good-will to the South, and Greeley tells us (*American Conflict*, 1864, Vol. I, p. 407) that in Wilmington, Delaware, a salute of a hundred guns was fired, at the news of the secession of South Carolina.

The *Memorial of the Public Meeting of the Christian Men of Chicago*, held September 7, 1862 (*Fund Publication*, No. 27, of Maryland Historical Society, p. 12), states that *Maryland, Kentucky, and Missouri* "have been kept in subjection only by overwhelming military force."

Dr. Holland gives (*Abraham Lincoln*, p. 289) an explanation of what he calls "Mr. Lincoln's pacific policy at this time." . . . "an early and decided war policy would have been morally certain to drive every slave State into the Confederacy except Maryland and Delaware, and they would only have been retained by force."

About the *Sons of Liberty*, J. Holt wrote to Stanton August 5, 1864, from the Bureau of Military Justice, a report as follows.[14] He calls it "a treasonable organization," and says: . . . "that its officers in Missouri all occupy high social positions;" . . . that it is successor to the *Knights of the Golden Circle*, and of the *Corps de Belgique*, and of the *Order of American Knights*; . . . that it is in complete sympathy with the rebellion, which it holds to be justified and right; . . . that it "exists alike in the North and in the South,

---

[14] *War of the Rebellion; Official Records of the Union and Confederate Armies*, Serial No. 125, pp. 577–579.

Vallandigham being its head in the loyal and Price its head in the disloyal States;'' . . . that ''the order is numerous in Indiana, Illinois, Missouri, Ohio, Kentucky, and New York, and exists in several of the other States. In St. Louis it is estimated that the membership amounts to 5,000; in Missouri to some 40,000 or 50,000. In Indiana a strength much beyond this is assigned to it. It is understood that Governor Brough supposes 25,000 of the order to be around in Ohio. They are believed to be armed in large proportion in Indiana, Illinois and Missouri, but in less proportion in Kentucky and New York.''

General Halleck, Military Adviser of the President, and General in Chief, wrote General Grant from Washington, April 12, 1864, the following,[15] which shows conclusively, considering the writer and the official he addressed, a very serious disloyalty in three States: ''I have just received General Heintzelman's report on General Burbaze's telegram in regard to arresting certain persons in Ohio, Indiana, and Illinois. General Heintzelman does not deem it prudent to make arrests at the present time, as a rescue would probably be attempted, and his force is not sufficient to put down an insurrection. He thinks there will be a forcible resistance to the draft, and greatly fears disturbances before that time. He does not deem the prisoners of war as secure, and thinks a combination has been formed to release them and seize the arse-

---

[15] *War of the Rebellion; Official Records of the Union and Confederate Armies,* Serial No. 125, p. 613.

nals. To provide against this, he wants 10,000 men in each of the States of Indiana and Illinois, and 5,000 in Ohio.

"General Pope and the Provost Marshal of Wisconsin report that there will be armed resistance to the draft in that State. . . . I think much importance should be attached to the representations of General Heintzelman in regard to the condition of affairs in the West."

CHAPTER XXVI

THE purpose and expectation with which Lincoln issued the Emancipation Proclamation has been questioned and discussed as follows: Burgess says (*The Civil War and the Constitution,* p. 16 or 118) of Lincoln's Emancipation Proclamation, "It contained paragraphs which might fairly be interpreted, and were so interpreted by the Confederates, as inciting the negroes to rise against their masters, thus exposing to all the horrors of a servile insurrection, with its accompaniment of murder and outrage, the farms and plantations where the women and children of the South lived lonely and unprotected." Burgess offers a labored defense (Vol. II, p. 16, *et seq.*) against the charge that Lincoln's purpose *was* slave insurrection, or "at least that Lincoln saw that the inevitable result of his act would be slave insurrection;" and Burgess fully concedes that the incitement of slaves to massacres of their masters would be not only immoral, but positively "barbaric." And Burgess adds (p. 118), still in the line of apology, "It is to be regretted that the questions at issue between the Union and the Confederacy could not have been fought out, when appealed to the trial of arms, by the whites only; but it is difficult to demonstrate the immorality of Mr. Lincoln's order upon this subject."

It is not difficult to understand why servile insurrection, with all its horrors, was expected by people
outside of the South. The slavery in the South had
been pictured to the world very falsely—notably by
Mrs. Harriet Beecher Stowe in *Uncle Tom's Cabin;*
nor is it difficult to explain why the expectation of
the horrors of servile insurrection was disappointed,
but the explanation is too long for this page, and will
be found in a note below.[1]

[1] It is a graceless task, in this twentieth century, to say anything that looks
like a defense, or even an apology, for slavery; but the proverb tells us to give
even the devil his due, and on that ground, at least, those who most hate the
memory of slavery may listen to the following suggestions. They are submitted that the children of slaveholders may be saved from being betrayed
into the error of regarding with reprobation the conduct of their parents in
holding slaves.

Those who rejoice most in the emancipation of the negroes must find a serious
check in their exultation if they open their eyes to some of the chief changes
in the condition of the negro race since its emancipation.

The negro slave was a highly valued member of the body politic; a tiller
of the soil, whose services could be counted on when the crop was pitched,
and a laborer who furnished to all his fellows, young and old, sick and well,
a more liberal supply of the necessaries of life than was ever granted to any
other laboring class in any other place or any other age. And in what the
Economists call the distribution of the wealth that was produced by the negro's
labor and the skill of the master who guided and restrained him, the share
the master took was small indeed compared with what the Captains of In-
dustry took in the free society of the same day. Compared with the share
those Captains take now, the modest share taken by the masters was what
the magnates of to-day would scorn to consider. The negro lived, too, in
cheerful ignorance of the ills for which he has been so much pitied. One is
startled now to hear the cheerful whistle or the loud outburst of song from
a negro that once was heard on every hand, night and day. Nor was his
attitude one of mere resignation to his lot. That it was one of hearty good-
will to the masters was conclusively shown during the war between the
States. A distinguished Northern writer has lately invited attention to the
indisputable fact that the negroes could have ended the war during any one
day or night that it lasted. And the kindly attitude of the negro to the
master was shown not negatively only, not by forbearance only. Not only did
a vast majority of them stay at their posts, working to feed and watching to
protect the families of the absent soldiers—when all the able-bodied white men
were absent soldiers—but after their emancipation ten thousand examples occurred of respectful and grateful and even generous conduct to their late
masters for one instance where a revengeful or a reproachful or even disre-
spectful demonstration was made. Of the few survivors of those who stood

Arming the slaves was one of the methods adopted to suppress "disloyalty." To arm slaves against their masters, with the horrors that may be expected to result, has been accounted barbarity. The French have been bitterly denounced by American historians for arming the Indians against the early English settlers in America. Did the people of the North and West approve of arming the slaves against their Southern masters? What was Lincoln's purpose and expectation in doing it?

Greeley says (*American Conflict*, Vol. I, p. 527) that the "repugnance in Congress and in the press, and among the people, to arming the blacks, was quite as acrid, pertinacious, and denunciatory as that which had been excited by the policy of eman-

in the relation of master and slave, a considerable number still maintain relations of strong and often tender friendship. John Stuart Mill worshipped liberty and detested slavery, but he confessed that the goodwill of the slaves to the master was to him inexplicable. And all this is none the less true, if all be granted as true about the abuses of slavery that Mrs. Harriet Beecher Stowe painted in *Uncle Tom's Cabin* and in the *Key to Uncle Tom's Cabin*. Abuses no less vile and on a far greater scale have occurred and still occur in England and in America, with all their boasts of freedom; not to speak of late occurrences in South Africa and in the Philippines.

To-day the negro is a formidable danger to the State and to society, and a danger that threatens only too surely to become constantly a greater danger. Elaboration of this proposition is unnecessary.

The curious may still see a manuscript letter (written late in the 18th century) in which Peter Minor, of Petersburg, Virginia, frankly tells his nephew, John Minor, of Fredericksburg, that the Virginia Legislature did right in rejecting a bill the nephew had proposed for the emancipation of the negroes, and says that they had as well turn loose bears and lions among the people. The Virginians of that day were as ardent lovers of all attainable liberty as the Virginians of the sixties, whose conduct in the war between the States has at last extorted high praise even from such a representative of the best product of New England as Mr. Charles Francis Adams, son of Mr. Lincoln's Minister to England. The Virginians of a still earlier day, with other Southern leaders, notably the Georgians, had striven often and in vain to get the importation of slaves stopped; but Parliament before the Revolution and Congress afterwards listened to the owners of the slave-ships of Old England and New England and continued the slave trade. Many of the for-cipation.'' We have seen how very *acrid* and *pertinacious* that repugnance was.

James C. Welling (*Reminiscences of Lincoln, &c.,* p. 521) quotes the diary of Secretary Chase to prove that on the 21st of July, 1862, in a Cabinet meeting, ''the President expressed himself as averse to arming the negroes . . . ;'' and Welling shows by the same diary of the 3rd August, 1862, that the President said, on the same question, that he ''was pretty well cured of any objection to any measure, except want of adaptedness to putting down the rebellion.''

It was a deliberate conclusion, for Holland quotes (*Abraham Lincoln,* p. 391) a letter of Lincoln's to

tunes that now startle us with their splendor in Newport, R. I., had their origin in the slave trade, and the social magnates who have inherited these fortunes might take with perfect right as their coat of arms a handcuffed negro, the design which Queen Elizabeth gave to Captain John Hawkins for his escutcheon, when she knighted him as a reward for the benefit that he had conferred on Christendom in originating the slave trade from the coast of Africa to America. John Fiske tells us the story.

But the Virginians knew the negro. Although his industrial education on the Southern plantations had raised him far above the bloody and cannibalistic barbarism of his home in Africa, the Virginians knew that to emancipate him as the chivalrous young legislator proposed would be to ''turn loose lions and bears among them,'' as old Peter Minor said. They foresaw one of the consequences of emancipation—the danger to which a hundred thousand husbands and fathers of the South must to-day leave their homes exposed if they leave them unguarded for an hour. Each day's newspapers make it impossible to deny this state of things. All Christendom is crying shame on the barbarous lynchings that are occurring in the States of the North as well as of the South, but even New England must concede that the provocation in the North is trifling compared with that in the South. Since President Roosevelt has twice suggested the barbarities practiced by Filipinos as palliation for the guilt of the tortures which so many of his soldiers have been convicted of using on ''insurgent'' Filipinos, none should forget the provocation, without a parallel in history, for the lynching in the Southern States.

A suggestion from Grover Cleveland has great weight with many good and wise men, but some curious and interesting recollections are suggested by his recommendation in a late address ''that technical schools for negroes be dotted all over the South.'' A very elaborate exposition of the need for technical education of the people in place of the kind that has been till now given was

A. G. Hodges, of Frankfort, Kentucky, April 4, 1864,
. . . "I believed the indispensable necessity for
military emancipation and arming the blacks would
come." . . . We have further light how it was
regarded in an extract given by Rhodes (*History
of the United States,* Vol. IV, p. 333), from an address of Major Higginson at Cambridge in 1897,
"for at that date (February, 1863) plenty of good
people frowned on the use of colored troops." We
have Lincoln's own statement of the public mind
about it, quoted by Rhodes (*History of the United
States,* Vol. IV, p. 334): "I was opposed on nearly
every side when I first favored the raising of colored regiments," said President Lincoln to General
Grant, "and no one can appreciate the heroism of

published in 1892 (this note was written in Jan., 1903) as a report of the
Department of Education at Washington with all the authentication that the
Government could give it, and its recommendations have been largely adopted.
In setting forth the need for this great change this report declares that the
existing public school system is such a failure that something radically different must be substituted for it. The concession of failure is hardly less complete than that lately made by another authority of the very highest rank,
President Eliot, of Harvard University, in addresses made to two great educational assemblies in two New England States. Incidentally the report makes
another concession, and it is, as is said above, curious and interesting to
compare it with what Mr. Cleveland now proposes as the cure for the country's grievous embarrassment about the emancipated negro.

The authoritative document referred to above, issued by the Government in
Washington for the instruction of the people of the United States (Bureau of
Education Circular of Information No. 1, 1892, "Southern Women in Recent
Educational Movements in the South," pp. 75, 93. 100 et passim, by the Rev.
A. D. Mayo) expressly declares that the best technical education that the
world has ever seen or can ever hope to see was the education that was given
by their masters to the negroes before their emancipation. There was good
reason why it should be so. Every boy and every girl was set to such work
as each was best fitted for and taught to do it well; for the teaching was not
done by a salaried official with the inefficiency so familiar to us all, but by
a person strongly prompted by interest to make the teaching successful and
having power to enforce exertion in the pupil, while he or she was at the
same time strongly restrained by self-interest from impairing the health of
the pupil by work at too early an age or too hard work or too dangerous work

Colonel Shaw[2] and his officers and soldiers without adding the savage threats of the enemy, the disapprobation of friends, the antipathy of the army, the sneers of the multitude here; without reckoning the fire in the rear as well as the fire in front.''

It seems impossible to refuse to Lincoln what he thus claims—all the credit that is deserved by any one for arming the slaves, and, as his own account shows the bitter reprobation it received from the people of the North and West, and from the army, no one should be surprised at Rhodes' report (*History of the United States*, Vol. IV, p. 344) that ''The governing classes in England could see in it''—the Emancipation Proclamation—''nothing but an at-

at any age. Is not this in strange contrast with the "free" labor of to-day, when such strong protests are urged every day against child labor, overwork and dangerous work in the factories and the mines of the North and South?

One of the worst of the many reproaches brought against the slave-owner by the abolitionist was the allegation that he denied his slave education. Is it not curious to observe that the highest authorities now say that it is necessary to change the existing system of education to one radically different, and to learn that the highest authority in the United States, the Department of Education, has conceded that the technical education to which we are turning had attained its highest perfection in the system of slavery which has disappeared?

Another truth about slavery seems to have escaped the observation of all. No one will deny that the evils of drunkenness are among the greatest that society has to encounter. It is needless to recite them. It is no less incontestable that nineteen-twentieths of these evils fall on the laboring class. The drunken laborer brings the miseries of cold and hunger and death from want upon mothers, sisters, wives, widows and children. Drink hurt the health of an exceedingly small number of the negro slaves and the life of almost none. And when disabling sickness or death from that *or from any other cause* did come, it made no difference at all in the supply of food, clothing, fire, doctors or nurses to the aged, the women or the children.

Some tender hearts who do not deserve to be called sentimental will be revolted at the claims suggested in this paper of such benevolent functions for slavery, but only by closing their eyes to the truth can they deny the claims.

[2] Shaw was a Boston gentleman who accepted the colonelcy of a regiment of negroes. There is a monument to Col. Robert G. Shaw in Boston. He is mounted and leading soldiers (Negroes?).

tempt to excite servile insurrection," in support of
which statement Rhodes quotes (p. 355) the following from the *London Times*: "President Lincoln
calls to his aid the execrable expedient of a servile
insurrection." Rhodes quotes the *Saturday Review,*
too, as making it a crime, and further says that
even friends of the United States in England sent
back "comments that were dubious and chilling,"
for which he quotes *The London Spectator* and the
Duchess of Argyle. The *Spectator* has not ceased
to this day—1903—boasting of its steady support
of the North against the South in this contest, and
of having been almost alone in supporting that side.
Rhodes further says that the *London Times* and the
Saturday Review represented the highest intelli-
gence of England.

How Negro Soldiers Were "Enlisted."

A romantic picture has been presented to the
world of the negroes enlisting—one hundred and
eighty thousand of them—in the Union army to
vindicate their liberty. See what the facts were.
We have Gen. W. T. Sherman's account of the way
the negro soldiers were enlisted and his estimate of
their value (*Memoir,* Vol. II, p. 249). At the end
of his *March to the Sea* he says, "When we reached
Savannah we were beset by ravenous State Agents
from Hilton Head, South Carolina, who enticed and
carried away our servants and the corps of pioneers [3] which we had organized, and which had done

[3] All negroes; he has shown that he used the negroes only as laboring
pioneers and as servants, not at all as soldiers.

such excellent service. On one occasion my own aide-de-camp, Colonel Audenreid, found at least a hundred poor negroes shut up in a house and pen, waiting for the night, to be conveyed stealthily to Hilton Head. They appealed to him for protection alleging that they had been told that they must be soldiers; that 'Massa Lincoln' wanted them. I never denied the slaves a full opportunity for enlistment, but I did prohibit force to be used, for I knew that the State Agents were more influenced by the profit they derived from the large bounties than by any love of country or of the colored race. In the language of Mr. Frazier, the enlistment of every black man 'did not strengthen the army, but took away one white man from the ranks.' ''[4]

Leland (*Lincoln*, p. 61, *et seq.*) quotes a soldier as saying, ''I used to be opposed to having black troops, but when I saw ten cart-loads of dead niggers carried off the field yesterday I thought it better they should be killed than I.''

Sherman's report above of State Agents kidnapping negroes to be shipped for enlistment from Hilton Head, on the coast of South Carolina, has light cast upon it by the two following extracts. *The War of the Rebellion*, &c., Serial 125, p. 631, gives a letter of the Mayor of Boston, H. Alexander, Jr., endorsed with urgent approval by Governor Andrew, August 22, 1864, as follows: ''From present indications, I believe it will be impossible for

[4] Sherman's authoritative professional opinion here antagonizes the often repeated allegation that "the colored troops fought nobly." The fact that "the enlistment of every black man took a white man from the ranks" was one temptation to vote for arming the slaves, to men eager to escape military service, as nearly all the people of all the States are shown to have been.

this city to fill its quota under the last call of the President by volunteers from its own citizens." Of the men enrolled he says, "More or less of these men are now leaving the city daily to avoid draft, and as the 5th of September approaches, the number leaving will be largely increased; . . . that more than 500 of the ablest-bodied young men . . . . . will have left. . . Now, what we want, and what I hope we may accomplish, is to get men from abroad to go as volunteers." In the next preceding volume of the record last quoted, sufficiently indicated as *Serial Number* 124, at p. 110, Governor Andrew, of Massachusetts, writes Secretary Stanton, April 1, 1863, . . . "If the United States is not prepared to organize a brigade in North Carolina, I would gladly take those black men who may choose to come here, receive our State bounty, and be mustered in."

General Sherman shows above how some of the negro soldiers were enlisted. Here is light upon another method. Leslie T. Perry [5] quotes from a letter of Lincoln to Lieutenant-Colonel Glenn, Henderson, Kentucky, of February 7, 1865: "Complaint is made to me that you are forcing negroes into the military service, and even torturing them," and Lincoln reproves it, though not severely, and forbids it. An examination of the orders of Major-General David Hunter, commanding the Department of the South, as found in the *War of the Rebellion,* will account for *all* the negroes that were en-

---

[5] Late of the War Record's Board of Publication. See *Lippincott's Magazine* for February, 1902.

listed. General Hunter gives orders (Series I, Vol. IV, p. 466) how to deal with "all fugitives who come within our lines. . . . Such as are able-bodied men you will at once enroll and arm as soldiers." Again, from headquarters, Department of the South, Hilton Head, South Carolina, August 16, 1864, General Hunter issued the order, "All able-bodied colored men between the ages of eighteen and fifty within the military lines of the Department of the South, who have had an opportunity to enlist voluntarily and refused to do so, shall be drafted into the military service of the United States, to serve as non-commissioned officers and soldiers in the various regiments and batteries now being organized in the Department." This order alone may account for the whole 180,000 colored volunteers.

CHAPTER XXVII

OPPOSITION TO LINCOLN'S RE-ELECTION

THE crowning proof of the attitude of a very large part of the people of the North and the West is the platform and the nominee adopted by the Democratic party for the presidential election of 1864 near the end of the war. It advocated the abandonment of the war, and the nominee was McClellan, an avowed opponent of emancipation. Colonel Theodore Roosevelt said in a speech at Grand Rapids, Michigan, September 8, 1900, "In 1864 the Democratic platform denounced the further prosecution of the Civil War." . . . The Chairman of the convention in 1864 made a speech in which "he declared that every lover of civil liberty throughout the world was interested in the success of the Copperhead party." Such was the issue adopted on which to appeal to the North and the West, and the framers of it were called by Lincoln's Secretary of the Navy[1] some of the most astute and experienced statesmen of their day. Nor was the appeal a failure, as has been so widely heralded. It is Ida Tarbell, Nicolay and Hay, Butler, Schouler, Holland, McClure, Lincoln himself, who have recorded as follows: That three months

---

[1] Welles' paper, *The Opposition to Lincoln in* 1864, in *The Atlantic Monthly,* Vol. XVI., dated 1878.

after his renomination they all despaired of his re-election.

Gilmore gives (*Personal Recollections of Abraham Lincoln*, p. 102) a long list of names, including "about all the most prominent Republican leaders, except Conkling, Sumner, and Wilson," who, with more or less full committal, joined in a solicitation to Rosecrans to run against Lincoln. Ida Tarbell concedes [2] only "a few conservatives supported Lincoln in his desire for a second term," while "there were more who doubted his ability, and who were secretly looking for a better man. At the same time a strong and open opposition to his re-election had developed."

Nicolay (*Outbreak of the Rebellion*, p. 475) says: "The evident desire of the people for peace was a subject of deep solicitude to the administration." Morse (*Lincoln*, Vol. II, p. 274) shows the general despair of electing Lincoln, in a letter to Lincoln from Raymond, chairman of the Republican National Executive Committee, August 22, 1864, which says: "I hear but one report—the tide is setting against us," speaking himself for New York, and quoting Cameron for Pennsylvania, Washburne for Illinois, and Morton for Indiana, "and so for the rest."

Nicolay and Hay (*Abraham Lincoln*, Vol. IX, p. 249) say that . . . by August, 1864, Weed, Raymond, every one, including Lincoln, despaired of his re-election. A. K. McClure says (*Our Presidents and How We Make Them*, p. 183), "But in

[2] *McClure's Magazine* for July, 1899, p. 268.

fact three months after his re-nomination in Baltimore his defeat by General McClellan was generally
apprehended by his friends and frankly conceded
by Lincoln himself.'' Several of his biographers
give copies of a memorandum sealed up by Lincoln
and committed to one of his Cabinet for safekeep-
ing, in which is recorded his conviction that Mc-
Clellan's election over him was certain, with a statement of his purposes how to act during the interval
before McClellan would take the presidency. It is
referred to by Welles in his papers in the *Atlantic
Monthly* under the heading, ''Opposition to Lincoln
in 1864,'' (pp. 266 and 366, *et seq.*) as ''Lincoln's
despondent note of August 23, 1864,'' Rhodes, too
quotes it.[3]

Allen Thorndike Rice quotes,[4] with his endorsement of its truth, W. H. Croffut's account of Lincoln's offering his withdrawal and his support for
the presidency to Horatio Seymour, and when that
failed, his offering the same to General McClellan,
because he despaired of being himself elected, and
asked in return from each his support for the rest
of his term. Nicolay and Hay, too, tell (*Abraham
Lincoln*, Vol. VII, p. 12) of Lincoln's offer to Seymour of the nomination. The nomination for vice-
president Lincoln had offered to Gen. B. F. Butler
(*Butler's Book*, p. 155, *et seq.*) before he procured [5]
the nomination of Andrew Johnson.

---

[3] Vol. IV., p. 522. See also Roosevelt's *Cromwell*, p. 208, where the note
is referred to.

[4] *Reminiscences of Lincoln, &c.*, Introduction, pp. 29 to 35.

[5] A. K. McClure's *Our Presidents and How We Make Them*, p. 185, *et seq.*

Rhodes says * that Thaddeus Stevens said that in the winter of 1863–4 there was but one single member of Congress who favored Lincoln's re-nomination, and Rhodes gives a long list of the names of leaders that opposed him, showing "a formidable discontent," and he says further, "Striking indeed it is to one who immerses himself in the writings of the time to contrast the almost universal applause of Grant with the abuse of Lincoln by the Democrats, the caustic criticism of him by some of the radical Republicans; the damning of him with faint praise by others of the same faction." All this was in the spring of 1864. Again Rhodes says (Vol. IV, p. 518), "Greeley wrote, August 8, 1864, 'Mr. Lincoln is already beaten.'" Rhodes gives evidence, like Nicolay above, of the hopelessness of success that prevailed among the leading Republicans (*History of the United States*, Vol. IV, p. 521), quoting the words of the above-mentioned reports from Thurlow Weed, E. B. Washburn, from Cameron about Pennsylvania, Morton about Indiana, and Henry J. Raymond, as chairman of the National Executive Committee. Governor Morton reported that "Indiana would go against us 50,000 tomorrow," and the Chairman, "that nothing but the most resolute and decided action on the part of the Government and its friends can save the country from falling into hostile hands." Morse, too (*Lincoln*, Vol. II, p. 247), gives Raymond's letter to Lincoln of August 22nd conveying the above reports.

Rhodes records (Vol. IV, p. 199, *et seq.*) that

* *History of the United States*, Vol. IV., p. 437 and p. 462.

Lincoln himself was conscious "that he was losing his hold on the people of the North."

What "resolute and decided action on the part of the Government" relieved it from this hopeless condition will be seen in the next chapter.

CHAPTER XXVIII

IT WAS under the conditions above described that Lincoln's second election came on. The way it was conducted explains why he no longer despaired of success, and why he was successful.

Despotic Control by the Secretaries of State and of War

The management of the election was committed in large measure to Seward, Secretary of State, and to Stanton, Secretary of War; the exercise of despotic power by both of whom has been described. Even a canvass for the presidency by Democrats was difficult, for an order of the War Department had made criticism of the administration treason, triable by court-martial.

Votes of Soldiers in the Field and Soldiers Sent Home to Vote

A. K. McClure (*Our Presidents and How We Make Them*, p. 195, *et seq.*) gives his answer to a messenger sent him "on a special message by Lincoln" about two weeks before the election, to learn the situation in Pennsylvania, as follows: "I had to tell him that I saw little hope of carrying the State on a home vote. The army vote would no doubt be largely for Lincoln, and give him the State, but it would be declared *a bayonet election,* and with such results in Pennsylvania, and New York lost, as was possible; . . . that I could go to Washington in a few days, if it should appear necessary to take extreme measures to save the State on the home vote. . . . As the political conditions did not improve, I telegraphed Lincoln that I would meet him . . . to discuss the campaign." . . . McClure then tells how he proposed, and Lincoln agreed, that five thousand Pennsylvania soldiers be furloughed by Grant for twenty days, . . . as that vote cast at home would ensure a home majority. Lincoln answered that he had no reason to think that Grant would favor his election—though he could count on Meade and Sheridan. The order was accordingly sent to General Meade, with directions *that the order be returned,* and, as soon as the furloughs were granted, it *was* returned, and so concealed. In connection with this disbelief of Lincoln in General Grant's friendliness to his re-election, it is interesting to consider General Wm. T. Sherman's statement (*Memoir*, Vol. II, p. 247) that Lincoln was "tortured with suspicions of my infidelity to him and his negro policy." McClure says, too (p. 162), that a constitutional change had been hurried through in Pennsylvania that same summer of 1864, that "was obviously intended to give the minority no rights at all in holding army elections." He says the law was "liable to grossest abuses, and without any means to restrain election frauds," and his description shows that it worked so. Allen Thorndike Rice tells the same story about Grant. (*Introduction to Reminiscences of Lincoln,* p. 43.)

Chauncey M. Depew describes (*Reminiscences of Lincoln, &c.,* p. 22, *et seq.*) the working of the new amendment in the Pennsylvania election; . . . how the soldier vote was polled— . . . "made out by the soldier himself, certified by the commanding officer of his company or regiment, and sent to some friend at his last voting place to be deposited on election day." Depew says that without the soldier vote, so managed, Lincoln would have failed to get the vote of New York.

Ex-President Buchanan wrote Mr. Leiper, October 26, 1864 (*Curtis' Life of Buchanan,* Vol. II, p. 627) . . . "and I now indulge the hope that we"—that is, the Democrats, in the Pennsylvania election—"may have a majority over the soldiers' vote and all."

Forcible Control of Elections by Armed Soldiers and by Suspension of the Writ

Gen. B. F. Butler tells more plainly than Depew above why Lincoln did not "fail to get the vote of New York." He says (*Butler's Book,* p. 753 to p. 762) that early in November, 1864—the November of Lincoln's second election—Stanton summoned him, and sent him to New York city to prevent an anticipated outbreak in the city, which was to give the whole vote of New York to McClellan by a far more widely extended and far better organized riot than the draft riot of 1863. At page 330, *et seq.,* Butler had before described how he put down those draft riots, as follows: "Ten thousand infantry and three batteries of artillery, picked troops, including regulars, were sent to New York city from the Army of the Potomac." By aid of these, Butler says, that "the draft was resumed, and proceeded with entire peacefulness." Not only General Butler, but Rhodes, too, describes,[1] with full particulars, the large force with which he occupied New York city, and shows how completely he controlled its vote and its opposition to the war that had lately been demonstrated in its great anti-draft riot. See how frankly Rhodes concedes that this despotic overruling of the will of the people was Lincoln's own doing. He says (*History of the United States,* Vol. IV, p. 417), "to meet the action of the judges who were releasing his conscripts and deserters, he stopped the writ of *habeas corpus,* but deferred till four days after the election his call for three hundred thousand more volunteers, with a draft to fill deficiencies." In considering what the consequences would have been of a failure to capture Vicksburg, Rhodes says (p. 183), "If nothing worse, certain it is that President Lincoln would have been deposed, and a dictator would have been placed in his stead as chief executive until peace could be assured to the nation by separation or elsewise."

Removal of His Chief Competitor

In the chapter headed *Estimates of Lincoln* it has been shown that he had from first to last the bitter

---

[1] *Butler's Book,* p. 752 to p. 773, and Rhodes' *History of the United States,* Vol. IV., p. 330, *et seq.*

and contemptuous hatred of his Secretary of the Treasury, Salmon Portland Chase, whom he finally made Chief Justice of the Supreme Court of the United States. A. K. McClure says (*Lincoln and Men of the War Time*, p. 123, *et seq.*), "Lincoln's desire for re-nomination was the one thing uppermost in his mind during the third year of his administration. He carefully veiled his resentment against Chase, and awaited the fullness of time when he could by some fortuitous circumstance remove Chase as a competitor"—his most formidable and conspicuous competitor for the presidency. At page 127, *et seq.*, McClure says, "Chief Justice Taney died the 12th of October, 1864. Within two weeks after, Chase declared himself in favor of the election of Lincoln." Warden says (*Life of Salmon P. Chase*, p. 630, *et seq.*) that Senator Sumner told him Mr. Lincoln once proposed to him to send for Mr. Chase, and frankly tell him that in his (Lincoln's) opinion he would make the best Chief Justice we ever had, if he could only get rid of his presidential ambition; . . . that Senator Sumner had to remind Mr. Lincoln that to do so would expose the President to imputations as to his motives, and would be offensive to Mr. Chase, as requiring in effect a pledge from the latter not to be, thereafter, a presidential candidate. Warden says [2] that Chase's own State—Ohio—made the most bitter

[2] Page 630. He says that it was told to him and to at least one other person by Sumner, that Chase's well known daughter, Mrs. Kate Chase Sprague, who was using all her powers to win him the Presidency, met Sumner, when he carried to Chase the news of his confirmation as Chief Justice, with the words, "And you, too, Mr. Sumner, in this business of shelving papa." . . .

objection, though it came from every part of the
country, and from many of the ablest and most
earnest of Lincoln's friends; that it was objected
that Chase was "without legal training," because
his life had been devoted almost exclusively to politics, as a United States Senator, as Governor, as
Senator again, in the Cabinet, and that "for many
years he had given no thought or efforts to the law."
McClure says further (*Lincoln and Men of the War
Time*, p. 130) of Chase, "His personal affronts to
Lincoln had been contemptuous and flagrant from
the time he entered the Cabinet until he resigned
from it, a little more than three years after, and I
am sure that at no time during that period did Lincoln ever appeal to Chase for advice as a friend;
. . . that Lincoln regarded Chase as his bitter
and malignant enemy during all that period cannot
be doubted; . . that it was not pretended (p.
130) that Chase had any claim to the Chief Justice-
ship on the grounds of eminent legal attainments or
political fidelity."

Use of Fictitious States

Explanation of Lincoln's re-election would be incomplete without details of his use of *fictitious
States,* and the details must be considered at some
length.

The New York *Times* of January 11, 1902, quotes
Ben Wade as denouncing President Lincoln's
"promise that whenever the tenth part of the people
of a State came back he would recognize them as a
State." And the *Times* goes on, meaning commen-

dation, not censure, of Lincoln, ''It was under this plan . . . that Union governments were inaugurated in Tennessee, Louisiana and Arkansas, the first two of which participated in the presidential election of 1864, and all before the close of the war elected members to Congress.'' This *plan* was denounced by the Hon. H. Winter Davis, stanchest of Republicans, and Abolitionist, as follows, in the House:

''It is not surprising, Mr. Speaker, that the President, having failed to sign the bill passed by the whole body of his supporters by both Houses, at the last session of Congress, and having assigned, under pressure of events, but without authority of law, reasons, good or bad, first for refusing to allow the bill to become a law, and therefore usurping power to execute parts of it as law, while he discarded other parts which interfered with possible electoral votes, those arguments should be found satisfactory to some minds prone to act upon the winking of authority.'' Then Winter Davis goes on, about Louisiana's then representatives, ''Whose representatives are they? . . . In Louisiana they are the representatives of the bayonets of General Banks and the will of the President, as expressed in his secret letter to General Banks.'' Then Winter Davis denounces with scorn the body sitting in Alexandria, pretending to be the legislature of the State of Virginia. He calls the pretended State ''a fringe along the Potomac and the sea,'' which, he says, ''has just sent two Senators to the other House, and has ratified the amendment of the Constitution of the United States abolishing slavery in all the rest of Virginia, where not one of them dares put his pretty person." And Davis goes on, "And so Congress has dwindled down to a commission to audit accounts and to appropriate moneys to enable the executive to execute his will, and not ours."

Usher shows (*Reminiscences of Lincoln, &c.*, p. 92 to p. 94) that when Montgomery Blair and Seward objected to omitting from the Emancipation Proclamation the thirteen parishes and the city of New Orleans in Louisiana, and the counties in Virginia near Norfolk, . . . which they said were the very heart and backbone of slavery, Lincoln explained that it was already arranged that Congressmen were to come to Washington from these regions, and that some of the Congressmen were elected. Mr. Chase then said, "Very true; they have elected Hahn and Flanders, but they have not got their seats, and it is not certain they will;" that Mr. Lincoln rose from his seat, apparently irritated, and walked rapidly back and forth across the room. Looking over his shoulder at Mr. Chase, he said "There it is, sir. I am to be bullied by Congress, am I? If I do, I'll be durned." Nothing more was said. Usher says, too, that a month or more thereafter Hahn and Flanders were admitted to their seats. Page 95 of the same book shows that a man named Hahn was the first Free-State Governor of Louisiana. Rhodes quotes (Vol. IV, p. 484) a letter from Lincoln to Michael Hahn, the new Governor of Louisiana, elected under Lincoln's "plan" above described. It reads as follows:

"Executive Mansion, Washington, March 13, 1864.
Hon. Michael Hahn:

My dear sir: I congratulate you upon having fixed your name in history as the first free State governor of Louisiana. Now you are about to have a convention which, among other things, will probably define the elective franchise. I barely suggest for your private consideration whether some of the colored people may not be let in as, for instance, the very intelligent and especially those who have fought gallantly in our ranks. They would probably help, in some trying time to come, to keep the jewel of liberty within the family of freedom. But this is only a suggestion, not to the public, but to you alone.

Yours truly,

A. LINCOLN.[3]

Nicolay and Hay (*Abraham Lincoln*, Vol. IX, p. 436, *et seq.*) describe the process of making a loyal State out of Virginia—not West Virginia—as follows: "The difficulty of effecting reconstruction strictly in conformity with any assumed legal or constitutional theories appears clearly enough in the case of Virginia, . . . when the spontaneously chosen Wheeling Convention of August, 1861, repudiated the secession ordinance of the Richmond Convention, the two Houses of Congress recognized the restored State government of Virginia, having Governor Pierpoint as its executive head, by admitting to seats the Senators sent to Washington by the reconstructed Legislature, and the representa-

[3] This letter is found in Nicolay and Hay, Vol. 8, p. 434.

tives elected by popular vote. Full reconstruction being thus recognized by both executive and legislative departments of the National Government, . . . West Virginia was organized and admitted to the Union as a separate State. . . . Governor Pierpoint, with the archives and personnel of the reconstructed State government, removed from Wheeling to Alexandria. . . . But while the constitutional theory was thus fulfilled and perfect, the practical view of the matter certainly presented occasion for serious criticism. The State government which Governor Pierpoint brought from Wheeling to Alexandria could make no very imposing show of personal influence, official emblems or practical authority. The territorial limits in which it could pretend to exercise its functions were only such as lay within the Union military lines; a few counties contiguous to Washington, two counties on the eastern shore, the vicinage of Fort Monroe and the cities of Norfolk and Portsmouth.''

Nicolay and Hay go on (*Abraham Lincoln*, Vol. IX, p. 438, *et seq.*) to show how Pierpoint ''ventured upon the expedient of authorizing the election of a State Convention,'' and of gathering a little Legislature about him at Alexandria; that this convention adopted and amended a constitution for Virginia which, among other things, abolished slavery. They tell how Winter Davis sneered at it, calling it ''the common council of Alexandria.'' They quote, without dissent or comment, a ''pamphlet,'' which deals as follows with the ratification by this convention of the 13th amendment to the Constitution of the United States: "And while this ratification may be said to have been, like Mercutio's wound, 'not so deep as a well, nor so wide as a church door,' it effectually served to make up the necessary number of twenty-seven States whose action made the amendment a vital part of the Constitution of the United States."[4] . . . "Under this ordinance and amended constitution Governor Pierpoint carried on his administration, clearly not with the normal health and vigor of an average State government, and yet, . . . that justified its continued recognition under the constitutional theory under which the President and Congress had recognized it before the division of the State."

Nicolay and Hay commend Gen. B. F. Butler's conduct in the matters for which he has been most denounced—his conduct in New Orleans—and they here quote (*Abraham Lincoln*, Vol. IX, p. 440) his characterization of Pierpoint as follows: . . . "a person who calls himself Governor, . . . pretending to be head of the restored government of Virginia." General Butler describes, himself (*Butler's Book*, p. 618), what a farce this fictitious State was. About the end of 1863, he says, "The army being much in need of recruits, and Eastern Vir-

---

[4] Nicolay and Hay can write as plain, good English as any one. The reader's attention is invited to the strait in which they find themselves to describe without censure this manufacture of *Fictitious States*. The cities— Norfolk and Portsmouth—were as stanchly faithful to the Southern cause as Richmond or Charleston, and were kept under by such methods as setting a "disloyal" clergyman to work on the streets, wearing the ball and chain of a convict. It was the Rev. Mr. Wingfield, afterwards Bishop of the Diocese of California. The use of these *Fictitious States* that might have been made in Lincoln's second election, if they had been needed, and the use that was made of one of them, is shown by Morse's account given later.

ginia claiming to be a fully organized loyal State, by permission of the President, an enrollment of all the able-bodied loyal citizens of Virginia within my command, was ordered for the purposes of a draft when one should be called for in the other loyal States. This order was vigorously protested against by Governor Pierpoint, and this was all the assistance the United States ever received from the loyal government of Virginia in defending the State. My predecessors in command of the Department of Virginia and North Carolina, with headquarters at Fortress Monroe, had endeavored to recruit a regiment of loyal Virginians, but after many months of energetic trial, both by them and by myself, the attempt was abandoned. A company and a half was all that State would furnish to the Union, and these were employed in defending the lighthouses and protecting the loyal inhabitants from the outrages of their immediate neighbors.''

Morse shows (*Lincoln*, Vol. II, p. 297) that Lincoln withheld until February 8th his approval of a bill passed by Congress in January, that forbade the votes of any of the eleven seceded States from being counted in the election. He says the 8th February was the very day of the count, and the votes of Arkansas and Tennessee, though offered, were not counted.[5]

Lincoln's veto, or his non-action, would have en-

[5] In answer to a question of the author, the Librarian of Congress says, in a letter of May 6, 1903, as follows: "On the 8th of February, 1865, the votes were opened by the Vice-President, Mr. Hamlin, and read by the tellers. The Vice-President had in his possession returns from the States of Louisiana and Tennessee, but did not present the doubtful votes."

abled him to use their votes, but the other methods described in this chapter had accomplished the purpose, and news of the success had reached him, so that there was no need for more votes. Morse, however, adds (Vol. II, p. 298), ''Yet the vote of West Virginia was counted, and it was not easy to show that her title was not under a legal cloud fully as dark as that of Arkansas and Tennessee.'' Dr. E. Benjamin Andrews says (*History of the United States*, Vol. II, p. 196, *et seq.*), ''When a handful of Virginia loyalists, in the summer of 1861, formed a State government and elected national Senators and Representatives, President and Congress recognized them as the true State of Virginia.'' Dr. Andrews says, further (Vol. II, p. 200), ''Every secession State but Tennessee rejected the amendment''—the fourteenth—of the Constitution. And here he gives, in a note, the number of States that voted for the three different amendments, and adds the following very significant comment: ''The States rejecting amendments, in every such instance, were either border slave States, not under military control, or those of the free North where public sentiment opposed the reconstruction policy of Congress.''

Andrew Johnson, Military Governor of Tennessee, wrote, January 14, 1864, to Horace Maynard about the organization of a loyal State of Tennessee as follows: (He owed Lincoln already his governorship, and soon after the Vice-presidency.)

---

* *War of the Rebellion; Official Records of the United and Confederate Armies,* Serial No. 125, p. 31.

"The voters in March should be put to the severest test. . . . if it should be thought advisable, two Senators could be appointed now who are sound as regards the slavery question and the Union. Will the Senate admit them? . . . I would give some of the fault-finders to understand that the real Union men will be for Lincoln for President. The war must be closed under his administration. . . I desire you to see the President in person and talk with him in regard to these matters."

See in the volume last referred to, at page 194, a very similar letter addressed to Lincoln, showing how a "loyal State" was set up in Arkansas. Lincoln's "plan" did not meet General Grant's approval, for we have in the same volume above referred to, at page 734, his letter to the Secretary, Stanton, September 20, 1864, from City Point, Va., "Please advise the President not to attempt to doctor up a State government for Georgia by the appointment of citizens in any capacity whatever."

This creation and use of fictitious States is plainly dealt with further by Morse also (*Lincoln*, Vol. II, p. 295 to p. 298), Lincoln's re-election by an exceedingly large majority has been triumphantly alleged and is adduced as proof that what he had done and was doing had the approval of the North and the West. That the vote of the electoral college should be recorded for Lincoln was quite inevitable in view of what the witnesses quoted in this sketch have recorded of the political and military management of affairs, at election-time and long before, in the border States, in Indiana, Illinois, Ohio, and New York;

in great cities like Chicago, New York, and Boston, and in the country at large, as far as Seward's "little bell" could reach. But with all the odds against McClellan that have been shown, the actual number of votes gotten by McClellan was more than eighty-one per cent. of the actual number of votes gotten by Lincoln,[7] although McClellan was fully committed against emancipation, and the Democratic platform said the war must cease.

---

[7] The figures by which this percentage is ascertained are furnished by the Peabody Library in Baltimore.

APPENDIX A

ADAMS, CHARLES FRANCIS (the father), was Minister to England during Lincoln's whole administration. He was of the family that had given two Presidents to the United States, and his father and his grandfather had been Ministers to England before him.

ADAMS, CHARLES FRANCIS, son of the above, served in the Union Army throughout the War between the States, and became brevet Brigadier-General of Volunteers—later *President of Massachusetts Historical Society*. His extreme partisan attitude is shown by the extract below from his address in Chicago, as late as June 17, 1902: "As to those who sympathized with the deliberate disunion policy, and in the councils of the government plotted for its overthrow, while sworn to its support, Mr. Adams held that it was unnecessary to speak. 'Such were traitors,' says he, and 'if they had had their deserts they would have been hanged.' That in certain 'well-remembered instances this course was not pursued is to my mind even yet much to be deplored,' " he adds.

ANDREWS, E. BENJAMIN, once President of Brown University, is still prominent in educational work. He shows in his *History of the United States* (Vol. II, pages 64, 77, 81 *et seq.*) that he is an ardent Abolitionist and an admirer of Lincoln; calls John Brown (p. **61**, *et seq.*) "a misguided hero," and perverts history so wildly as to say (p. 89) that "Virginia and Tennessee were finally carried into secession by the aid of troops who swarmed in from the seceded States, and turned the elections into a farce. Unionists in the Virginia Convention were given the choice to vote secession, leave, or be hanged. Missouri, Kentucky, Delaware and Maryland resisted all attempts to drag them into the Confederacy." . . .

ASHE, SAMUEL A'COURT, who condensed the article "Lincoln and Democracy" by Paul S. Whitcomb, appearing as Appendix C in this edition and supplied the footnotes thereto, is recognized as an authority on North Carolina and Southern history. He is the author of "A History of North Carolina" in two volumes. He edited six volumes of Van Noppen's "Biographical History of North Carolina." Capt. Ashe was for several years editor of The Raleigh (N. C.) News and Observer. He has been throughout life a close student of history and has written much on historical subjects. He lives at Raleigh, N. C.

BURGESS, JOHN W., Ph. D., LL.D., is now (1904) Professor of Political Science in Columbia University. He says in his *Civil War and Constitution* that "absolute truthfulness was the fundamental principle of his (Lincoln's) character," and that "he was on the inside a true gentleman, although the outward polish failed him almost completely."

BUTLER, GENERAL B. F., was made by Lincoln Major-General and one of General Grant's corps commanders, and was Lincoln's first choice for Vice-President in his second election.

BEECHER, REV. HENRY WARD, brother of Harriet
Beecher Stowe, was a strong Republican and Abolitionist, and a very prominent supporter of the war.

BOUTWELL, GEORGE S., was in Congress from Massachusetts, aided in organizing the Republican party in
1854, and in procuring Lincoln's election, and was
made by Lincoln the first Commissioner of the Internal
Revenue. (See name of Rice.) Boutwell's whole
paper, and notably in the last pages, is full of the
most ardent eulogies of Lincoln, strong and unqualified as any other.

BROOKS, PHILLIPS, Bishop of the Protestant Episcopal
Church in Massachusetts, His Life and Letters by
Alexander V. G. Allen (New York, E. P. Dutton,
1900) Vol. II, p. 9 says, ''In Philadelphia he had appeared almost as a reformer and agitator, with a work
to do outside of the pulpit, which rivalled in importance and popular interest his work as a preacher. He
had thrown himself into the cause of the abolition of
slavery with an intensity and rare eloquence which was
not surpassed by any one. He had espoused the cause
of the emancipated slaves, pleading in most impas-
sioned manner for their right to suffrage in order to
complete their manhood. . . . From his activity
in these moral causes he had become as widely known,
as by his eloquence in the pulpit.'' For evidence (*Life
and Letters* by Allen, Vol. I, p. 531) of his partisanship, see a prayer he made in the streets of Philadelphia on the downfall of the Confederacy. In the
large page and a half there is not a reference to
the miseries of the defeated nor an aspiration for the
amendment of their condition, physical or spiritual.

CHANDLER, ZACHARIAH, SENATOR, was one of the organizers of the Republican party in 1854; United States Senator from 1857 to 1877; Secretary of the Interior. Appleton's Cyclopaedia of American Biography calls him "a firm friend of President Lincoln."

CHANNING, EDWARD, Professor of History in Harvard, and author of *Short History of the United States,* quotations from which show his partisanship.

CHASE, SALMON P., was Lincoln's Secretary of the Treasury till made by him Chief Justice.

CHESNEY, CAPT. C. C., Royal Engineers, Professor of Military History, Sandhurst College, England, published in 1863 *A Military View of Recent Campaigns in Virginia and Maryland.*

COFFEE, TITIAN J., says of Lincoln (*Reminiscences of Lincoln,* p. 246) . . . "The better his character and conduct are understood, the brighter will he shine among those names that the world will not willingly let die."

COGGINS, DR. J. C., author of "Abraham Lincoln a North Carolinian, With Proof" (see chapter III) native of Buncombe county, N. C., attended school in his father's still house on Bee Tree, educated Milligan College, Tenn., Grant University and American University, receiving his Ph. D. from last named institution. Was licensed to practice law by Supreme Court of North Carolina. First president Atlantic Christian College and author of "A New Philosophy, or the Soul of Things," "Christ's Place in the Old Testament, or

Voices of Hebrew Prophets'' and ''The Star Crowned Woman.''

CURTIS, GEORGE WILLIAM, long editor of *Harper's Weekly*, was a widely known scholar and author. The quotations from his pen show how he stood towards the war and Abolition. His prejudice was bitter enough to make him institute (*Orations and Addresses*, Vol. III, p. 10) a parallel between Robert E. Lee and Benedict Arnold; and he must be accounted an *unwilling witness*, since he adds (Vol. III, p. 219), ''Heaven knows I speak it with no willingness,'' after his testimony that is quoted of his own people's resistance to emancipation and to coercion.

CRITTENDEN, L. E., was Register of the Treasury. The words quoted show his attitude toward Lincoln.

DANA, CHARLES A., was long managing editor of the New York *Tribune*, took an important part in procuring Lincoln's election and was his Assistant Secretary of War. See his book, *Recollections of the Civil War, with the Leaders at Washington, etc.*, N. Y. Appleton & Co., 1898.

DANA, RICHARD H., was a distinguished author and law-writer, was nominated by President Grant for Minister to England, and was a representative of the best culture of Massachusetts. It was he who proposed, in Faneuil Hall, to hold the Southern States ''in the grasp of war for thirty years.''

DAVIS, HENRY WINTER, though a Marylander, was an ardent supporter in Congress of the war and of emancipation.

DAVIS, DAVID, is named by McClure in his *Lincoln* with
Leonard Swett, Ward H. Lamon and William H. Herndon as one of the four men "closest to Lincoln before
and after his election." He was made by Lincoln one
of the Supreme Court Justices, and finally executor
of his estate.

DAWES, HENRY L., represented Massachusetts in the
House for nine sessions, beginning in 1857; succeeded
Sumner in the Senate, and continued there till he de-
clined re-election in 1893.

DEPEW, CHAUNCEY, says in *Reminiscences of Lincoln,
etc.*, that Lincoln was "among the few supremely
great men this country has produced."

DOUGLASS, FREDERICK, was one of the most honored
and respected colored men during his long life, with
everything to prejudice him in favor of Lincoln.

DUNNING, E. O., was chaplain in the Union army. His
words quoted show his attitude.

DUNNING, WILLIAM ARCHIBALD, Professor of History in Columbia University, in his *Essays on the Civil
War and Reconstruction*, pictures with merciless exultation (pages 247 to 252) the years of humiliation and
torture imposed on the South during the "reconstruction."

EVERETT, EDWARD, had been Minister to England,
and was such another man as Richard H. Dana, rank-
ing even higher; was in the House or the Senate, or

Secretary of State, or Governor, or President of Harvard for twenty-nine years, and then candidate for Vice-President.

FISKE, JOHN, historian and lecturer. His *Old Virginia and Her Neighbors* shows his Northern bias.

FOWLKE, WILLIAM DUDLEY, shows in his words quoted his partisan attitude.

FRÉMONT, J. C., ran against Buchanan as "Free-Soil" candidate for the presidency. As Major-General he proclaimed freedom to the negroes in his command before Lincoln's Emancipation Proclamation. Schouler attributes to him (*History of the United States*, Vol. VI, p. 98) "patriotism, integrity and humane sentiment." The title page of the pamphlet quoted is as follows: "Fund Publication, No. 27. President Lincoln and the Chicago Memorial on Emancipation; a paper read before the Maryland Historical Society of December 12, 1887, by Rev. W. W. Patton, D. D., LL. D., President of Howard University, Baltimore, 1888."

FRENCH, WILLIAM M., shows in his words quoted his partisan attitude.

FRY, MAJ.-GEN. JAS. B., provost marshal of United States. See Allen Thorndyke Rice, chapter III.

GARRISON, WILLIAM LLOYD. The *Dictionary of the United States History*, 1492–1894, by J. Franklin Jamison, Ph.D., says, "Garrison's influence in the anti-slavery cause was greater than that of any other man;" started Liberator newspaper in 1831, and ran it till 1865.

GAY, SIDNEY HOWARD, became, in 1844, editor of the *Anti-Slavery Standard.* Senator Henry Wilson speaks of him as the man who deserved well of his country because he kept the *New York Tribune* a war paper in spite of its owner, Horace Greeley.

GILMORE, JAMES R. Appleton's Encyclopaedia says that a mission to Jefferson Davis made by Gilmore had the effect of assuring the re-election of Lincoln.

GODKIN, E. L., was long and until lately the able and useful editor of the *Nation,* but was utterly intolerant as to all that concerns secession and slavery.

GORHAM, G. C., author of a late life of Stanton, which shows in what is quoted his partisan attitude.

GRANT, U. S., General and President, is obviously the most trustworthy of all witnesses in the matters about which he is quoted.

GREELEY, HORACE. A. K. McClure calls (*Our Presidents and How We Make Them,* p. 243) Greeley "one of the noblest, purest and ablest of the great men of the land;" calls Greeley's *Tribune* (p. 155) "then the most influential journal ever published in this country," and says (*Lincoln and Men of the War Time,* p. 225 and p. 295), "Greeley was in closer touch with the active, loyal sense of the people than even the

President (Lincoln) himself," and that "Mr. Greeley's *Tribune* was the most widely read Republican journal in the country, and it was unquestionably the most potent in modelling Republican sentiment. It reached the intelligent masses of the people in every State in the Union." Again McClure says (p. 300), "Greeley was one of the founders of the Republican party, and did more to make it successful than any other one man of the nation." . . . Dr. E. Benjamin Andrews says,[2] "Greeley and his party were the chief founders of the Republican party, and the most effective moulders of its policy. The influence of the paper before and during the war was incalculable, far exceeding that of any other sheet in America. Hardly a Whig or Republican voter in all the North that did not take or read it. It gave tone to the minor organs of its party, and no politicians upon either side acted upon slavery without considering what the *Tribune* would say." Gilmore (*Recollections of Lincoln,* p. 54) has a letter from Lincoln to Robert J. Walker, which says of Horace Greeley: "He is a great power; having him firmly behind me will be as helpful to me as an army of an hundred thousand men." Channing (*Short History of the United States,* p. 300) calls Greeley "one of the ablest men of the time."

HALE, EDWARD EVERETT, of Boston, well-known author and editor; a strong partisan of the North.

HAMLIN, HANNIBAL, was Lincoln's Vice-President.

---

[1] Edward Everett Hale in *James Russell Lowell, His Friends, &c.,* pp. 174-5.
[2] *History of the Last Quarter Century in the United States,* Vol. II., p. 58.

HAPGOOD, NORMAN. His *Abraham Lincoln* is the latest important biography, published in 1899. It shows the author's attitude of admiration for Lincoln in the first page of the preface, declaring that he was "unequalled since Washington in service to the nation," and quoting the verses—

He was the North, the South, the East, the West;
The thrall, the master, all of us in one.

See under names of Herndon and of Lamon his endorsement of their "revelations."

HAY, JOHN, Secretary of State under McKinley and Roosevelt, came from Springfield with Lincoln, and was his private secretary, as Nicolay was, to his death. Their joint work, *Abraham Lincoln,* in ten large volumes, makes the most favorable presentation of Lincoln of all that have been made. They are the editors, too, of the only collection of Lincoln's complete works. See the name of Nicolay in this Appendix.

HERNDON, WILLIAM H. His *Lincoln,* dated 1888, sets forth on the title page that Lincoln was for twenty years his friend and law partner, and says in the preface (p. 10) : "Mr. Lincoln was my warm, devoted friend; I always loved him, and I revere his name to-day." He quotes with approval and reaffirms Lamon's views as to the duty to tell the faults along with the virtues, and says in the preface (p. 10) : "At last the truth will come out, and no man need hope to evade it;" and he betrays his sense of the seriousness of the faults he has to record by calling them in the preface (p. 9) "ghastly exposures," and by saying in the preface (p. 8) that to conceal them would be as if the Bible had concealed the facts about Uriah in tell-

ing the story of King David; and the very latest
biographer, Hapgood, writing with all the light yet
given to the world, says in his preface (p. 8) : "Herndon has told the President's early life with a refreshing honesty and with more information than any one
else." Morse, the next latest biographer, also commends Herndon's dealing in this matter. See, too, on
page 2 of this book, Horace White's testimony, that
"The world owes more to Mr. Wm. H. Herndon, for
this particular knowledge"—that is of his life before
he was President—"than to all other persons." See,
in this Appendix, under Swett's name how Herndon's
extraordinarily close relations with Mr. Lincoln are
shown, and see under Lamon's name how Herndon's
testimony and Lamon's have gone uncontradicted.
Students need to be warned of a discovery made by the
author since the first edition of *The Real Lincoln* was
published. The genuine book of Herndon about Lincoln is still (1902) to be found in the Pratt Library
and the Peabody Library of Baltimore, and in the
Congressional Library in Washington, in three volumes, and is entitled as follows: "Herndon's 'Lincoln;
The True Story of a Great Life.' (*Etiam in minimis
major.*) 'The History and Personal Recollections of
Abraham Lincoln,' by William H. Herndon, for
Twenty Years His Friend and Partner, and Jesse William Weik, A. M., Chicago, New York and San
Francisco. Bedford, Clarke & Co., Publishers, London. Henry J. Drane, Lovel's Court, Paternoster
row." The quotations above given of Herndon's
avowal of his purpose to conceal nothing, come from
this book. In place of this genuine book another has
been substituted, in two volumes, with the same title
page, except that it is published by D. Appleton & Co.

There is an introduction by Horace White, but no intimation of the suppression of any part of the work of Herndon, and his avowals of his purpose to tell all, good and bad, about his hero, are copied as above from the genuine book. Every word, however, of the "revelations" and "ghastly exposures" is suppressed. Without acknowledgment of any omission, five pages of the genuine book (beginning with the second line of fiftieth page of the first volume) are omitted. In these pages Herndon records a satire written by Lincoln, called "The First Chronicle of Reuben," and describes the exceedingly base and indecent device by which Lincoln brought about the events which gave opportunity for the satire and adds some verses written and circulated by Lincoln which he considers even more vile than the "Chronicle." Of these verses Lamon says, "It is impossible to transcribe them." Leland (*Abraham Lincoln, etc.*, pp. 12 and 13) quotes Lamon and Herndon, and calls (p. 42) Herndon "a most estimable man, to whose researches the world owes nearly all that is known of Lincoln's early life and family." Yet Leland gives a list of the authorities he uses and omits from it both Lamon and Herndon. In like manner some influence has caused the American Encyclopaedia of Biography to omit Herndon and Lamon.

HOLLAND, J. G., was a popular author, and was long editor of *Scribner's Magazine.* For his ardent admiration of Lincoln, see the last page of his *Abraham Lincoln.*

HUNTER, DAVID, was made Major-General by Lincoln, and was one of the most ardent Abolitionists.

JULIAN, GEORGE W., says (*Reminiscences of Lincoln, etc.*, p. 64), "Every lineament of his grand public career should have the setting of his rare personal worth. In all the qualities that go to make up character, he was a thoroughly genuine man. His sense of justice was perfect and ever present. His integrity was second only to Washington's, and his ambition was as stainless."

KASSON, JOHN ADAMS, was a conspicuous Republican in Congress, honored by Lincoln with important assignments at home and abroad in the Post-Office Department.

KEIFER, JOSEPH WARREN, was Major-General of Volunteers; was member of Congress from Ohio and Speaker of the House; in 1900 wrote *Slavery and Four Years of War*, G. P. Putnam, publisher, which book shows his partisan attitude.

LAMON, WARD H.; published his *Life of Lincoln* in 1872. He appears in the accounts of Mr. Lincoln's life in the West as constantly associated in the most friendly relations with him. He accompanied the family in the journey to Washington, and was selected by Lincoln himself (see McClure's *Lincoln*, p. 46) as the one protector to accompany and to guard him from the assassination that he apprehended so causelessly (see Lamon's *Lincoln*, p. 513) in his midnight passage through Baltimore to his first inauguration. He was made a United States Marshal of the District in order (McClure's *Lincoln*, p. 67) that Lincoln might have him always at hand. Schouler (*History of the United States*, p. 614) says that Lamon as Marshal "made

himself body-guard to the man he loved." Though
Lamon recognizes and sets forth with great clearness
(p. 181) his duty to tell the whole truth, good and bad,
and especially (p. 486, *et seq.*) to correct the statements of indiscreet admirers who have tried to make
Lincoln out a religious man, and, though he indig-
nantly remonstrates against such stories as making his
hero a hypocrite, the book shows an exceedingly high
estimate of the friend of his lifetime. Dorothy Lamon
(*Recollections of Abraham Lincoln,* p. 168) quotes
Lamon's own words as follows: "It was my good fortune to have known Mr. Lincoln long and well—so
long and so intimately that, as the shadows lengthen
and the years recede, I am more and more impressed
by the rugged grandeur and nobility of his character,
his strength and intellect and his singular purity of
heart. Surely I am the last man on earth to say or
do aught in derogation of his matchless worth, or to
criticise the fair fame of him who was, during eighteen
of the most eventful years of my life, a constant, con-
siderate, and never-failing friend." Both Morse and
Hapgood commend Lamon and Herndon for their
"revelations." The careful search in many records
for the material for this book has not found a single
attempt to deny the truth of Herndon's testimony, or
of Lamon's. But the search did find a curious proof
of the strait to which some one has been driven to
conceal Lamon's testimony. In the Pratt Library in
Baltimore, Maryland, is a book with a title as follows:
"*Recollections of Abraham Lincoln,* 1847–1865, by
Ward Hill Lamon, edited by Dorothy Lamon, Chicago,
A. E. McClurg & Co., 1895." Nowhere in this book
of several hundred pages is found an intimation of the
fact that the same Ward Hill Lamon published in

1872 the *Life of Lincoln* quoted frequently in this book, or that he had published any book about Lincoln, and although these *"Recollections"* do contain the avowal that appears in the *Life of Lincoln,* that Lamon thinks it his duty to conceal none of the faults of his hero, every word is omitted of the "revelations" and "ghastly exposures" about Lincoln's attitude towards morals and religion that are recorded in Lamon's genuine book. Bancroft, in his very lately published *Life of Seward,* quotes (Vol. II, p. 42) Lamon from this late book, making no reference to the genuine book, and a paper in the Baltimore *Sun* of February 25, 1901, does the same. See in this Appendix what is said under the names of Herndon and Swett.

LELAND, CHARLES GODFREY, is author of a book once very popular, *Hans Breitman's Ballads.* In his *Abraham Lincoln,* and the *Abolition of Slavery in the United States* (G. P. Putnam's Sons, New York, 1881), he says (Author's Preface, p. 2), "Lincoln's career also proves that extremes meet, since in no despotism is there an example of any one who governed a country so thoroughly in detail as did this Republican of Republicans." For Leland's bitter partisanship, see pp. 109, 121, 122, 186, 200, 202 and 220 to 222.

LOCKE, DAVID R. (Petroleum V. Nasby). Born in New York in 1863; an American political satirist; author of Nasby's letters, after 1860, in Toledo *Blade.*

LOGAN, JOHN A., Major-General. His book about the war, *The Great Conspiracy,* shows throughout, as in its title, his partisan attitude. He served under Grant at Vicksburg, and under Sherman in Georgia; was unsuccessful Republican candidate for vice-presidency in 1864.

LOWELL, JAS. RUSSELL, long professor in Harvard; editor of *Atlantic Monthly*, 1857 to 1862, and of the North American *Review*, 1863 to 1872; Minister to Spain and to England.

MARKLAND, A. H., was a supporter of Mr. Lincoln for the presidency the first time; was in charge of the army mail service, and was Commission-Colonel on General Grant's staff in November, 1863. He was the only person besides President Lincoln and General Grant who ever had authority to pass at will through all the armies of the United States, thereby showing the confidential relations between him and the President and General Grant.

McCARTHY, CHARLES H., is author of *Lincoln's Plan of Reconstruction*. Page 497 in eulogy of Lincoln nowhere surpassed.

McCLURE, A. K. In his *Lincoln and Men of the War Time,* and in his *Our Presidents and How We Make Them,* the author's intimate association with Lincoln is shown in many places (*Lincoln,* p. 112, *et seq.*), and his attitude towards his hero may be measured by the following tribute (p. 5 *et seq.*): "He has written the most illustrious records of American history, and his name and fame must be immortal while liberty shall have worshippers in our land."

McCULLOCH, HUGH, author of *Men and Measures of Half a Century*, was Secretary of the Treasury under

Lincoln, Johnson and Grant. He attributes to Lincoln (*Reminiscences of His Associates,* p. 424) "Unwavering adherencee to the principles which he avowed— . . . personal righteousness — . . . love of country— . . . humanity— . . . "

MORSE, JOHN T., published in 1892 by Houghton, Mifflin & Co., his *Lincoln,* one of the American Statesmen Series. It shows throughout, but notably in the last four pages, as ardent an admiration for Lincoln as any other biography. It concedes (Vol. I, p. 192) the truth of the "revelations of Messrs. Herndon and Lamon" and the duty and necessity that rested on them to record these truths. Morse is next to the latest of the biographers. The Harvard Graduates' Magazine said of the book: "As a life of Lincoln it has no competitors; as a political history of the Union side during the Civil War, it is the most comprehensive and, in proportion to its range, the most complete."

NICOLAY, JOHN G. (like John Hay), came with Lincoln from Springfield, and was his private secretary to the end. In the Author's Preface to the great work— *Abraham Lincoln*—written by him and John Hay (see his name in this Appendix), is found the following (Vol. I, p. 9): "It is the almost unbroken testimony of his contemporaries that by virtue of certain high traits of character, in certain momentous lines of purpose and achievement, he was incomparably the greatest man of his time. . . . The voice of hostile faction is silent or unheeded; even criticism is gentle and timid (p. 12). We knew Mr. Lincoln intimately before his election to the presidency. We came from

Illinois to Washington with him, and remained at his side and in his service—separately or together—until the day of his death. . . . The President's correspondence, both official and private, passed through our hands, he gave us his full confidence. (p. 14) . . . each of us has written an equal portion of the work. . . . We each assume responsibility, not only for the whole, but for all the details.''

PARIS, THE COUNT OF, was a volunteer in the Union army. See *History of Civil War in America,* translated by Tasiastro, Philadelphia, 1875, Vol. IV, pages 2 to 7, for his partisan attitude.

PATTON, W. W., was President of Howard University, for negroes, in Washington, D. C.

PIATT, DONN, GENERAL, in *Reminiscences of Lincoln* (p. 449), refers to Lincoln as ''the greatest figure looming up in our history,'' and as one ''who wrought out for us our manhood and our self-respect,'' and says (pp. 499–500), . . . we accept the sad, rugged, homely face and love it. . . . Clara Morris describes Piatt (in her *Life on the Stage*), as a gentleman of delightful social and domestic traits. (See name of Rice.)

PHILLIPS, WENDELL. Appleton's Encyclopaedia says he ''began as Abolitionist leader in 1837 . . . made a funeral oration over John Brown . . . had the *Anti-Slavery Standard* for his organ.''

POORE, BEN PERLEY, was a distinguished editor, but best known as Washington correspondent; was Major in the Eighth Massachusetts Volunteers. His book, *The Conspiracy Trial for the Murder of Abraham Lincoln,* shows his partisan attitude. (See name of Rice.)

RAYMOND, HENRY J., assistant editor of the New York *Tribune,* and founder of New York *Times;* Republican Member of Congress from New York 1865–1867; author of *Life and State Papers of Abraham Lincoln.* Known in his day as "the Little Villain of the N. Y. *Times.*"

RHODES, JAMES FORD, is author of an exceedingly valuable six-volume *History of the United States* that (Vol. IV, p. 50) eulogizes Lincoln ardently.

RICE, ALLEN THORNDIKE, was long editor of the *North American Review,* a leading Republican organ. He is editor, too, of *Reminiscences of Lincoln by Distinguished Men of His Time,* frequently referred to in this book. Rice supplies the *Introduction* and is more or less responsible for all that is quoted from Piatt, Usher, Boutwell, Poore and Depew and Maj.-Gen. James Bosnet Fry.

RIDPATH, JOHN CLARK, professor in Indiana Asbury University, published his *History of the United States* in 1883, of which see page 522 to learn his attitude.

ROPES, JOHN CODMAN, author of the *Story of the Civil War,* which eulogizes Lincoln. No historian of his day ranks higher.

RUSSELL, WILLIAM HOWARD. His *My Diary, Nortl. and South,* published in the London *Times,* shows a bitter aversion to slavery, and to almost everything he saw in the South, and he shows plainly his judgment that it was the right and duty of Lincoln to crush secession. George William Curtis says in his *Orations* (Vol. I, p. 139) about Russell, that ''Europe sent her ablest correspondent to describe the signs of the times, and that Russell saw and gave a fair representation of the public sentiment.'' Adam's *Life of Adams* (p. 151, *et seq.*) speaks of Russell's *Diary* as ''the views and conclusions of an unprejudiced observer through the medium of the most influential journal in the world.''

SCHOULER, JAMES. His *History of the United States* (p. 631, *et seq.*) shows that no biographer is more eulogistic of Lincoln. Volume VI begins with, ''The further we recede from the era of our great civil strife, the more colossal stands out the figure of Abraham Lincoln.'' . . . See also Vol. VI, page 624 to end. He calls the John Brown raid (Vol. VI, p. 437) ''a sporadic and nonsensical movement;'' says ''the pitiful and deluded assailants'' were not treated ''with the decent magnanimity for which so good an opportunity was offered, and that (p. 438) ''the slave master showed on this occasion his innate tyranny and cruelty towards an adversary.'' He likens to Brown, Charlotte Corday, saying the difference was that her action was ''reasonable,'' Brown's ''unreasonable.''

SHERMAN, JOHN, President McKinley's first Secretary of State, was a very prominent Republican leader during the war, and served in the Union army with sword, tongue, pen and purse, raising largely at his own expense a brigade known as Sherman's Brigade.

SHERMAN, GENERAL W. T., the man who next after Grant was "Conqueror of the Rebellion."

SEWARD, WILLIAM H., was Secretary of State during Lincoln's whole administration, and accounted one of his ablest supporters.

SMITH, GOLDWIN, a distinguished historian and publicist; professor of History for two years in Oxford, and for three years in Cornell. In his *United States, an Outline of Political History* (p. 221, *et seq.*), it is claimed that Lincoln was a Christian. A dreadful picture is given (p. 222 to 225) of master and slave— of the slave "overworked and tortured with the lash—" . . . of "fetters and blood-hounds"— . . . of "constant dread of slave insurrections;" that "it is not amongst whips, manacles and blood-hounds that the character of true gentleman can be trained;" . . . that "with slavery always goes lust;" . . . of "a clergy degraded by cringing to slavery."

STANTON, EDWIN M., was often called Lincoln's "Great War Secretary." Appleton's Encyclopaedia says: "None ever questioned his honesty, his patriotism or his capability."

STANWOOD, EDWARD. His *History of the Presidency* is a recognized authority, with no Southern leanings.

STEVENS, THADDEUS, entered Congress in 1858, and from that time until his death was one of the Republican leaders, and the chief advocate for emancipating and arming the negroes.

SUMNER, CHARLES, was long Senator from Massachusetts, and was a leader in support of the war and emancipation.

SWETT, LEONARD. See his very close relations to Lincoln, shown under the name of David Davis in this Appendix.

TARBELL, IDA, shows constantly in her histories the most ardent admiration for Lincoln.

TRUMBULL, LYMAN, United States Senator, declined to oppose Lincoln for the nomination in 1860, and was one of the first to propose in the Senate the abolition of slavery.

USHER, J. P., was in Lincoln's Cabinet as Secretary of the Interior. He says, in *Reminiscences of Lincoln by His Associates,* page 77, "Mr. Lincoln's greatness was founded upon his devotion to truth, his humanity and his innate sense of justice to all."

WAR OF THE REBELLION. Official Records of the Union and Confederate Armies. We have a very extraordinary light upon the history of that period in a publication made by the Congress of the United States which, beginning in 1870, has now grown to more than 100 large volumes, "The War of the Rebellion, Official Records of the Union and Confederate Armies." The history of the war that has been written since the war by Jefferson Davis or U. S. Grant,

Alexander Stephens or Charles A. Dana, Joseph E. Johnston, John Codman Ropes, and all the rest who have undertaken it, may be distrusted as the work of partisans, or of men too near in time to see things correctly. But we are getting down to the real truth of history when we have the very words used by Mr. Lincoln and his Cabinet members, by General McClellan and his subordinates in their proclamations, orders, reports and correspondence during the months when active "disloyalty" was being repressed in all the States of the Union that were within reach of Secretary Seward's "little bell," and especially in Maryland, Kentucky, Missouri, Indiana, Illinois, Ohio, and New York. It will be seen that none of the extracts are taken from the Confederate record, they are all from the Union records and in all cases the volume and page are referred to. How the publication of these Records has helped the cause of the South in setting history straight and keeping it that way is shown by the admission of an honest old Union veteran who was heard to say: "The damned Record ought never to have been published."

WADE, BEN, was one of the most prominent Republican leaders. Ohio Senator from 1851 to 1869. Anti-slavery leader. Favored confiscation in the war, and emancipation.

WEBB, ALEXANDER S., LL.D., professor in College of City of New York, says, as follows, in his *Campaigns of the Civil War*, III; *McClellan's Campaign of 1862*, preface, page 6, that "In speaking of the President of the United States and his advisers, he (the author) must not be considered as rescinding or changing at any time his constant and repeated expressions of admiration, affection and regard for the President himself. He appeals 'to the closing chapter . . . to prove that he is as loyal to that noble man's memory as ever he was to him in person, and is but doing the work of an honest historian in recording the sad tale of the want of unity, the want of confidence, the want of co-operation between the Administration and the General commanding the Army.' "

WELLING, JOS. C., editor of *National Intelligencer* at Washington during the Civil War; afterwards President of St. John's College, Annapolis; then President of Columbia University.

WELLES, GIDEON, was Lincoln's Secretary of the Navy.

WHITCOMB, PAUL S., author of the article "Lincoln and Democracy," used in an abbreviated form in this edition, is a resident of Gladstone, Oregon. His forbears were New Englanders, moving across the plains in 1852 to settle in the Northwest. He says, "I do not know when I was attracted to the critical study of Lincoln but that study was intensified subsequent to the late war by the fact that De Valera, the Irish leader, used the principles of the Declaration of Independence as a basis for argument tending to show Ireland's right to complete independence and, in rebuttal, Mr. Lloyd-George quoted Lincoln's arguments against secession. Only a bigot acting in bad faith could fail to see that Lincoln's position did not square with the principles of the Revolution and of Democracy."

WHITE, HORACE, had a distinguished career in journalism for forty-years; was editor of Chicago *Tribune* and of the New York *Evening Post*.

WHITNEY, HENRY CLAY, shows his exceedingly high estimate of Lincoln in the last page of his *On Circuit with Lincoln*.

WILSON, WOODROW, was long a distinguished and popular professor in Princeton, and is now President. For his admiring attitude towards Lincoln, see pages 216 and 217 of his *Disunion* and *Reunion,* and Vol. IV, page 256 of his *History of the American Peoples*.

WINTHROP, ROBERT H., was eminent as a scholar and statesman; was ten years in the House, and then in the Senate from Massachusetts.

YOUNG, JOHN RUSSELL, had a distinguished career in journalism, especially in the *Tribune* group with Horace Greeley.

APPENDIX B

ABRAHAM LINCOLN, A SUPPORTER OF JOHN BROWN[1]

Sir:

As bearing on a statement made by Dr. Mary Scrugham, in an article that appeared in the September issue of your magazine, as to the pro-John Brownism of President Lincoln, I submit for your consideration several interesting items which have come under my observation and which may prove of interest to your readers.

(1). His law partner testifies to the fact that Lincoln made a contribution to John Brown's activities in Kansas. In the recent edition of the Herndon-Weiks *Lincoln*, published by the Jefferson Printing Co., of Chicago, Vol. II, page 379, we find the following:

"In Illinois an association was formed to aid the cause of 'Free-Soil.' We recommend the employment of any means *however* desperate to promote and defend the cause of freedom. At one of these meetings Lincoln was called on for a speech. He counselled moderation—We raised a neat sum of money, Lincoln showing his sincerity by joining in the subscription and forwarding it to our friends in Kansas."

(2). In a recent correspondence that I had with Dr. W. T. von Knappe of Vincennes, in regard to his History of the Wabash Valley, I received the following letter, to

[1] This article is reprinted verbatim from *The Libertarian*, a magazine published at Greenville, S. C., in its issue of October, 1924. It appeared there as a communication from M. D. Carter, editor of this edition of "The Real Lincoln."

which you will see he has made affidavit. Dr. Knappe tells me he is Head of a Masonic Memorial Hospital, the son of the well known journalist, Horace Knappe, editor of the Cincinnati *Enquirer*, Fort Wayne *Times* and *Sentinel* and other papers, and the grand-nephew of Gov. Silas Wright of New York. His letter is as follows:

Office of the Presbyterian Hospital of Wilhelm T. von Knappe, A. M., M. D., Homeopathic Physician and Specialist. Office Cor. Sixth and Perry Streets, Telephone 604, Vincennes, Ind., November 3, 1922.

M. D. Carter:

I thank you for the $3.00, and I am sending the history by registered mail. They would not print the other side in the U. S. is the reason of the expense. I expect to sell the plate of the saloon license to a Georgia Professor for cost and if you wish his address I will give it to you.

When John Brown was collecting cash to buy pikes to arm the slaves of Virginia to murder their masters, he came from Oberlin, Ohio, south to Ashland, where my father, H. S. Knappe, had me in an Abolitionist's shoe store buying me a pair of boots. His name was Wassen. A crazy-looking fellow came to the door and enquired for the boss. I told him he was back at his desk, talking advertising with my father. When Brown produced his subscription paper, my father wanted me to witness to the fact that this document was headed by "A. Lincoln $100.00."

Well, when Governor Wise hung John Brown, my father wanted A. Lincoln and every traitor that gave a dollar given the same dose, and, if President Buchanan had taken his advice, there would have been no war between the North and South.

Respectfully,
(Signed) Wilhelm T. Knappe, A. M., M. D.

AFFIDAVIT TO THE ABOVE LETTER

State of Indiana
County of Knox.   *S. S.*

Subscribed and sworn to before me, a Notary Public, in and for said County by W. T. von Knappe, this third day of November, 1922.

      My Commission expires February 2, 1925.

Seal   *Address of Notary Public,*
Notary Public   *R. N. Foulks, Asst. Cashier,*
Knox County, Ind.   *American National Bank,*
           Vincennes, Indiana

(3). Dr. Lyon G. Tyler makes the following statement on this subject in his treatment of the Federal Period, in the six-volume *History of Virginia*, published by the American Historical Society, in vol. II, page 402:

The abolitionists united in praise of Brown, and Wendell Phillips declared that he was not at all surprised at his action. He boasted that it was "the natural result of the anti-slavery teaching," and said: "For one I accept it, I expected it. On the banks of the Potomac—history will visit that river more kindly because John Brown has gilded it with the eternal brightness of his deed than because the dust of Washington rests on one side of it."—If it be said that the abolitionists constituted a small factor of the Northern people who regarded them as crazy, the answer is, that while uttering sentiments inciting to further murders they were approved by many and interfered with by none. None of them were arrested or put in hospitals for the insane.—We are bound to believe that the condemnation of Brown by Lincoln and other politicians was sincere in no degree, that in fact they secretly honored and believed in him; and this was shown by their after talk when there was no need for policy.   When hostilities at last began, the most popular song of the Federal soldier was "John Brown's Body," and for many years after the war his name held first place in the affections of the Northern writers.

M. D. Carter.

APPENDIX C

LINCOLN AND DEMOCRACY [1]

By Paul S. Whitcomb, *Gladstone, Oregon*

Nothing so intrigues the mind of the people of the Northern States of the American Republic as the personality of Abraham Lincoln and the imperial American Union. For sixty-two years the crescendo of laudation of Lincoln has been steadily rising, and the end is not yet. For Lincoln was the central figure and the dominating personality in one of the greatest wars of history and, in spite of all the theories of democracy, nothing so appeals to the emotions of men, which are the well springs of eulogy, as martial and imperial glory. People are not given to repudiating the wars they wage or those who lead them into war. Lincoln, himself, was retired from Congress for eight years because of his opposition to the Mexican War.

It is an interesting question as to what Lincoln's place in history would have been if there had been no Civil War with its lurid glow to silhouette his eccentric personality for future generations. At the time of his election to the Presidency he was scarcely more than a local character. He had served in Congress without rising above medi-

---

[1] This article was first published in *Tyler's Quarterly Magazine* for July, 1927, and is reprinted here in somewhat condensed form by permission of the author. The editor is indebted to Capt. Samuel A. Ashe, well-known North Carolina historian, for condensing this article to a compass that would permit of its reproduction in this volume. The force of this article is increased by the fact that the writer is of Vermont stock and professes entire change in his opinions as formerly entertained. For additional facts regarding both the author and Capt. Ashe see Appendix A.

ocrity. He had played fast and loose with the questions of slavery and secession without contributing anything original or constructive to the discussion, and what he said only served to further agitate the South and to so compromise his own public position as to make secession inevitable when the Black Republicans came into power.

He has been called a great thinker but his attitude toward both slavery and secession was at once doctrinaire and the result of mechanistic logic which failed to recognize the distinction between the laws of physical science and the laws of human action. With regard to the slaves he appealed from their legal status to the 'higher' law, but with regard to secession and the rights of the free and highly civilized white people of the south he argued their rights on the basis of those maxims of despotism which were invented for the express purpose of denying to the people their rightful liberties. He argued that the principles of the Declaration of Independence applied to the negro but denied that they applied to the free white inhabitants of the States in whose favor they were originally promulgated. He failed to discern that the independence of the slave and the independence of the states involved the same fundamental principle, that the right of secession was absolute and unqualified and no more required oppressive acts to justify it than did the right of the slave to secede from his master. He failed to see that those same class of arguments which denied freedom to the South also denied freedom to all men "and undermined the very foundation of free society."

The indiscriminate and uncritical eulogies which have been heaped upon Lincoln have been pronounced in the face of all but the most superficial facts and as though all the rest of the world was composed of brutes, knaves and fools. There is no evidence that Lincoln was any more honest, kind, accommodating or sagacious than the ordinary run of men. His waging of the Civil War was the very antithesis of common sense and statesmanship. There was no catastrophe potential in secession that in any way justified the waging of the war, viewed simply as a matter of state policy, without reference to the moral and human aspect of the war. It was one of the most colossal bankruptcies of common sense and humane statesmanship known to modern history. As the situation stood in 1860 it were better for the North and the South both that they should separate. The prosperity which followed in the wake of the Civil War was not due to keeping the South in the Union but to the development of the West. But even if it was, it is a Prussian, and not an American, doctrine that War is a legitimate agent of national progress, that the end justifies the means. We have no right to do evil that good may abound.

Lincoln has been acclaimed the great democrat,[1] yet the greatest act of his career was the very antithesis of democracy. Washington was infinitely a greater statesman and a greater democrat. Robert E. Lee was greater in all around character. It has been too readily assumed that lowliness of birth is evidence of greater democracy. But the man of lowly birth can be no more than a democrat and it is no particular credit to him that he is. But the man of aristocratic birth, who has the privilege and opportunity of being more than a democrat, and yet who remains one, not only in simulation but at heart, can truly claim the title of being a great democrat. The purpose of democracy is not to drag the few down but to lift the many up. It is not to make all common but to make all aristocrats, to diffuse the benefits of culture and good breeding throughout the community. And Washington,

[1] In politics Lincoln was a Whig. (Ashe).

who was an aristocrat by birth, because of the largeness of his heart and the breadth of his character became the first democrat through choice and affection. Never can it be truthfully charged against the man who subordinated the military to the civil through seven long miserable, heartbreaking years of revolutionary struggle and at the finish scornfully spurned a crown, that he was lacking in all the great qualities of a democrat.[2]

When Lincoln said that the question of union or disunion could only be settled by war, and ridiculed those who decried force as a legitimate and lawful means of maintaining the union, arguing that "their idea of means to preserve the object of their great affection would seem to be exceedingly thin and airy" and compared them to free lovers, Washington said "Let us erect a standard to which the wise and the just can repair,—the result is in the hands of God"; and of the accomplished Union he said that it was "the offspring of our own choice, uninfluenced and unawed, adopted upon full investigation and mature deliberation, completely free in its principles." Washington based the Union upon the democratic principle of free consent. Lincoln ridiculed the basis of democracy, spoke of it as exceedingly thin and airy, likened it to a free love arrangement and asserted that force was the only sound basis of government. He appealed from the basis of democracy to the basis of despotism, from the ballot to the bullet. The Civil War was the result of the putting the new wine of democracy into the old skins of despotism.

The responsibility for the Civil War has been laid at the

[2] It is a remarkable confirmation of this character in Washington that Col. Landon Carter, of Sabine Hall, Va., used the following language on May 3, 1776, before Washington had been called to the command of the American armies: "I never knew but one man who resolved not to forget the citizen in the soldier or ruler, and that is G. W., and I am afraid I shall not know another."—(Tyler).

door of the South on the grounds that they fired the first shot against Fort Sumter. But the grounds beg the question and the responsibility for the war must await the determination of the question as to whether or not the South had a right to secede. If South Carolina had a right to secede she had the right to take Fort Sumter. Lincoln's policy in sitting tight and forcing the South to make the first move was identical with that of Bismarck. "Success," Bismarck said, "essentially depends upon the impression which the origination of the war makes upon us and others; it is important that we should be the party attacked."

But the attack of South Carolina upon Fort Sumter was not an attack upon the North in any such a sense as the attack which Bismarck maneuvered an all too willing Napoleon into making upon Prussia. Fort Sumter was historically and geographically an integral part of the soil of South Carolina. It was there, as Lincoln said in his special message to Congress, for the protection of the people of South Carolina. It was an integral and vital part of their system of common defense. It symbolized the right of these people to defend themselves, a right which is basic to all other rights and which is the very test of manhood. Deny a man or a group of men the right to defend themselves and you deny them all other rights, for what a man has not the right to protect it cannot be reasonably and intelligently argued he has a right to at all.

Fundamentally and vitally the fort belonged to the people of South Carolina. The site of the Fort had been ceded to the Federal government for the protection of the City of Charleston, and the moneys with which the fort had been constructed were drawn by taxation from the people of the States by methods to which all the States had agreed in ratifying the Constitution. South Carolina had contributed her share and was morally entitled to a division of the common property. As to the legal phase of it there was none, for there was no law governing the subject, regardless of the fact that no technical, legal grounds can justify such a social catastrophe as war. War defeats the very end of law and government, which is the conservation of human values.

In spite of the persistent attempt, carried on through school histories and by partizan historians in general, to brand the people of the South in general, and of South Carolina in particular, as so many hell-bent hot heads, the fact is that the secession movement was done 'decently and in order.' They did not wantonly and in undue haste fire upon Fort Sumter. They sent a commission to Washington to negotiate a peaceful settlement of all questions arising from secession.[1] The assertion that secession was an essentially war-like act was a federal doctrine and not a southern doctrine. It was not until this commission had been snubbed on the narrow, childish legalism that the people of the South had no right to speak for themselves, that the people of South Carolina took the only other course open to them and asserted their rights by force of arms.[2]

[1] They offered to pay the cost of construction of the fort, etc. (Ashe)

[2] This does not state the full case. Not only were commissioners snubbed and denied audience, but no attack took place till Lincoln sent an armed squadron to supply the Fort with men and provisions. On this very question he took the advice of his cabinet, on March 15, 1861 and only one of them favored the movement. The rest in effect declared that the measure would inaugurate civil war, and it must be remembered that Mr. Hallam in his constitutional History of England states that "the aggressor in a war is not the first who uses force, but the first who renders force necessary." (Tyler)

It is proper to add that Mr. Lincoln and his cabinet had agreed that there should be no war and that the troops would be withdrawn from Fort Sumter, until he was persuaded by nine governors to bring on a war and to have it started by getting South Carolina to fire on Fort Sumter. Nicolay and Hay, close to Mr. Lincoln as brothers, wrote as of April 1st, p. 442, vol. 3: "Congress had neglected to provide measures and means for coercion. The conservative sentiment of the country protested loudly against everything but

In general principle the right of the people of South Carolina to dispossess the Federal Government of Fort Sumter involves no more than the right of any property owner to discharge a watchman hired to protect his property. The Federal Government had no more reasonable or moral right to wage war against the people of South Carolina and destroy their lives and property than a discharged watchman would have to destroy the property he was hired to protect. The authority of government is not an end in itself but a means to an end. The attempt to give to civil authority a special extra moral status is without ethical or social warrant and is simply one of the superstitions invented by despots as a means of awing the people and maintaining themselves in power.

Unionists would deny that two times two make four if it were necessary to vindicate the Civil War. To them no statement of principle is valid in favor of the independence of the South and against the War. Secession itself is a true principle when exercised in favor of the Union as Lincoln declared in the case of the secession of the forty-nine counties of Old Virginia.

The issues involved in the Civil War were not of concern solely to the generation which fought the war but are questions of eternal right and wrong and are subject to the law of Lincoln's doctrine that no question is settled until it is settled right. The objection that the war is water over the dam and that the problems of the present demand

concessions. His own cabinet was divided in council. Public opinion was 'awry.' Treason was applauded and patriotism rebuked." Then the President determined on war and with the purpose of making it appear that the South was the aggressor, he took measures. He sought to bring about the Confederate attack on Fort Sumter. "The President was looking through and beyond the now inevitable attack and the response of the awakened and united North. . . . He was looking through Sumter to the loyal states— beyond the insulted flag to the avenging nation." (Nicolay and Hay, IV, p. 28, p. 45). So Fred Seward, the Assistant Secretary of State, records that the firing on Sumter "was not unexpected" (p. 587). (Ashe) our attention is valid providing that history is all bunk and that there is nothing to learn from our past. But the problems of the present are largely the legacy of the past, and if the past had settled them right they wouldn't confront us at the present time. It has only been since the late war that an English Premier has quoted the arguments of Lincoln against secession as an answer to the principles of the Declaration of Independence as put forward in defense of the right of the Irish to freedom. And the struggle of Ireland for freedom antedates our Revolutionary War by a century and a half and involved and involves the same questions.

It is thus that our past rises up to meet us and, as Lincoln said of slavery, "deprives our republican example of its just influence in the world." In setting up the sovereignty of the Union as a basis for making war against the seceding States and as a fence against European interference he was acting upon the same principle that if one man chooses to kill another, neither that man nor any third man has a right to object. The logic of the Civil War was that the right to govern is paramount over the right to live, that man is made for government, rather than that government is made for man, and that for men to claim the right of self-government is to deserve and incur the death penalty.

Lincoln's arguments against the right of the South to independence were drawn from baseless exaggerations, the fatalistic sequence of mechanistic logic, an imperial and authoritarian interpretation of the Constitution which ignored its humanitarian purpose, a strange hodge podge of the maxims of monarchical political science, and an instinctive metaphysical attitude toward government.

Lincoln said of slavery that it was the only thing that endangered the perpetuity of this Union and that it was the *sine qua non* of secession, but from the Constitutional and historical standpoint this is not true. Slavery, as he admitted, was "indeed older than the Revolution." It existed previous to the Constitution and the Union was formed in spite of it. Both from the standpoint of the Constitution and sound statesmanship it was not slavery but the intemperate fanatical Abolition movement that endangered the Union.

These Abolitionists proposed to apply all the principles of the Declaration of Independence to a race of people that were totally unprepared for self-government.

It was the intemperate, arrogant, self-righteous and academic attitude of the Abolitionists that made any constructive solution of the slavery question impossible and led the six cotton states to withdraw from the Union. The right to withdraw was early claimed.

As a matter of historical fact South Carolina had threatened to secede over the tariff. The Colonies seceded from Britain over a question of local self-government. Belgium seceded from Holland and Norway from Sweden, where no question of slavery was involved.

Lincoln said of secession that it was the destruction of the country, of the Union, of the nation and of the liberties of the people and of the institutions of the country. He said "we have, as all will agree, a free government, where every man has a right to be equal with every other man. In this great struggle, this form of government and every form of human right is endangered if our enemies succeed." The argument was absolutely senseless. One would think to read the argument that some Napoleon, Caesar or Alexander the Great were attempting to conquer the Southern people and set up a despotism and that Lincoln was waging a war in aid and defense of those people, rather than that those people were seeking to do nothing more than govern themselves and that Lincoln was warring to conquer them, to keep them from exercising their rightful liberties.

Secession was not, in any substantial sense, the destruction of the nation, nor was it in a proper sense the destruction of the Union. A nation is simply a corporation through which men exercise certain of their rights, just as they exercise other of their rights through their other organizations.

Secession did not destroy the nation, but merely altered it. The Union existed when there were only thirteen states composing it,[1] and it would have continued to exist when there were twenty states left with a boundless public domain.

As for the liberties of the people, all their liberties would have remained intact. Furthermore in spite of the gravity of the situation as it existed in 1789, Washington never proposed to use force to compel a Union.

In his Missouri Compromise speech Lincoln said: "I trust I understand and truly estimate the right of self-government. My faith in the proposition that each man should do precisely as he pleases with all which is exclusively his own lies at the foundation of all the sense of justice there is in me. I extend the principle to communities of men as well as to individuals. I so extend it because it is politically wise, as well as naturally just; politically wise in saving us from broils about matters which do not concern us— The doctrine of self-government is right,—absolutely and eternally right."

No argument could give any stronger support to the right of secession than this argument in favor of freedom for the slave. If the inhabitants of the states are men, is

---

[1] As a matter of fact it existed when only eleven states were members of it— before North Carolina and Rhode Island joined.

it not to that extent a total destruction of self-government to say that they shall not govern themselves? When the people of the North govern themselves that is self-government; but when they govern themselves and also govern the people of the South, that is more than self-government —that is despotism.

The negro was the beneficiary rather than the victim of slavery as Booker T. Washington has admitted. Lincoln's talk about ''unrequited toil'' ignores the fact that the condition of the negro was better under slavery than it was in Africa, it ignores the fact that as compared to white laborers of equal mentality he was not deprived of any substantial rights, it ignores the economic and social status of northern so-called ''free'' labor which bordered closely upon serfdom, and it ignores the contribution of management to production. The strong probability is that the negro received at least as great a share, in proportion to what he contributed to production, as did the technically free northern laborer.

In any event civil war was no more a legitimate remedy for slavery than were the reputedly revolutionary methods of the I. W. W. a proper remedy for the wrongs inflicted upon free labor by northern capitalists.

In his first inaugural address Lincoln said:—''I hold that in contemplation of universal law and of the Constitution, the Union of these States is perpetual. Perpetuity is implied, if not expressed, in the fundamental law of all national governme ts. It is safe to assert that no government proper ever . ad a provision in its organic law for its own termination. Continue to execute all the express provision of our National Constitution, and the Union will endure forever—it being impossible to destroy it except by some action not provided for in the instrument itself.''

The argument views States simply as political abstractions. It ignores "States" as denoting an organization of men. It assumes that there is some authority capable of making a contract binding upon all generations of men which shall, throughout the course of time, inhabit a certain territory. It assumes that a few hundred thousand voters living along the Atlantic seaboard a century and a half ago possessed authority over all generations of men which may throughout the course of time inhabit all the country from the Atlantic to the Pacific seaboard.

The Southern people of 1860 had never entered into "a clear compact of government." It is true that a generation of men previously inhabiting the same territory had done so, but that was not their affair. One generation possesses no such authority over future generations. Political theorists may call this anarchy, but they take their theories too seriously. Men do not maintain government because their granddaddy said they should any more than they live in houses, or eat three square meals a day, or go to church because their granddaddy said they should. In some notes on government Lincoln said: "Most governments have been based, practically, on the denial of the equal rights of men, as I have, in part stated them; ours began by affirming those rights.

In asserting that if we continue to execute all the express provisions of the Constitution the Union will last forever Lincoln asserted no more than is true of any institution whose charter runs in perpetuity. But the assertion contains no argument against secession. Theorize, as men will, with regard to the basis of government it must conform to rational and moral reasoning, and there is no rational and moral reasoning to support the assumption that one generation can bind another generation in any such a way as is implicit in Lincoln's interpretation of the idea of perpetuity as applied to the Union.

Lincoln neglected to draw the distinction between the right to dissolve an organization and the right to withdraw or secede from it. The one is a right which belongs to the members as a whole while the other is a right inherent if not expressed in the laws of any organization except as membership therein partakes of the nature of a contractual obligation involving a consideration. But the Union is not of such a nature and there is no authority by which such a perpetual obligation could be established.

In arguing that secession was the essence of disintegration and anarchy Lincoln asked "why may not any portion of a new confederacy—arbitrarily secede again"—"Is there such perfect identity of interests among the States to compose a new union, as to produce harmony only, and prevent renewed secession?"

"Plainly, the central idea of secession is the essence of anarchy. A majority, held in restraint by constitutional checks and limitations—is the only true sovereign of a free people."

Grant has admitted in his *Memoirs* that if the Southern States had been allowed to secede, they would have set up a government that would have been real and respected, and the assertion that secession was the essence of anarchy was purely academic.

The essence of secession is not anarchy but freedom, independence and nationalism.

Lincoln asserted that "All who cherish disunion sentiments are now being educated to the exact temper of doing this (continuous disintegration)." He could have better argued that all who cherish warlike sentiments are being educated to the temper of conquest. His argument that secession was the essence of anarchy and that the movement could end only in the complete disintegration of society is answered by his own words that "Happily the human mind is not so constituted."

But while the central idea of secession is not the essence of anarchy, war is anarchy. "It is the essence of war to summon force to decide questions of justice—a task for which it has no pertinence."

After being brought up to the idea that the Southern leaders were so many hasty hotheads, it is disconcerting to read in the speeches of their real leaders the fairness, calmness and friendliness with which they faced the situation. And this attitude was not only in their speeches but in their actions as well. They took only those measures which any people who had determined upon their course, would have taken as a matter of good judgment and precaution.

Lincoln asked, "Why should there not be a patient confidence in the ultimate justice of the people" and again, "Will you hazard so desperate a step while there is any possibility that any portion of the ills you fly from have no real existence?" He had better have asked why he should not have a patient confidence in the ultimate justice of the Southern people and why he should hazard so desperate a step as war while there was any possibility that the evils of secession had no real existence. He had said of the Southern people that in point of justice he did not consider them inferior to any people and that devotion to the Constitution was equally great on both sides.[1]

The South in seceding did not take anything that by any moral principle belonged to the North, and if the Civil War is to be justified, either upon policy or principle, it must be upon a showing that secession was an invasion of

[1] At this point the author overlooks the circumstance that only the cotton states acted on their rights of secession prior to President Lincoln's making war on them—then the other states united in resisting the invading armies. —(Ashe)

the rights of the people of the North that justified the taking of human life.[2] No abstract, highly synthetic and controversial theories of sovereignty can justify the taking of human life. Man acting gregariously possesses no other right to take life than is possessed by the individual. Murder is murder whether it is committed by one man or twenty millions of men and the empiricisms of political so called "science" constitute no authority for murder. The idea that a "nation" can commit murder in order to achieve a fancied destiny is the essence of immorality and imperialism.

Lincoln said "This country, with its institutions belongs to the people who inhabit it. Whenever they shall grow weary of the existing government, they can exercise their constitutional right of amending it, or their revolutionary right to dismember or overthrow it." His theory was that the territory of the United States belonged to the people as a whole as sovereign proprietor. That the soil of South Carolina did not belong to the people of South Carolina, who inhabit it, but to the people of the United States as a whole.

The theory is a legacy from feudalism and monarchy and as applied to a republican union or state is the essence of communism. Democracy is an association of equals.

Under monarchy or feudalism the title to both person and property ultimately resided in the monarch or lord. It was this principle which was the cause of the War of 1812 when England asserted that once a subject always

[2] The *New York Times*, in a remarkable editorial September 9, 1864, justified the war not on slavery or the restoration of the Union, but on the threatened danger to the Northern people. It passed a tremendous eulogy on the resistance which had distinguished the Southern people beyond any in the world, rendering their conquest absolutely necessary, lest in the future the Northern States themselves might become subject to their terrible neighbors. In other words, the more evidence the Southerners gave of their right to self-government, the more it was denied to them.—(Tyler)

a subject, just as Lincoln claimed that once a state in the Union always a state in the Union.

The right of expatriation, which is simply a right of personal secession, is an acknowledged American right and has been ever since Jefferson directed the affairs of the nation. We fought for it in the War of 1812 and incorporated it in the Burlingame treaty with China. This right is absolutely inconsistent with the description of the Southern peoples as rebels and traitors and the calling of them to return to their "allegiance" to the Federal Government. The idea of "allegiance" is that of the relation of an inferior to a superior and not of the citizens of a republic to their republican society.

Certainly there is a territorial consideration in the formation of civil society, but that consideration is born of practical necessity and must end with the necessity. But no such consideration was involved in the secession of the Southern States. They were as able to govern themselves as were the people of the North or of England or of France or any other state. There are however no Constitutional grounds for the pretense of territorial sovereignty on the part of the United States government. The government of the United States is simply the joint and common agent of the States, members of the Union, just as a farmers co-operative is the agent of its members. The basic principles involved in the union of States are the same as those involved in the agricultural co-operatives. And as I have previously observed the United States cannot, under the Constitution exercise exclusive legislative jurisdiction over the site for its own capitol, or the sites for forts, dockyards or other needful public buildings without first getting the consent of the legislature in which the site is situated. To call such a government a territorial sovereign is absurd.

The people of South Carolina possess exactly the same natural, moral and fundamental rights as against the people of the State of New York that the people of Canada do.

Lincoln spoke of the people as possessing a revolutionary right, but such talk is to deny their sovereignty and imply the sovereignty of the Constitution. Revolution is the overthrow of the sovereign, not of the Constitution or of the government. The people do not derive their sovereign authority from the Constitution. It is not the Constitution of the people but of the Federal government and is also the record of a compact between the States.

Lincoln admitted that the government could be overthrown and the Union dismembered. A successful rebel becomes a revolutionist and his success vindicates his rebellion. It is a curious doctrine that success vindicates what would otherwise be a crime.

As a matter of historical fact these rebellions were generally efforts on the part of the people to regain their rightful liberties. As to whether or not secession was revolution depends upon whether the people of the seceding states possessed the right to run their own business.

Lincoln said of secession that "It recognizes no fidelity to the Constitution, no obligation to maintain the Union," but the fact is, there is no obligation on the part of the States to maintain the Union. He said "Surely each man has as strong a motive now to preserve our liberties as each had then to establish them," but in order to justify war he must have a stronger motive, for the Union wasn't established by force and the war overthrew those very liberties for which the Revolutionary War was fought and the Union created—the right of each state to govern itself. He said "This Union shall never be abandoned, unless the possibility of its existence shall cease to exist without the

necessity of throwing passengers and cargo overboard.''
A more accurate analogy would be to compare the Union
to a fleet of ships sailing in voluntary convoy for mutual
protection and Lincoln's act in waging war to the act of
the elected commander of such a convoy in sinking any
ship that seceded from the convoy.

Of the States Lincoln said they ''have their status in
the Union, and they have no other legal status. If they
break from this, they can do so only against law and by
revolution. The Union, and not themselves separately,
procured their independence and their liberty.—The Union
is older than any of the States and, in fact, it created them
as States. Originally some dependent colonies made the
Union, and, in turn, the Union threw off their old depend-
ence for them, and made them States, such as they are.''

Lincoln here pretends to be arguing upon legal grounds.
The force of his argument lies in the implication that the
Union had the legal authority to create those ''dependent
colonies, states, such as they are.'' But the Union of which
he speaks possessed no legal status or authority whatever.
It was purely an illegal, revolutionary Union whose acts
depended for their force upon ratification by the respective
colonies represented in the Continental Congress or tacit
consent. It was ridiculous for Lincoln to impute legality
to such a Union while denying it to the Confederacy which
was established upon the same legal authority as was the
United States.

Lincoln hypostatizes the Union and speaks of it achiev-
ing the independence of the States. But the Union was
not a personality or an entity but simply a condition of
co-operation.[1]

---

[1] There was no union in existence before 1781. There was a congress of
delegates who acted as allowed or directed by the several colonies or states.
In 1781, Maryland having agreed, the congress then became a Congress of
the States—and the confederation became operative. Then by Article VII of

Water cannot rise higher than its source; derived power cannot be superior to the power from which it is derived and the Federal Union cannot be superior to the States that created it. The Constitution is supreme only in the sense that the laws of any organization are supreme over its members, so long as they remain members.

Contrary to Webster's assertion and the language of the enacting clause of the Constitution, it was not ratified either by the authority of the people of the United States or directly by the people of the States.[1]

The phrase, "people of the United States," does not bear out the argument of Webster and the imperialists, that the people of the United States are united. The phrase is not "united people" but "united states." The present Constitution was ratified when the union was still based upon the Articles of Confederation. The mode of ratification ignored the Articles entirely and referred back to the prime authority of the State legislature.

It is only in a subjective or administrative sense that the people of the United States constitute one people. In the exercise of their sovereign powers they do, and always have resolved themselves into sovereign states. Marshall argued that the United States was sovereign to the extent of its authority, but it is no more sovereign than any agent is sovereign. Its powers are delegated powers. In waging the Revolutionary War the men of 1776 were fighting for

the proposed constitution, "The ratification of nine states shall be sufficient for the establishment of the constitution between the states so ratifying the same"; and, when nine states ratified, it went into effect between them; and it went into practical effect, leaving out some of the states. The ratifying states had broken up the old confederation—agreed to be "perpetual." (Ashe)

[1] The Constitution was to take effect between the states just as the "perpetual confederation" of 1781 was—not "over" the states but "between" the states—and Virginia and each other state was, by the Treaty of Peace with Great Britain, declared to be—each separately—"free sovereign and independent states"; and so in subsequent treaties. Nor was their condition altered by the Constitution of 1788. (Ashe)

everything that Webster and Lincoln argued against. The men of 1776 denied the rightfulness of the asserted British sovereignty. They asserted that they were men with all the rights of men, and Englishmen with all the Constitutional rights of Englishmen, and that their colonial situation had no political significance, that it was not a crime for which they could be punished by depriving them of their rights of self-government.

They claimed for their colonial legislature a constitutional parity with Parliament, possessed of exclusive legislative jurisdiction within its respective colony and that the Empire was bound simply by the theoretical sovereignty of the crown. They did not fight for union, but for the right of each colony to complete self-government.

The question as to whether the Union is a league, confederation, federation or nation, is not a vital one but is purely technical and is simply a matter of the mode of administration, of the extent of organization, not of obligation. Because it employs some machinery of government also used in national organizations is no more reason for calling it a "nation" than there would be for calling a gasoline engine a steam engine because of certain features they possess in common.

The assertion that secession is treason is not borne out by the nature of the Union, by the Constitutional definition of treason or the nature of treason itself, or by the principles of democracy. Treason is a crime against the "sovereign." The Union is an association of co-equal states and the Federal Government is simply the common agent of those states. The Constitution says that "Treason against the United States shall consist in levying war against them, or in adhering to their enemies," etc. It uses the plural "them" and "their" denoting an association of sovereigns rather than a unitary sovereign. It was Lincoln who committed treason and not the States. Lincoln overthrew eleven sovereign States and State governments, which even according to Webster were the equal of the Federal Government. The idea of the sovereignty of the whole people of the United States is purely an imperialistic dogma. Analyzed, it means that the people of Oregon are sovereign over the people of South Carolina and that the people of South Carolina are sovereign over the people of Oregon. The people of Oregon possess no more sovereign rights in the government of the people of South Carolina than they do in the government of the people of Canada or Mexico. The doctrine is indefensible by the principles of democracy.

Lincoln has been put forward as the great exemplar of Christianity, but the Civil War was fought in diametrical opposition not only to every principle of democracy, but of Christianity. What he said of John Brown may also be said of Lincoln that "It could avail himself nothing that he might think himself right." That cannot excuse violence, bloodshed and treason.

Like the enthusiast, of whom Lincoln said that he "broods over the oppression of a people till he fancies himself commissioned by Heaven to liberate them," so Lincoln brooded until he fancied himself commissioned by Heaven as a modern Moses raised up to lead the "oppressed" slaves to freedom, and when the war had brought such misery and destruction that it could no longer be justified upon the original object of saving the Union he then attributed to it the added character of a Divinely appointed means of punishing the North and the South for "the bondsman's two hundred and fifty years of unrequited toil."

But, regardless of the fact that slavery was in no sense a unique crime, Christ said that he "came, not to judge the world, but that the world through him might be saved." The Civil War was a greater crime than slavery. Both were a denial of the right of self-government, but where slavery simply took away the unrestrained barbaric freedom of the negro and put him to constructive employment, the war destroyed the very lives of those who had been previously denied the right of self-government. Lord Morley has said that it is not enough that we should do good. We must do it in the right way. War was no more a righteous method of perpetuating the Union than it would have been a righteous method of originally forming the Union. It was no more a righteous method of keeping the Southern States inside the Union than it would be a righteous method for bringing Canada into the Union or the United States into the League of Nations. The end does not justify the means.

Lincoln would have been a true democrat if he had perpetuated the Union by the method by which Washington formed it. He would have been a true Christian if he had followed the example of that other Abraham who said to his kinsman, "Let there be no strife I pray thee between me and thee—for we be brethren. Is not the whole land before thee? Separate thyself, I pray thee, from me; if thou wilt take the left hand, then I will go to the right, or if thou depart to the right hand, then I will go to the left."